African Friends and Money Matters

Observations from Africa

Second Edition

SIL International®
Publications in Ethnography 43

Publications in Ethnography (formerly International Museum of Cultures Series) is a series published jointly by SIL International and the International Museum of Cultures. The series focuses on cultural studies of minority peoples of various parts of the world. While most volumes are authored by members of SIL International who have done ethnological research in a minority language, suitable works by others will also occasionally form part of the series.

Series Editor
Mike Cahill

Volume Editor
Dirk Kievit

Managing Editor
Bonnie Brown

Compositor
Lois Gourley

Contributing Artists
Côme Mbringa
Mbanji Bawe Ernest
Momar Touré, Cover Illustration

Cover Design
Barbara Alber

African Friends and Money Matters

Observations from Africa

Second Edition

David E. Maranz

SIL International®
Dallas, Texas

© 2015 by SIL International®
Library of Congress Catalog No: 2015948502
ISBN: 978-1-55671-277-7
ISSN: 0-0895-9897

Copies of this and other publications of SIL International®
may be obtained through distributors such as Amazon,
Barnes & Noble, other worldwide distributors and, for
select volumes, www.sil.org/resources/publications

SIL International Publications
7500 W. Camp Wisdom Road
Dallas, Texas 75236-5629 USA

General inquiry: publications_intl@sil.org
Pending order inquiry: sales_intl@sil.org
www.sil.org/resources/publications

Contents

Acknowledgements

I have benefited from the suggestions, comments, and experiences of many people. They have all been either Africans or expatriates who have spent years working or living in Africa.

Fred West heads the list as it was first his idea to ask me to talk about my experiences—something I had not thought of doing. After him, the history is hard and tortuous, as is often the case during the gestation of a book. Discussions with individuals and groups, and more life experiences in Africa, fattened the file until it turned into this book. Hence, extensive and varied contributions from many people have provided valuable material and comments. I would like to thank all these friends and colleagues who have collectively made this book possible. It could not have been written by me alone. In the final analysis, of course, I was the one who put all these contributions together, so any blame for misrepresenting Africa or Western viewpoints falls on me. I do trust, however, that the book contains no misrepresentations.

In the space available I can thank certain friends who have been involved. Those who made substantial contributions or reviewed the text at various points include the following (in alphabetical order): Elinor Abbott, Grace Adjekum, Kwashie Amenudzie, Victor Azelenkor, Jules Badji, Pierre Boly, Oumar Diallo, Viking Dietrich, Mandé Diop, Joseph Diouf, Marilyn Escher, the late Djibril Fall, the late Mbengue Fall, Salifou Fall, George Foryoh, Yatta Foryoh, Karl Franklin, Glenn Gero, Fritz Goerling, Stephen Graham, Mafatim Guèye, Irene Haibucher, June Hathersmith, Marian Hungerford, Jim Leonard, the late Karen Lewis, Steven Maranz, Eddie Mungai, Emmanuel Njock, Stephen Payne, Clinton Robinson, Richard Shawyer, Duane Troyer, Bert Visser, Katy Wienecke, Gordon Williams, and Sara Williams.

John Watters, Africa Area Director of SIL International during much of the period in which the research and writing of the book took place, provided invaluable encouragement. Some early versions or excerpts were sent to colleagues in several countries from Senegal to Kenya, who used the materials in various seminars, courses, and training sessions. Their positive reports as to the helpfulness of the material have been a stimulus to keep pressing on. Barbara Moore and Harriet Hill have been special encouragers.

My wife, Louise, has from the beginning been a major supporter. In fact, together we lived many of the examples presented in the work.

I must thank the countless African friends and acquaintances who are really the subject of the book. Almost without exception I have found Africans to be friendly, accepting, and personable. The book is really about them and "us" Westerners, and how we can better understand and appreciate each other.

A few contributors have asked to remain anonymous, so they are cordially thanked anonymously.

The names of some who gave me a good word, or suggestion, or encouragement along the way may have been left out. I ask their indulgence; no one has been omitted intentionally.

I finally thank the academic editorial staff of SIL International for their interest in the book and for bringing it to light of day. In particular my sister, Bonnie Grindstaff, did the heavy editing for which I'm most grateful, followed by Bonnie Brown. Others were part of the process, in the editing and business sections headed by Mary Ruth Wise and Larry Salge, respectively. Many cordial thanks to all.

Westerners who give money and economic advice to Africa, as well as those who write about the continent, spend far too much time looking in the wrong direction. We concentrate our energies on semifictional, barely functional, frequently irrelevant Western imports: central bureaucracies, ministerial policy papers, macroeconomic statistics, and the "sincerity" of leadership commitment to free-market reform. All of which can be condemned, applauded, or made fun of within easy walking distance of a four-star hotel. Meanwhile, we are ignorant of the indigenous system that helps hold the whole...together.

Blaine Harden[1]

---

[1] Harden 1990:63–64.

"Buy from me!"

Introduction

Several years have passed since the first edition of *African Friends and Money Matters* was published. The author and publisher have been gratified at its reception and from the comments received. Expatriate and national workers across Africa have been using it. It has gone through several printings. Now we present a new edition including two completely new chapters. We believe this added material will add to the usefulness of the book.

The first edition attempted to contrast two main types of behaviors, those African and those Western. It was pointed out in the first edition that what was described were observed to be typical behaviors, seen often across the African continent, but that there are many local, regional, and individual differences. The same was noted as true for "Western" behavior, with differences, for example, between Europe and America, and within countries. Also noted in the first edition was the fact that even though the "observations" have been discussed and revised with African friends from West to East, they should be taken as starting points or hypotheses when living and making friends with Africans in any particular country or location. They are not absolute and invariable across the huge continent that is Africa.

In mathematical terms two sets of behaviors are discussed. A set is defined as "a number of things of the same kind that belong together." Sets can be complete, where all possible variants are included, or incomplete, where only a partial listing is included. In our discussion, the observations of both African and Western behaviors are incomplete sets. Behaviors are discussed that have been seen widely across Africa, but of course they are only a sampling. Many readers have commented that the observations have been useful, in helping them to see things differently from what they are used to, even if there is not a 1:1 correspondence with what they see and experience in their personal or local environment.

Comments over the years have been overwhelmingly positive although a few have been negative. The range of comments can be seen on *www.amazon.com*. One of those favorable was:

> *African Friends and Money Matters* is essential reading for
> anyone working in Africa, particularly for short term NGO
> and mission workers. Unfortunately, I didn't read it until af-
> ter my second trip. I'll be better prepared on my next trip,
> after having read it. It will save me from some embarrassing
> and occasionally quasi-confrontational moments as I relate
> to people I really care for. For you who have been deluged
> with requests for money and financial help, during and af-
> ter your visit, it will explain some cultural issues, and will
> help you to better deal with these issues. I regard it as es-
> sential reading for mission organizations, mission workers,
> and other NGOs working short term or long-term in Africa.

One of those negative comments:

> Informative, but very redundant. Author repeats himself
> over and over. Everything in the book could have been writ-
> ten in two chapters.

A mixed response was received from a university professor:

> If I were to review the book...would have to raise questions
> of methodology and terminology. Your observations for the
> most part seem based on anecdotal evidence, but you ap-
> ply them to the entire continent of Africa. Such a procedure
> immediately generates resistance...When I showed an ear-
> lier version of this book to...a professor of classical civiliza-
> tion...his immediate response to reading it was that it needs
> a broader, more systematic basis of inquiry.

> One reason for this comes from the broad sweeping terms
> "African" and "Western." In my field of literature, the terms
> are nowadays almost taboo. In a contribution I made on "Af-
> rican" literature to a recent book...I had to be very, very
> careful about definitions and point out that the term "Afri-
> can literature" is an oversimplification.

> So for a review, I would have to take these methodological
> and terminological issues into account. I would of course put
> the best face I could on them. I would insist that what you
> have given us is a set of hypotheses that need further proof
> and refinement. (That is also how I will introduce the book
> to my students.)

I accept these as valid criticisms—from a strictly academic point of view.
But this book is not presented as an academic text; rather, it is meant as a
practical book for anyone living or traveling in Africa. It is built on anecdotes,

rather than on detailed surveys of every point tested as to whether each observation is accurate over a wide area or not, etc. Furthermore, the observations have been informally tested over large parts of Africa, from West to East.

Besides that, the introduction to the first edition (Maranz 2001:10) attempted to be clear about the generality and the limitations of the text:

> The "observations" are just that. Africans, and Westerners in the descriptions related to them, have been observed countless times using their resources in the ways described. Some of the observations seem to contradict others. That is natural. People from all cultures behave differently at different times and in different moods. Emotions, recent experiences, family conflicts, health, and many other factors influence behaviors at any one moment. People in all cultures also always have many possible behaviors to choose from at any one time but they tend to follow certain patterns of behavior in similar circumstances. These patterns are distilled in the "observations" found in the following pages. So these "observations" represent behaviors that have been observed across Africa. Some have regional or local variations, or are more typical of one region than another.

Some African readers have pointed out that the dichotomy African/Western is too simple. African culture is fast changing and a cultural gap is widening between rural/traditional and urban/modern. Young people especially realize this is happening, as many of them have to straddle this divide. One wrote:

> We are people who have been deeply affected by Christianity and globalization. Therefore while we are Africans, our mindset is different from that of our forefathers. We see certain things from a mixed point of view; not Western, but not traditionally African either.

As for terminology, as referred to by my professor friend, I realize words can involve sensitive issues. He mentions "Africa" and "Westerner." There are many others. "Tribe" or "tribal" are a common pair. I have personally observed that in some African areas or countries, tribe and tribal are taboo terms, to be avoided at the risk of incurring bad relations. Yet I have also been in areas where, for example, people readily refer to themselves or others by tribal designation. I hope the reader will give the author the benefit of the doubt—that in no instance is a term used with any intent whatsoever to denigrate or to be prejudicial. Political correctness, and keeping up with all local and regional sensitivities, exceed the limitations of the author.

Addressing overgeneralization: from the beginning this was recognized as a liability. Of course, with such a vast continent as is Africa, describing any behavior as "African" will result in misrepresenting some of its many behaviors. Likewise, "Western" covers such a broad area that inaccuracies will result from using such a broad umbrella term. Still, as many observers have noted, much behavior seen in Africa will not be confused with what is seen in Asia. Although there are differences across Africa, there are many things that are African in a unique and identifiable way. It is the latter that this book tries to describe. Many expats and nationals have found the down-to-earth approach followed in this book to be helpful and applicable to the situations within their experience. We hope that the added material will be at least as helpful.

Another criticism has been the tediousness in referring to "African" and "Western" countless times. One reader suggested using a variety of synonyms, such as foreign worker, volunteer, visitor, or outsider. When I attempted to use such alternative terms the result seemed confusing, with referents often becoming unclear. So repetition was chosen over confusion. Sometimes the described contrasts between Western and African behaviors may seem to be greater than what Westerners experience while living in Africa. This comes not from the differences being exaggerated but from long-time residents adjusting to and better understanding African cultures. New arrivals see the differences more keenly.

Two new chapters have been added. New chapter one is an introduction to African society. The first edition jumped right into financial matters. Starting now with general characteristics seems like a better way. A broad collection of topics is provided to try to paint a balanced picture of interpersonal behaviors. With this, the reader should be better able to understand how financial matters fit into society as a whole. Some of the topics covered can be found in the many travel books available. While there may be overlap with some travel books, this chapter goes into more depth than is found in them. Besides, many of the topics presented here are not at all addressed in the travel texts.

New chapter two continues to address everyday topics, but largely those whose significance are more "below the surface." For example, consider decision-making. An expat involved with a committee tasked with making certain decisions, may not understand the process involved and be frustrated with delays he or she observes. So the section on decision-making processes may be of help. Many behaviors in any culture have meanings that are not obvious to an outsider. One section, describing clientelism, will be seen to be much longer than the others. Clientelism has been much studied in Africa and many scholars agree that it is practiced across the continent and is very important. Hence the detailed description, in the hope that this will help expats understand many behaviors they will observe but often with little understanding of the underlying system they represent.

1

Interpersonal Behavior

Introduction to African society

One hand alone cannot wash itself.
Tamasheq proverb (Mali)[1]

Although the African continent encompasses many countries, ethnic groups, languages, and histories, there are many commonalities. These allow for continent-wide generalizations. The likenesses and differences are similar to those described by Daniel Pipes for a different context: "The Muslim world can be compared to playing cards. Each hand that is dealt is different from the others, yet all the hands clearly come from the same deck."[2] There are differences between hands, i.e., individual African cultures, yet there are commonalities that distinguish them from all other cultures.

Some authors have treated elite families separately from the general population, but we will here treat elites and non-elites together, since they have much in common. As most people who fall into the elite category have come from the masses in the current or a recent generation, they carry with them behaviors described here that are common to most Africans. Therefore, in this chapter we will present behaviors and characteristics common to both the general population and the elites.

African cultures focus on human relationships, developing them to great complexity. This chapter describes some of the many social relationships common in Africa.

Success in any endeavor that involves Africans requires building good personal relationships. This applies in business as well as with individuals. Showing respect is a salient theme in most African contexts. It carries a high

[1]A. Savage 1997:12.
[2]Pipes 1985.

1

value that many Westerners are not accustomed to. This applies especially to those who come from societies which have ideals of equality and "fairness." In Africa, respect must be shown in relation to individuals, hierarchies, titles, ranks, positions, and age.

Africans traditionally lived materially simple lives. This was typical of pre-industrial subsistence agricultural societies everywhere, not only in Africa. Although African societies were materially simple, they developed very complex relationships, with both kin and non-kin. With urbanization and the expansion of roads, electrification, public transportation, the market economy, and, more recently, television and cell phones, life has become more complex, even in rural areas. In urban contexts, African life has become as complex as life anywhere. Yet, in spite of life becoming increasingly complex materially, African society has maintained social relationships as the primary focus and interest. "Within [this] complexity, interpersonal relations take precedence, in everything from working with government officials to making purchases from vegetable vendors."[3] For expatriates in Africa, connecting with people on a human basis is the key to success, whether in business, development work, or in any other field.

One way to become more "human" is to suggest in some contexts that your friends give you a name in the local language. This applies especially to village or neighborhood situations where the expatriate will have a continuing presence. I have several times been given a name in the local language when doing anthropological research. This has had several benefits. My name placed me within the kinship system, placing me in the social hierarchy so that people knew where I fit in their society. I was now part of a particular kin group. My name was also easily pronounced and remembered. It conferred on me the obligations and privileges that accompanied my status. People enjoyed playing the game of calling me by my local name, knowing full well it was a fiction and any kinship it afforded me was not real, yet it really did give me a place in their society. I had become part of it, as I had a meaningful name and was a member of a clan. To a significant degree, people knew how to relate to me as one of themselves, not as a mere foreigner.

Expatriates often misconstrue the emphasis and time spent on socializing by Africans as a sign of laziness or lack of purpose. This is far from the truth. Richmond and Gestrin explain that social relationships build personal understanding and trust that are requisite to any on-going endeavor. This is especially important in Africa, where interdependence is an ideal. Mutual obligations are required for success. Thorough discussion and understanding of the matter at hand is necessary for achieving the desired long-term outcomes. This too requires socializing. Often, in such cases, there is really no dividing line between the social and business aspects of a program. "In

---

[3]Richmond and Gestrin 1998:90.

the village Africans sit under a tree and chat before deliberating or doing business. In the city they also sit and chat prior to doing deals, not under a tree but at their offices or over food and drink."[4]

Greetings and conversation

Greet all people one meets—even complete strangers.
Yoruba proverb[5]

Greetings are of supreme importance in Africa. The travel literature repeats this point for all countries across the continent. Especially in villages where life is more leisurely than in cities, greetings between two individuals can last many minutes. The value placed on greetings is perhaps best illustrated by short stories in which a character fails to greet others, and it is taken as a demonstration of ill will, or even a curse against others. Expatriates become easily annoyed at this practice, as people seem to go on endlessly about health, all family members, the household, job or work, and children. In some areas, greetings include the well being of relatives and close friends, and even of livestock, if appropriate! There are times and places where some subjects are not enquired about: husband, wife or wives, the number of children in the family, or pregnancy (even if obvious) are common examples. Such taboo subjects sometimes are thought to be related to bad luck or the evil eye.

Judith Irvine found greetings to be formulaic among the Wolof of Senegal. That is, predictable routines were followed to the extent that she could write formulas and rules that people unconsciously followed, often repeating phrases and news that were already well known to both parties.[6] The main point of such greetings is to demonstrate mutual respect and concern. Extended greetings are also a source of pleasure to those who grow up with them, much to the amazement of expatriates.

Among the Igbo of Nigeria, Nwoye writes:

> Not greeting, or even greeting in culturally inappropriate ways, can lead to a negative assessment of a person's character. Such a person is regarded as either 'proud' or not a good person. It can also be said of him/her that *na azuro ya azu* 'he/she is not properly socialized'. Part of the early socialization of the Igbo child consists of the proper ways of greeting...Perhaps, because Igbo culture does not operate non-verbal demonstrations of respect or deference like bowing...it makes up for this by insistence on the proper

[4]Ibid., 127.
[5]Ibid., 91.
[6]Irvine 1989.

> execution of verbal greetings....Failure to greet is indicative
> of pride, bad manners or an expression of ill-will towards
> one party or the existence of a strained relationship between
> the two parties. The warmth of a greeting, its duration and
> content, are all indexical of the degree of relationship exist-
> ing between the interactants.[7]

To rush a greeting, or to fail to adequately greet someone, can be extremely rude. Greetings are necessary even when asking directions, when
traveling, or shopping. Before asking a passerby or shopkeeper for directions or information, the enquirer needs to greet the individual. Even when
simply asking someone for directions, or buying tomatoes in the market,
start with a greeting.

Handshakes are closely tied to greetings. One of the first and most important things to know when traveling or living in Africa is the importance of handshakes. Older people are greeted first, seated first, and given
precedence when entering a room. Westerners are typically surprised at
the frequency and seeming importance both men and women attach to
handshakes. Whereas Westerners may greet friends and colleagues with a
handshake when they have not met for some time, or when congratulating
someone on a special occasion, Africans typically shake hands when coming and going during the course of a given day. One thing to note about
handshakes in Africa is that they may be very light, even flaccid, sometimes
practically just a touch of hands. The degree of firmness varies from one
culture to another, but it is never a sign of a lack of sincerity or character,
as such is often interpreted in the West.

The American "group wave," where one looks around at everyone and
waves a greeting to all present, is not appropriate or appreciated. It is too
impersonal, showing that one is not taking the time for individual relations.
This applies to initial greetings and also to farewells. When it is time to
leave a group, farewells are said to everyone present. This includes shaking
hands with everyone.

Many Muslim men, especially those older or of higher position, will not
shake hands with a woman. Women who meet Muslim men should always
wait for the man to initiate any handshake; otherwise it will be awkward for
all present if the woman holds out her hand with the man not responding.
Christians and adherents to African traditional religion are generally open
to handshakes between the sexes.

In some countries it is good to smile at the person being greeted. In other
countries "over smiling" may raise suspicions about the person's sincerity.
In all situations and cultures it is good to frankly explain to your counterparts that you are ignorant of appropriate etiquette and culture (which they
are doubtlessly aware of but they would say nothing if you didn't bring up

---

[7]Nwoye 1993:37, 47–48.

the subject). The degree to which direct eye contact is encouraged, prohibited, or limited varies widely, but is integrally associated with ideas of respect. Whereas Westerners may associate looking directly into people's faces with respect or honesty, in African societies, avoiding direct gaze with social superiors, older people, or high status individuals may demonstrate "power distance" or respect for the social order.

It is always a good idea to have a "cultural guide" when living in another society. Humbly explain your need of their advice and counsel regarding cultural matters, including the proper way to greet people. Admit your need for instruction. With people who consider you socially or economically superior, it may be necessary to emphasize your seriousness about wanting their opinions; otherwise they may be hesitant to offer counsel to a superior. It will take a good bit of courage for them to do this, because to correct someone above you in the social hierarchy breaks the rules of etiquette. Basically, you're asking them to be impolite to you, so you'll need to beg and plead, and be very humble and accepting of any remark they might make.[8]

And make sure that you do not shame or anger them if they tell you something they do not appreciate about your behavior. Be prepared to be stoic and not react visibly to uncomplimentary opinions. I have had several occasions when I asked for opinions and received unflattering, but very valuable, responses.

Introductions

Follow the customs or flee the country.
Zulu proverb[9]

In urban contexts people want to be introduced to a stranger or visitor. Introductions can vary a great deal from country to country. Sometimes last or first names are used; often the inclusion of a person's title is mandatory. If an introduction is not forthcoming within a few minutes, a stranger may introduce himself. "It is critically important to take time when you greet someone to make many inquiries into their health and (that) of their relatives...It is considered very rude not to take a considerable amount of time when meeting someone to make these inquiries and express understanding of their responses; he or she will do the same in kind."[10] Africans consider relationships to be an essential part of business.

After introductions in many situations, seating comes next. A stranger to a gathering should never seat himself. Ordinarily the stranger will be

---

[8]Hill 1996a:4.
[9]Richmond and Gestrin 1998:90.
[10]Foster 2002:117.

told where to sit. Proper seating involves position or role, rank, gender, and age. Depending on the occasion, men, women, and children may be seated separately.

Conversation topics

If you want to keep your workmen, keep your temper.
South African proverb[11]

An expatriate may wonder what subjects are appropriate to talk about. Neutral subjects include sports, especially soccer in most African countries. Music, food, art, the country's history—these are always welcome subjects. If the expat is at least somewhat knowledgeable about these subjects concerning the country involved, this will be received very positively. In business meetings discussion of one's company and industry will usually be most welcome, as Africans are anxious to better understand the wider world.

In some African cultures it is acceptable to make relevant comments while a person is speaking. In others, it is very impolite to interrupt or interject comments before the person finishes. I did not always recognize this and sometimes noted that people became deeply irritated with me when I tried to interject a comment. Instead of interrupting, there is a constructive way to enter into the conversation: "give the other person signals that he or she is being listened to rather than chime in quickly with your own thoughts."[12] This is part of the rules of conduct found in all societies. They are often highly developed, even ritualized acts, to which people attach great value, even moral value.

There are also subjects that the expat should not bring up or express an opinion on. These include politics, current events that are sensitive within a country, neighboring countries that are in conflict with the host country, current tensions between religions, poverty or slums, and ethnic rivalries. Asking local people about their occupation may not be welcome. On the other hand, expats may be asked about their occupation or even income. When such issues are raised it typically indicates a desire to better understand the Westerner's country, rather than prying into personal matters. While sex may be an offensive subject, physical features or actions that are taboo for Westerners are by no means identical to those perceived that way by African cultures. Don't assume that what you can talk about easily will be deemed acceptable. Likewise, suspend your judgment of Africans based on what they joke about or talk about with ease. Bring up subjects that you think you have in common with your acquaintance. Conversation on such

---

[11]Richmond and Gestrin 1998:145.
[12]Foster 2002:121.

topics will help forge personal relationships that will be good for both you and your organization.[13]

Although this is not exactly a subject of conversation, in many African cultures, verbal communication often involves flowery, effusive, even exaggerated speech. To the typical Westerner this may seem extreme and insincere. Contrary to the Westerner's thinking, this may actually be speech designed to demonstrate the sincerity of the speaker. In some cultures professional "praise singers" are used at weddings, ceremonies, and other occasions. People may actually pay to be spoken well of, or even be praised in verse, extemporaneously. As a Westerner myself I have not been able to understand how this pleases people, but Africans I have talked to have had as hard a time understanding my incomprehension as I have had in understanding how it gives them pleasure. Maybe a little pop psychology can be enlightening. The Westerner thinks paying someone to praise you cannot involve sincerity. Perhaps to the African, the praise singer is actually giving the truth in expressing the fine qualities of the person that ordinarily go unrecognized. Church offerings provide a good example:

Most African societies expect the wealthy to contribute generously, both to the church and to the public benefit at celebrations. An usher may break into praise when a wealthy person contributes a large sum, a wealthy person may dance joyously down the isle waving a large bill in the air, or a pastor may encourage an expatriate or an elite member to give generously, much to the astonishment of a Westerner, who has been taught, "Don't let your right hand know what your left hand is doing." However, as long as they are humble, local Christians are encouraged by such displays of generosity, and will doubtless break into celebration (personal communication, 2014).

Formality

It is not bad to love the king, but it is even better to be loved by the king.
Wolof proverb (Senegal)[14]

African society tends to be formal in many everyday environments. For Americans and probably to a lesser degree for other Westerners, it is important to recognize this. If Americans are not aware of the formalities expected in many situations, they risk embarrassing their African counterparts and other Westerners who are tuned in to the formal requirements of the moment. Formality can be expressed in several ways. Terms and mode of address, posture, gestures, dress, and attitude, are a few of the elements involved.

---

[13]Ibid., 207.
[14]Shawyer 2009:404.

In practical terms, when in new social situations, it is best to use people's last names and titles, including academic titles, until there is indication from Africans that the foreigner should be less formal. When in doubt it is better to err on the side of formality. The higher value to keep in mind is showing respect and refraining from doing or saying anything that will be interpreted as disrespectful. This is important for building and maintaining healthy relationships with others. This is good advice especially if the foreigner is young.

> People are respected because of their age, experience, wealth and/or position. Older people are viewed as wise and are granted respect. In a group one can always see preferential treatment for the eldest member present. With respect comes responsibility and people expect the most senior person to make decisions that are in the best interest of the group.[15]

In French-speaking regions it is best to avoid the familiar pronouns, like *tu*, until rapport is established and the African begins to use them with the expat. Even then, if the African person is older, it is often good to ask how they prefer to be addressed. Because Americans value equality, perhaps as a reaction to the English class system under which they were poorly treated, they tend to be quick to address people by their first names. They should be very careful to not do this without assurance it is acceptable to people.

> Each group has its own way of honoring the hierarchies, establishing respect and deference, and following (or not following) through on their responsibilities. There are formal ways that guests (outsiders) and hosts (insiders) must act toward one another, in order to preserve the honor of all groups and individuals.[16]

There are, of course, times when informality is called for. The foreigner needs to distinguish between leisurely talking and being formal. A general rule is that personal conversation may be informal but group meetings are formal.

Formality is an especially important concern when the expatriate is meeting and interacting with persons of rank, such as government and business officials. They need to be treated with the respect and protocol due to them because of their positions. Familiarity should be avoided. Appropriate dress needs to be worn to show respect. In all these matters Westerners should inform themselves ahead of time as to the requirements that are mandated by local custom.

---

[15]www.kwintessential.co.uk
[16]Foster 2002:203.

Names and titles

A goat's head is not lost in the soup.
Ibibio proverb (Nigeria)[17]

As is probably true worldwide, names are important in Africa. Local usage varies, but there are elements that are common to all or most of Africa. In most countries, titles are important and are used when addressing the individual. When the family is discussed, kinship terms are used. Whatever the local usages are regarding name, titles, family and kinship, and various honorifics, they should be taken as matters of importance to the people involved.

In some African cultures names have special meaning and significance. They are not chosen at random or picked out from a published list of possibilities. In most Western countries names are used to individuate children, giving them personal identities. While names are used to individuate children in African societies as well, the identity of a person is centered more in their wider context of relatedness, their lineage, their clan or tribal identity, or their religious heritage, rather than their individuality. Boys in Muslim families are named using one of many variants of Muhammad, or for other Muslim personages of note, while girls are more likely to be given names which sound pretty, or are associated with highly valued virtues or characteristics, much like the "Christian virtue" names Westerners give. Roman Catholics often name children, both boys and girls, after a saint. However, many Africans have multiple names, but lack an apparent "surname." People in Christianized or Islamized societies frequently carry at least two names, a name that associates them with their parents' religion, and a vernacular name that associates them with their lineage, an historic event, or a social, historic event or circumstance surrounding their birth. Many people, especially men, also carry nicknames, by which most villagers know them, but which they prefer not to be introduced by formally. Knowing which name to use in which context can be a matter of showing respect.

Some names relate to the kinship group and so serve to identify more than just the individual. Sometimes they relate to events surrounding the child's birth. An example from Kenya shows just how important an individual's name may be, and therefore, how important it may be to take a person's name seriously. Under certain circumstances where the newborn is believed to be at risk, it is intentionally "lost," and then ritually "found." Upon being thus "found," the child will be named after the container in which it was ritually abandoned. It may be called Atonga (basket), Odheru (tray made of straw), or Adita (small basket). The child may also be named after the person who "discovered" it on the path.[18]

[17]Clasberry 2010:127.
[18]Owin 1995:4–5.

A number of societies give "commentary names" through which people voice their opinion, or the way they experienced an event, or problem, even a family dispute. This should not be interpreted as "airing dirty laundry," for even once the problem is resolved, it serves to correct bad behavior and instruct people on proper interpersonal relationships. They welcome visitors to ask about the specifics, for through such names one can learn a great deal about a person's, or a family's, internal dynamics.

Other societies name children for living or deceased relatives, give them names that correspond to colors of cattle, anomalies of birth (breech, covered, wrapped cord, etc), omens, deities that a parent prayed to for a child, or answers to prayer. New names may be given at certain junctures, like initiation, circumcision, birth of a child, death of a parent, etc. It is important to understand the social meaning these names carry, the way they integrate a child or person into society, or the category they place an individual in.

Vernacular names may be difficult for outsiders to pronounce or even to spell. In such cases it will be much appreciated if a serious attempt is made to master a person's name. Asking the person to pronounce his or her name slowly and even coaching the outsider in its pronunciation will be much appreciated as it shows a real concern for something important to that person. Writing down the name for future reference and practice in pronunciation is also a good habit. A child of a Cameroonian acquaintance of mine named one of his children after me. I felt honored until I asked the father why he had chosen my name. He said because it was the most difficult name to pronounce that he knew. I never understood the thinking involved or if my friend had given me the true reason behind the naming.

Referring to individuals or groups as "Africans" is offensive in some areas. This comes from the perceived colonial history when Africa was called the Dark Continent and Africans were considered to be primitive or backward. It is much better to refer to people as Cameroonians or Kenyans, as the case may be, and so avoid any negative connotations. On the other hand, when the subject refers to regions or the whole continent (as is the case in this book), the general term "African" may be appropriate and unavoidable.

Social space

When you are eating with the devil use a long spoon.
Igbo proverb (Nigeria)[19]

Typically people live and work in close proximity to one another in Africa. In many occupations they prefer to work in groups. While Africans certainly can work alone, they seldom express the need to "be alone," the way that Westerners, including extroverts, sometimes talk. So expats living in an

---

[19]www.gambia.dk.

African context may feel they have little privacy and even wonder about Africans' sense or need of privacy. Many rural Africans typically live in small houses with many people sleeping in the same room. They seem to always be in close proximity to one another. Africans certainly have and value privacy, but privacy in Africa is very different from what it is in the West. The boundaries of African privacy are not defined by space, as in the West; but rather, boundaries are defined by rules of interactions with others. "African social life involves institutionalized restrictions on social contact between age and sex groups."[20] "Privacy" in African terms means freedom from unwanted interpersonal involvement—it does not mean being apart from other people in physical separation. Privacy can be thought of as being left alone in your space rather than being in a separate space. In fact, in many African cultures, going off to be alone is suspect behavior. Those who want to be alone are looked at as possibly dangerous, or even accused of being greedy, or of being witches.

Privacy includes limits on conversation, e.g., not bringing up subjects that are off limits in particular situations and between particular categories of people. The rules governing this kind of privacy may vary greatly from one African culture to another. They are often very formal and may involve avoidance patterns between individuals of certain relationships. They may include segregation by sex or age, and many other prescriptions and pro-scriptions that constrain people in the ways they interact. Westerners are of-ten surprised at the formalities that apply even within families. I once asked a young man how old his father was. He said he did not know and could not ask. His father had never told him and he was not allowed to inquire into such personal matters. One African man invited an expat to eat with him, complaining that he was tired of eating alone. He was surrounded by his family at meal times, but avoidance rules prohibited his wife or his children from eating with him.

Probably most surprising to Westerners are the seeming barriers to intimacy between individuals, even within a family. Unwritten rules that govern African behavior, even within families, would seem normal only in organizational or bureaucratic settings in the West. Such formal rules limit free and personalized behavior. There is little "sharing of innermost thoughts and feelings, the giving and taking of emotional support....It seems that intimacy in this sense, and the individualized relationships that accom-pany it, are of less importance to Africans than other goals of interpersonal relations."[21] The kind of intimacy in personal communications now so com-mon in the West was not always the norm. In many ways, this is a modern development, even in the West, and even now, is not found in all families.

---

[20]LeVine 1970:284.
[21]Ibid., 286.

Social distance

If you climb up a tree, you must climb down from the same tree.
African proverb[22]

Social distance and space can also be thought of as systems of communication even though we don't usually think of them in this way. On an individual level people sense the proper distance others should maintain with them. The "proper" distance is determined by the level of the relationship and also by culture. The distance in an intimate relationship is shorter than one that is formal, in all cultures. Likewise, for any degree of intimacy or formality, different cultures unconsciously set different distances that seem natural and comfortable for those who grew up in that culture. Edward Hall considers the use of space by humans to be a "hidden dimension."[23] He points out that humans' use of space can be better understood if thought of in terms of the distances typically maintained in different social settings: intimate, personal, social informal, social formal, public, and psychological. This discussion will not pursue the details Hall associates with each of these; suffice it here to alert the reader of the need to be sensitive to how space or distance is being used by Africans with whom he or she is interacting. Any sense of uneasiness that develops may stem from their different uses of space. For example, at a reception, if one party is backing away from the other, it may mean that they have different culturally determined senses of the proper distance that should be maintained in that circumstance.

Power distance

A man who pays respect to the great paves the way for his own greatness.
African proverb[24]

Another type of "distance" has been described, unrelated to the physical space between individuals. This is "power distance." It can be defined as "the extent to which the less powerful person in society accepts inequality in power and considers it normal."[25] Cultures can be placed on a continuum from high to low power distance, in effect evaluating the influence and sway that leaders and followers of a particular culture exert on one another. For foreigners living and working cross-culturally, the concept can help them focus their attention on those who may enable their project or work to succeed.

---

[22]www.worldofquotes.com.
[23]Hall 1966.
[24]www.allgreatquotes.com.
[25]Mani 2010:4–5.

Joseph Mani describes marked differences in how power is exercised in different cultures. In some cultures, those who hold the power and those who are affected by power are significantly far apart in many ways (high power distance), while in other cultures, the power holders and those affected by power holders are significantly closer (low power distance).[26] For expats working in a foreign culture, this raises questions such as: Is power distributed equally or unequally (whether by individuals or institutions)? Do individuals accept the exercise of power by leaders as normal, or do they resent it? Do superiors consider others to be different from themselves, or do they consider everyone to be intrinsically equal, leaders only occupying their positions under temporary or fortuitous conditions? Do leaders believe they are entitled to their positions? Etounga-Manguelle finds that in many African societies, people in subordinate positions accept their superiors as being different from themselves and having a right to privilege.[27] In other words, these are cultures of high power distance.

Individuals from high power distance cultures accept power as part of society and regard power and authority as facts of life. With low power distance cultures, laws, norms and everyday behaviors make the power distances as minimal as possible. To low power distance societies hierarchy is an inequality of roles established for convenience; subordinates consider superiors to be the same kind of people as they are and superiors consider their subordinates the same way.

The Kamba culture of Kenya, like many age-graded societies, exhibits a high power distance, especially in the relationship between the old and the young. Young members of the society must observe all protocol while addressing elder members of the society. Elders have power over the young; any elder from the society can punish any child or youthful member of the community found engaging in inappropriate behavior irrespective of whether he or she is the biological parent. In high power cultures leadership is normally limited to those who are accepted as leaders.

In high power distance societies people with special skills, such as leaders, warriors, wealthy individuals, or people with unique talents, are considered to have a right to privileges as a fact of life.[28] If a foreign development agent attempts to put someone from a "powerless" stratum into a leadership role in such a society, a successful outcome will be in doubt.

Robert Thornton reports that in South Africa respect and power occur in an inverse relationship. That is, when people who are in respected positions, such as priests or healers, become politicians or executives in a development project, they lose respect. "In general, then, respect is not accorded to those in power, nor is power accorded to those who are most

---

[26]Ibid., 5.
[27]Etounga-Manguelle 2009.
[28]Ibid., 5.

respected."[29] This seeming contradictory view of respect, where persons in higher positions are afforded less respect, is interpreted by Thornton as a reaction to jealousy, jealousy of the haves by the have-nots. He writes:

> The process of counteracting jealousy with diffusion of wealth and power generally means that respect and power are exchanged against one another. In other words, those with most respect often have little real power....Chiefs who are most respected are those who seek only to 'help' their communities.[30]

Respect in this context can be thought of as a kind of capital or disposable resource. When a respected person moves into a higher office, he in effect does so by "spending" his capital. In this culture if a person of wealth wants respect, he must distribute his wealth. Although this dynamic may be pronounced in South Africa, it does seem doubtful, however, that this generally results in a loss of respect.

Stratification

Everyone is a sheep to someone and a lion to another.
Wolof proverb[31]

Another way to look at power and influence in society is to consider how it is organized on social, economic, or kinship levels, that is, its stratification. This approach is concerned with the ways in which people perceive their relationships with classes of others, rather than those that are individual-to-individual. Three types of organization will be looked at briefly: authoritarian, individualistic, and collective.

The first type of organization is authoritarian. In parts of Africa, people believe that there are some individuals or families or kinship groups that are born to lead while others must follow. This is in some ways parallel to the discussion above, where this was called high power distance. In Europe and elsewhere this was distilled in the phrase "the divine right of kings." The Arabs cite a proverb that refers to the same concept, even if not quite so clearly: "The eye cannot rise above the eyebrow."[32] In these societies those from the ruling family or other elite stratum, are accepted, and even expected, to lead. This applies in political, religious, and military domains.

The second type of organization is individualistic. American society is generally referred to as individualistic. There, it is believed that all people

---

[29]Thornton 2005:25.
[30]Ibid.
[31]Sylla 1978:96.
[32]Samovar, Porter, and McDaniel 2007:157.

should have equal rights and equal opportunities. To hold an opposite view is to disregard the constitution, and some would say, violate the will of God and the dignity of fellow man. Probably few if any African societies could be identified as individualistic, at least not to a significant degree, although people are free, or even encouraged, to express themselves individualistically, such as the way they paint their houses, decorate their personal items, invent personalized victory calls, and so forth.

The third orientation to consider here is called collective. Probably a majority of African societies come under this heading. Some are very collective and even anti-individualistic. The Maasai of East Africa are so strongly collective that "attempts to get Maasai students to raise their hands and participate in formal classrooms are often futile."[33] Children, as well as their elders, do not want to be distinguished from their peers. Although men and women will decorate their jewelry or spears in individualistic ways, the group is more important to them than the individual. The family or other group entity heavily influences decisions regarding marriage, education, and occupation, among others. Children are trained to be sensitive to the larger context to which they belong beginning at a very young age. They are not supposed to eat by themselves, try to do projects by themselves, or make decisions for themselves. Besides Africa, many examples of collective cultures are found in China, India, Native America, Korea, and Latin America.

Like many other African cultures, the Kamba culture, mentioned previously, emphasizes the collective orientation. A striking example of collective behavior is cited by Joseph Mani: "When someone from the Kamba community killed a person, let's put it accidental in this case, he is not made to bear full responsibility for his act alone, his respective clan takes responsibility for the action and matters of compensation and apologizing to family members of the deceased."[34]

One common effect of rigid stratification is "where social rank was sharply defined, for the lowly farmer to be too ambitious or too successful was to risk punishment by social superiors for attempting to rise above his station and thereby to threaten more highly placed persons."[35]

The way the local society is organized—whether authoritarian, individualistic, or collective—will have profound effects on how Westerners should go about establishing rapport with local people, and with project planning and execution. Many specialized publications dealing with these issues are available. This discussion only touches on some of the considerations involved.

---

[33]Ibid., 158.
[34]Mani 2010:12.
[35]Pennington 1990:130.

Respect

The dignity of a man is without price.
Wolof proverb[36]

Respect is a critically important consideration across Africa. It is probably present, if just below the surface, in most interactions. This applies whether the interactions are personal, informal, or formal. It is the basis of all relationships. Because it is such a central consideration, foreigners living or working in Africa need to pay close attention to it. This is doubly true because respect is treated so differently in Western countries and in Africa. One result of this is that Westerners may be seen as acting disrespectfully without ever intending to.

A person who does not show respect will find it difficult, if not impossible, to build healthy relationships.

Respect is shown in many ways:

- The manner in which a person greets others.

- Using the appropriate names or titles that reflect the social rank of others, both in face-to-face interaction and in public reference.

- Being clean and respecting the personal space of others.

- Dressing appropriate to your social position, and to the social position of others.

- Showing deference to people of age.

- Appropriately showing or refraining from showing emotions.

- Following social conventions at time of illness and death.

Most of these items will be taken up in separate sections. In this introductory section, some generalities are described and some examples given in an attempt to show Westerners how important respect is, yet how difficult it often is to know how to show respect.

Many air travelers from America and Europe are accustomed to handling their own luggage at an airport. When they arrive in Africa local baggage handlers often irritate them. They often don't have local currency and if they do, they don't know the local fee. The handlers may insist on carrying luggage, to the further irritation of the traveler. Local baggage handlers depend on tips for much-needed cash, and the self-sufficient traveler may appear selfish or greedy by withholding pay from a porter, and doing a job which is theirs. Additionally, local baggage handlers think it beneath the status of the air traveler to carry his or her own luggage. Rather than

[36]Sylla 1978:91.

respecting the foreigner who can do his own work, they feel overlooked and disrespected. The observant traveler will do well to note the number of African travelers who (don't) carry their own bags.

Another way expatriates unintentionally show disrespect is when they talk about money matters that are completely beyond the possibilities of their African friends. They might mention how they expect to buy a certain vehicle, or a motorcycle, or the latest in electronic gadgets—any item that their friend could never consider for himself. Owning these things is not the issue. Being sensitive to the relative wealth or lack thereof is the issue. I have found that even mentioning a pending trip by air to someone for whom such travel is beyond his dreams, causes discomfort and shows a degree of disrespect, unless it is necessary to talk to that person about one's plans. Conspicuous consumption is also disrespectful of others. Most shoppers will cover the goods they buy, rather than let others see. They do not openly display valuables, but conceal them in their personal room. To place them where others can see them may be considered prideful, and tempting others to the point of jealousy. Since jealousy is considered as morally wrong as anger or bitterness, those who provoke others to jealousy by their behavior may be considered guilty of creating dissension, or "poisoning society."

A personal example illustrates the gap that may exist between Western and African expectations regarding respect. I hired a young man to key into the computer my research notes. The first day of work he addressed me with the title *Doctor*. I told him I preferred that he not use that title but could just use my name. Although he worked for me for over a year, he never again addressed me with *any* name or title. He always found a way to interact with me without using my name. Why? My conclusion was that he was unable to show me the respect I deserved and could not bring himself to treat me in a way that for him would have been disrespectful. Our difficult working relationship was, I believe, partially tied to the respect issue. As an employee he vacillated from being overly respectful to impudent, because he could not determine how to interact respectfully with me.

Sometimes a Westerner develops a personal friendship with an African colleague. The African may even suggest that they address each other by first names. They may joke and be very relaxed together in private. However, the Westerner needs to remember to show adequate respect when in public. When Africans observe familiarity shown by the Westerner, if they do not know of their personal relationship involved, they may well interpret it as a lack of respect. Even if they do know of their friendship, they may in any case consider the informality to be humiliating. This is especially true if the person involved is of high status or position.

Americans value informality as a way of showing humility, and so tend to be very informal in the way they use names, overlook titles, and behave in other areas of relationships. For instance, some American parents encourage their children to address them and other elders by their first names. Few American men would have any reservations about singing a duet with their daughter, playing on the same team as their son, or sharing food with their children. Many Africans may interpret this informality as a refusal on the part of children to show proper respect.

So for Westerners coming from a background of informal personal interactions, not only must they learn how to show respect, they must also learn to graciously receive and accept respect from others. Most Americans are uncomfortable when someone kneels in front of them when they greet them, or when they request something. But they do not realize that to deny others the ability to show due respect, is itself a kind of disrespect.

Following are examples of Westerners misunderstanding issues of respect. The domestic help (read maid) of a Western woman told her that as the employer she should not be in the kitchen, that doing the cooking was too difficult for her. The Western woman took this to mean that the domestic help considered her weak or not a good cook, and she reacted negatively. But the domestic help was only trying to show respect to her employer. She thought that cooking and kitchen work were beneath the dignity of the Western woman, that she should not be doing menial work, but office work or other "higher status" activity. The domestic help's implicit compliment was misunderstood, as the Westerner was not attuned to African issues of respect.

Another example is when the domestic help told a Western woman who had been out bike riding that she looked sweaty from the bike trip and didn't handle the heat very well. Again, the Westerner took this negatively, assuming that the comment was meant to imply that the Western woman was frail and inferior. The reality was quite the opposite. The comment was just a recognition that the Western woman was of status, and such women do not exert themselves physically, and should not expose themselves to conditions they are not used to. The domestic help was merely expressing respect.[37]

Sometimes the issue of respect appears in unexpected situations. Another domestic account is a case in point. Expatriates often hire domestic workers to do a variety of household tasks, including the laundry. Often there is no clothes dryer so clothes are hung outdoors on a clothesline, including underwear, and bras. In many African countries underwear is never hung where others may see it as this may be very offensive. In fact, in some African cultures men and children are responsible for washing their own underwear. Underwear is considered to be so personal that others should not handle it, above all if it is spotted with blood. The seriousness of this taboo

---

[37]T. Savage 1996:2–4.

becomes apparent where touching blood requires a sacrifice to the spirits to restore ritual purity.

Often the domestic help is male. If so, their tasks usually include doing the laundry, including underwear. They may go along with this in order to maintain employment, but it can be shameful for them. They may lose the respect of their peers if they become aware of it. In one instance where a man hung out underwear, he was treated with scorn. His friends said, "Not even women hang out underwear, but you do it. You are less than a woman." One way to determine if these customs and taboos apply to any locale is to observe the clothes that are put out to dry in the neighborhood, and see if underwear is ever shown in public.[38] People may not tell you directly about such sensitive subjects, so personal research may be more accurate than the answers people give you.

A final example illustrates an aspect of African ways of doing things which Westerners would never imagine could be a matter of "respect":

> The law of the Luo people states that sons must build their houses in order of seniority. That is, older sons must build before younger sons can build. This is justified by saying that this is a way of showing respect. The law is underpinned by magical powers, which will bring misfortune or a curse should it not be upheld.[39]

Robert Thornton writes of an interesting aspect of respect. Although he writes about South Africa, he states that it applies to Africa in general. All members of a community deserve to be respected, yet this is not derived from a liberal notion of "equality." Equality in the liberal or Western sense basically refers to "equality of access to the market, to rights, security and to justice."[40] African equality is better thought of as "equivalence," which represents the value that all members of the community are, in principle, equivalent as human beings and as brothers and sisters. In real life terms, this means to be at one with the community and not think that because of position or other attainment, one is better than another since ultimately all deserve (equivalent) respect, while some are worthy of special respect as long as it does not transgress equivalence. Such an attitude toward others is realistic and healthy in my estimation. It means that although special respect and deference are shown to those in positions of authority or prestige, Africans recognize that all humans are subject to the good and the bad, they have strengths and weaknesses—in a word, no matter who they are, they are just basically human.

---

[38]Haibucher 1999b:10.
[39]Harries 2000:495, citing Mboya 1938.
[40]Thornton 2005:25.

It is important to keep in mind that respect should be mutual or two-way. Respect must not only be given, but also received. For foreigners coming from egalitarian societies, this may require some adjustment of attitudes. Richard Dowden, with long experience in Africa at all levels of society, gives some pointers. These apply in business and in personal relations. He writes:

> I learned how to get by without causing offence. That meant, first,
>
> • Avoid confrontation. Tease, joke, cajole, don't demand or command.
>
> • Don't always seek a definite resolution of a problem; sometimes it is better to leave things unresolved.
>
> • Don't expect the truth and don't blurt it out. Hint at it, work round to it, leave it understood but unspoken.
>
> • Never, never get angry. Anger never works and loses you respect.
>
> • Above all be patient. Everything takes more time in Africa than elsewhere.
>
> Good-hearted outsiders, idealists who truly want to help Africa, often find themselves mysteriously impeded by Africa because, in their enthusiasm to get things done, they come across as rude or domineering.[41]

We have discussed respect as an overarching subject somewhat isolated from its social context. Actually, it is very difficult to adequately consider it in isolation. In many ways it is inseparable from social status, hierarchy, deference, authority, power, and more. Besides, each of these concepts is lived out in human interactions that are particular to each of the hundreds of African languages and cultures.

To underline the fact of great cultural differences across Africa, note how this one concept, respect, can be considered in such a different way from one African culture to another. Thornton describes respect in terms of suffering. (Suffering is a common subject in many African cultures, where it is thought to be essential to human development.)

> (Suffering) can be compared with the notion of achievement in liberal democratic politics. It elevates the sufferer to a status of respect in a community of suffering. Those who suffer most achieve respect, while those who manage to

---

[41]Dowden 2009:29–30.

transcend their suffering are held to possess special virtue or power *(amandla).*[42]

A very different attribute of respect is observed by Mani:

> When a young member of the community is addressing an old member of the community, respect is paramount, for it is believed that old people hold immeasurable power in their tongues and when not addressed as appropriately, or are addressed in a disrespectful manner, they can curse someone; people are afraid of curses, as they heighten the already high uncertainty avoidance.[43]

In fact, more than one African society uses the generic phrase "without respect" as a metaphor of bad character.

Respect for age

It is the duty of children to wait on elders, and not the elders on children.
Kenya proverb[44]

Open disagreement with someone who is elderly should be avoided. Any use of harsh words will be especially offensive. Communications and interactions are very sensitive to age and seniority in an organization. Even when a younger person is recognizably more able and competent than an older superior, the younger will still show deference to the older. This keeps the elder from publicly being shamed or losing face, which is a very important consideration. Job security may be jeopardized with open disagreement. Instead of resorting to open disagreement with a person of senior status, sensitivity and subtleties need to be used when expressing differences. Otherwise these may well be interpreted as personal attacks rather than constructive criticism. Prudent subordinate employees will find a tactful means to circumvent a "blockage" created by an incompetent or inattentive superior.[45] In extreme cases they will have to wait until the superior is no longer in his position. Of course these dynamics are not limited to Africa. Superiors are everywhere deferred to, but the consideration of age is much more salient in Africa than in the West.

---

[42]Thornton 2005:26.
[43]Mani 2010:4.
[44]www.allgreatquotes.com.
[45]Amoako-Agyei 2011.

Respect and children

When the child falls the mother weeps; when the mother falls the child laughs.
Rwandan proverb[46]

Better the problem that makes an infant cry than one that makes an adult cry.
Wolof proverb[47]

African children tend to be more quiet and submissive than their Western counterparts who happen to be in Africa. Children should always be polite and respectful in the presence of African adults. They need to be taught to greet guests and visitors in a polite and respectful manner. After greetings ordinarily they may leave. They should not ask questions of adults, but answer them when asked. "Forward" children will be considered disrespectful. Children should not bring out their toys for a guest to look at. Even if African guests bring children with them, the expatriate child should not display too many toys at once. If the African child is from an economically disadvantaged family, not knowing how to use certain toys, or the sheer number of toys may leave a child or their family feeling embarrassed.[48]

One common reaction of children to an accident or a mishap often seems jarring to expats. I have many times seen children in Africa laugh and jeer when one of their own tripped or was hurt. On one occasion I was driving a vehicle that had just been in an accident. The side of the vehicle was caved in although it was drivable. As I passed along several streets, children who saw the vehicle laughed derisively, pointing to the vehicle. This sort of behavior has been explained in these terms: "When a child falls down, other children may laugh. It's their way of reducing the fright associated with pain."[49] A Westerner is surprised at seeing laughter when he or she expects a more appropriate reaction would be one of some sympathy.

Here is another explanation of this behavior:

> (People) laugh because they are frightened by the situation. They panic and use laughter as a defence. Laughing is...a way for the brain and body to cope with situations. Humour reduces the intensity of a situation, and places a cushion of laughter between the person and the awkward emotions they feel....That is our defense mechanism.[50]

---

[46]www.allgreatquotes.com.
[47]Sylla 1978:117.
[48]Haibucher 1999a.
[49]Devine and Braganti 1995:18.
[50]Mohammed, Nadia. 2013. www.asmallvoicewithbigtoughts.blogspot.com.

A Westerner may be equally surprised to hear expressions of sympathy for what one considers normal events of life. It is not unusual in Kenya or Tanzania for people to say, "Pole" (meaning "Sorry") when someone trips or something breaks. This is not meant to express culpability or guilt, but simply to commiserate, acknowledging that one understands the unpleasantness the other has endured. One American couple related that while on home leave one of their daughters tripped and fell while playing with her friends. She sat on the ground, waiting until someone asked why she didn't get up. "Because no one has said 'Sorry,'" she replied, to which the other children quickly pointed out that they were not guilty. Names that signify that a preceding child died accomplish the same purpose. Ma'di women, from northern Uganda, claim that when someone hears a name like "Tears," "Termitarium (termite mound)," or "The Father is down," then they know you have suffered loss and can sympathize with your situation.

Public anger

Arguments between ants are settled underground.
Ibibio proverb (Nigeria)[51]

Anger shown in public or directed toward an individual is a serious issue in much of Africa, much more so than in the West. An example from my experience in a central African country points to the differences. It seemed to me that to local people sexual activity outside of marriage was not of great concern even to religious people there. For example, I was told that at the local Christian seminary, numerous women would be seen leaving the dormitory in early mornings, having spent the night with a seminarian. On the other hand I saw that displaying anger in public was taken very seriously, and when seen, would upset people. I asked a local person about this. He told me that local Christians were scandalized at the anger sometimes expressed by Christian missionaries. He said some local people even doubted whether these missionaries were Christians because they frequently were seen to be angry. Often the anger was "righteous indignation" directed at the sexual laxity they saw. American Christians rate sexual sins as especially bad, while local Christians were not nearly as concerned about them. On the other hand, Americans rated anger near the bottom of sinful acts, like a minor infraction, while for Africans, anger was seen as a serious moral fault, perhaps in part because it threatens interpersonal relationships. In terms of the teaching of the Bible, both anger and sexual immorality are sins. The Bible openly and clearly condemns them both, so it does not serve the missionary well to condemn the sins of other societies while minimizing the severity of their own.

---

[51]Clasberry 2010:115.

A friend tells of the experience of a Westerner who was riding a motor-cycle along a country road. When a man flagged him down, he stopped at the side of the road, thinking there was an urgent need. The man just asked him for money. In the meantime the motorcycle fell over and was dented. The combination of events made the Westerner angry and he expressed it in strong terms. Upon seeing the angry reaction, the African man showed real fear and said, "I'm sorry, please just go." To the Westerner the man over-reacted in a way that he didn't understand.[52]

So one could ask, "Why is anger so serious in many African cultures?" One reason is that for many Africans, being angry at someone is tantamount to cursing them, and a curse is feared. The fear is related to the action or re-venge that a spirit might inflict on the one cursed. A friend of mine told me of a great fear he had. His mother was old and wanted him to marry a woman he was not interested in. He feared that in her anger his mother would put a curse on him for not heeding her wishes. Then, if she died, there would be no way to have the curse lifted. Another example is a language group that has long declined in population. The people who speak this language told us that they attributed their decline to the actions of one of their chiefs a century ago. He was accused of some serious crime and the punishment was to bury him alive. As he was in the grave hole and his people were throwing dirt on him, he cursed them. They continued with the burial and consequently the one who instituted the curse was not available to have it lifted.

In modern culture "cursing" has been reduced to the use of bad language with no thought of its literal meaning of calling down malediction or mis-fortune from the gods. In many African societies curses are taken seriously and literally. People avoid expressing anger for fear that they will suffer the consequences, and they fear there will be consequences when others are angry. Assane Sylla writes that the Wolof individual "strongly believes that if a person commits an offense against the moral law or violates a taboo, inevitably a severe misfortune will fall on him, brought on by the village or family familiar spirit."[53] Maintaining peace with others is an essential part of the Wolof moral code. Anger and resentment are emotions that everyone knows are normal human reactions, but they must not be revealed openly, or at least the individual must express displeasure in some other way. In the West, by contrast, even those who are religious do not fear punishment in this life. Any punishment they are due will await them after death. John Mbiti, a recognized authority on African religion, states that in Africa

> the majority of African peoples believe that God punishes in this life. Thus, He is concerned with the moral life of mankind, and therefore upholds the moral law. With a few exceptions there is no belief that a person is punished in the hereafter

---

[52]Haibucher 1999b:45.
[53]Sylla 1978:156.

for what he does wrong in this life. When punishment comes, it comes in the present life.[54]

A number of African societies feel that pent up emotions can have negative effects on other people, a form of unintentional witchcraft. Directly voicing these emotions risks being interpreted as a curse, but they must be dissipated and released somehow. Instead of openly expressing anger, many societies dissipate anger, jealousy, displeasure, intense grief or bitterness through a number of permissible means. A person may act in an antisocial way, temporarily withdrawing from social norms. They may stage a drama in which they take on the persona of another, and through that masquerade express what they are unhappy about. Other people may sing lament songs, releasing their hard feelings. "Commentary names" which mention social tensions within extended families also give a person a legitimate venue through which to say things indirectly.

As a consequence of their beliefs about how anger can affect others, Africans may interpret verses like "Be angry but sin not," "Don't let the sun go down on your anger" or "Anyone who hates (is angry with) his brother has committed murder in his heart/mind" much more seriously than Americans. They are very concerned that their anger might harm others, while Americans assume that being angry will only affect the person who is angry psychologically.

Hierarchy

An important man may be wrong, but he is always right.
Bambara proverb (Mali)[55]

Across Africa, people are ranked according to different social criteria. The most basic ranking puts men at the top above women, with children below women. Each of these categories may be further divided. "Men" may be subdivided into men who are senior, men with children and those without, unmarried men, and so on. The scheme is broader than just humankind and includes both animate and inanimate components of creation. Most Africans believe in a High Creator God, and that it is He who has established the cosmic hierarchy, which is:

1. God
2. Man
3. Woman
4. Child
5. Animals, nature

---

[54]Mbiti 1989:205.
[55]Richmond and Gestrin 1998:143.

This list does not include ancestors and spirit beings such as angels and jinn, which most Africans believe are present and active in the world of humans. The consideration of such unseen beings and forces is outside the purview of this book.

Most African societies hold that placing people in hierarchies is not only proper and represents the way things should be, but is even cosmically ordained. This contrasts greatly with the Western ideal of equality of persons. Foster describes the importance of hierarchy from Kenya in the east to Senegal in the west:

> Secular life and ethic group membership...is rigidly stratified.... Individuals...play their roles—children, women, and men in relation to one another, hosts in relation to guests, religious leaders and other elders in relation to the community. Defining for others one's rank is important and status symbols (for example, the jewelry that women wear, the ritual scarification imposed by the ethnic group, the pattern used on the traditional robe and, most especially, the property that one owns, which is typically land or livestock) are traditionally important. It is critical that everyone show respect for elders and devout (religious) observers.[56]

Some of the differences between the ways Africa and the West deal with hierarchy are revealed in an experience of an African student:

> A Malian student attended Texas AandM University as an intern. He went on an extended field trip from College Station to far West Texas and New Mexico. The trip included a tour of Carlsbad Caverns, many large cattle ranches, vast cotton fields, countless oil wells with their derricks and pumpjacks, and lush irrigated farmland. At the end of the trip he was asked what impressed him most. He replied, 'I could never tell who was in charge of the trip.' So throughout the long trip, he was disoriented because everyone was treated as virtual equals. Authority structures were hidden, without outward deference shown to those in leadership positions. He was uncomfortable to the extent that the lack of deference shown to whoever was supposed to be the leader, stood out to him as the most memorable part of his trip (personal communication, 2012).

Three basic elements that manifest the hierarchy of human interactions are deference, respect, and precedence. Of course these elements are well known in the West. What makes them different in Africa is their required expression in settings that in the West would call for informal interactions.

[56]Foster 2002:115.

That is, there is generally more formality required in African social intercourse than with similar settings in the West. These three elements of prescribed behavior are defined as follows, according to Merriam-Webster.

> Deference: Proper respect and esteem due a superior or an elder or persons of particular positions or categories.
>
> Respect: A high or special regard.
>
> Precedence: The right to superior honor...on a formal occasion.[57]

Often these three elements exist together in ways that are difficult to separate. So, for example, showing respect may involve deferring to a superior in giving him precedence in a particular situation. A common expression of respect is refraining from open disagreement with a status-superior person, or with a person of advanced age. To openly disagree is a very serious breech of decorum. I found this out on one occasion when I had ordered panes of glass to close in a porch. The man who came to install the glass was a bit elderly, but not much older than I. He came with a stack of custom-cut panes and began to install them. They clearly did not fit, yet he continued to try, breaking one pane after another. The stack of panes was disappearing while the pile of shards was growing. I told him to stop. I don't recall my exact words. To me I maintained my cool, but told him it was useless to continue. Afterward several Africans, who had witnessed the scene, severely criticized me for my disrespectful behavior toward an elderly man. I asked them if I was supposed to let the man continue to break all the panes, or what? They told me that nothing mattered, compared with showing respect to a man of age. Upon reflection, I am sure I could have found, or at least tried to find, a face-saving pretext when telling the man to stop but in the exasperation of the moment I did not think to do so.

Ketil Hansen writes of a recent experience involving multiple facets of deference in Cameroon.[58] A local man returned for the first time from the capital where he recently had been named a government minister. A delegation received the minister and speeches followed. The delegation included the governor of the state in which the town is located, the prefect and sub-prefect ("county" heads), the city mayor and deputies, the traditional ruler of the area, the chief of the militarized police, the most important businessmen and cattle owners, and the wealthiest man in the area. All these important people went to the airport to receive the minister.

Certain aspects of this delegation and the ceremonies that followed illustrate deference and some general characteristics of African culture.

---

[57]*Merriam-Webster's 11th Collegiate Dictionary* 2003.
[58]Hansen 2003:204.

1. The governor, other regional officials, and the traditional ruler (lamido), arrived later than the announced time, thus indicating their high status. A general rule is, "the later one arrives for an appointment, the more people who await one's entrance, then the more excellent one must be."[59]

2. As it happened, the lamido was fortunate in the timing of his arrival. Had he actually arrived after the minister's plane, which happened to be late, it would have been seen as extremely impolite or worse—a refusal to acknowledge his importance.

3. The late arrival of the lamido created tension, as by the official hierarchy, the governor and other governmental officials outranked him. The lamido asserted his importance, and the others honored him in allowing his affront to pass.

4. When greeting the lamido, the governor took off his shoes and shook hands with both hands, while kneeling and looking into the eyes of the lamido. These actions communicated many signals. By taking off his shoes and kneeling, the mayor showed respect. But as no one should ever shake hands with a lamido, who was virtually "untouchable," the mayor signaled they were peers and both were modern men. That the lamido accepted a handshake showed the influence of the modern world. Yet by using both hands, the mayor showed extra respect.

5. The new minister arrived and was greeted by the dignitaries present, the entire event being filmed for national television. When he greeted the lamido he used both hands, thus honoring the lamido. The lamido accepted the handshake but put his hand on top of the minister's hands, showing himself to be a superior with fatherly concern.

In sum, the arrival of the minister was a small event, yet the participants took it seriously, giving much attention to the pomp and circumstance, and to many symbolic details. Expatriates would probably have missed most of the significant details, of how deference was shown and even contested in nuanced ways by the various actors in what could be called a drama. It would have been very difficult for an expat to navigate how he or she should have acted, and the symbolic meanings certain behaviors would have carried, whether or not they were even conscious of their existence.[60] A lesson provided by this episode is just how complex African social interactions can be and how difficult it is for outsiders to recognize, let alone understand, them.

---

[59]Dealy 1992.
[60]Hansen 2003:202–208.

Giving and receiving

Sharing brings a full stomach: selfishness brings hunger
Bekwel proverb, Congo-Brazzaville[61]

Giving and receiving material goods and services feature far more importantly in personal relationships with Africans than is the case in the West. LeVine even goes so far as to write, "Relationships are frequently characterized by Africans primarily in terms of the type of material transaction involved: who gives what to whom and under what conditions. Even premarital sexual liaisons and courtship are discussed in these terms." While Westerners define friendship largely in terms of mutual interests and emotional support, Africans "are frankly and directly concerned with the material transfer itself as indicative of the quality of the relationship."[62] I experienced this on a number of occasions. For example, over a period of a couple of years I was able to funnel funds from an international aid organization to a small project an African friend had established. The man frequently "hung out" at my house. He said people were constantly coming to his house to ask for money and assistance while it was peaceful at my place. When I no longer had access to funds, he stopped coming to the house and had no further dealings with me. I had thought we were friends, but it turned out that to him material interest was inseparable from friendship. No issue had developed between us, but without monetary implications the friendship was no longer a priority in his busy life. I do not believe he consciously ditched me; rather, the lack of material involvement took me off his list of current contacts.

The Zambian scholar Mwizenge Tembo takes strong issue with LeVine's description of the African personality. He places LeVine among those who attack

> the African past as retrogressive and reactionary. This school of thought does not entertain at length any questions about why Africans behave and think as they do. Implicitly, this school of thought emphasizes Westernization as the "solution" to Africa's lag in electronic technology without recognizing Africa's superiority in spiritual and cultural sectors.... He (LeVine) states that evidence indicates that the African society is distinguishable from societies elsewhere.[63]

Tembo continues his criticisms, writing that LeVine provides "at best, highly subjective value judgments of the African society." The criticisms seem more emotional than factual. For instance, he says that LeVine's

---

[61]Phillips 1999:2–4.
[62]LeVine 1970:288.
[63]Tembo 1990:196.

description of African society, emphasizing material transactions as it does, cannot be true. Africans are too poor for this to be so. "How many material goods do Africans have which could generate a reliance on their exchange? A few cattle, a couple of chickens, several goats perhaps."[64] But having few possessions does not in any way rule out their being important to the people involved. Tembo's critique does not deny the validity of LeVine's descriptions, but he insists that these should be understood in their African context, suggesting that anyone in similar circumstances acts the same way.

Africans who visit other people, or call on an official or important figure for help almost always take a gift of some sort with them. This should never be interpreted as a bribe, but as an acknowledgement of the status of the person on whom they are calling. The quality, substance and amount of the gift carry a great deal of importance. Even when invited to a friendly call or meal, it is not unusual for an African visitor to bring a small gift, such as tea, sugar, fruit, some delicacy, or a highly valued artifact. In return, the host will quite often send the visitor back with a gift, such as a hen, or even the leftover roast meat.[65]

Diffuse roles

Wisdom is like a baobab tree; no one person can encompass it.
Ghanaian proverb[66]

In the West the exercise of an occupation is usually restricted to one function: a buyer buys, an employer employs, a teacher teaches, with little professional involvement outside their field of specialization. In much of Africa, both traditional and modern, occupations are not so concentrated in separate roles or specializations. Sellers enter into personalized relationships with buyers (for example, charging loyal customers a higher price, so that business overlaps with charity), employers are expected to provide for employees' personal needs, and teachers often expect personal services from pupils and students. "In schools all over English-speaking Africa, primary and secondary school pupils are pressed into service by the teachers as domestic servants in their houses and seasonal laborers in their fields and gardens."[67]

An egregious example is the following: "When Nigeria's education minister faced an audience of 1,000 schoolchildren, she expected to hear complaints of crowded classrooms and lack of equipment. Instead, girl after girl

---

[64]Ibid.
[65]Personal communication, May 8, 2014.
[66]www.afritorial.com
[67]Tembo 1990:297.

spoke up about being pressured for sex by teachers in exchange for better grades. One girl was just 11 years old" (personal communication, 2013).

Another example involves a teacher who made demands of his pupils that are far beyond anything related to the classroom and learning. A South African reports on the demands of one of his teachers with a surprising outcome. He had a teacher who required his senior students to wash his car every Friday during break.

> In the process we had to remove the wheels to clean the inside of the mudguards and the backs of the wheels. One Friday we left his car with bricks under the rear axle just high enough that they almost touched the ground. We ran for the gates and hid in a nearby ditch to observe the fun. He started his car, engaged a gear...and nothing happened!...He tried again and again...[68]

The above examples may seem to single out teachers, but only because they were the ones at hand. However, in other dyadic relationships laden with power, such as employer-employee, and religious leader–follower, actors have diffuse roles, so that the employees and followers become much more than nine-to-five workers or purely religious disciples. This ties in with patron-client relationships, discussed in chapter 2. An employer may be held responsible for the moral conduct of his employees. One missionary in northern Uganda hired a man to serve as a night guard, and as part of his pay, helped send his wife to school. The missionary observed a woman leaving the compound early in the morning, but when he asked the guard, was told that she was a relative who was bringing him breakfast, so he did not investigate it further. But church elders alerted him the guard was sleeping with a woman he was not married to, and that his own reputation was being sullied because he was ostensibly allowing it. When the wife came back from school and heard the gossip, she confronted the missionary, accused him of being an immoral person, and demanded to know why he would have allowed her husband to sleep around while working for him (personal communication, 2014).

Blame

One who blows on the fire swallows the smoke.
Ibibio proverb (Nigeria)[69]

When misfortune overtakes individuals, typically they search for causes outside themselves rather than examining their own behavior. This applies

---

[68]Personal communication, May 31, 2013.
[69]Clasberry 2010:179.

to modern urbanites as well as to those living in traditional, rural areas. In general, people do not readily accept that their own actions or decisions might have led to unfavorable outcomes. Nor do they readily accept that impersonal natural randomness might have been the cause of illness, accidents, mischance, personal setbacks, and failures. Every significant event, positive or negative, is believed to have a cause that originates in the spirit world, which is acting in the visible world. Instead of following what Westerners consider a rational analysis, traditional Africans typically assume that most such events have a personal origin, and thus follow a different path to find answers: First, such adverse events are assumed to originate with unseen (spirit) forces, or personal metaphysical powers rather than from "natural," empirical causes. Second, other people are accused of provoking or instigating these malevolent forces to act against the individual.[70] Humans do this by engaging sorcerers, who they believe have the knowledge and power to entice malevolent spirits to act according to their wishes. Consequently, they try to ascertain who caused a problem, whether by contravening a taboo, or hiring a sorcerer.

"Bad luck" or "randomness" are often used to explain adverse events in the "scientific" West. These do not provide convincing explanations to traditional or animistic peoples. So, for example, in answering the question of why my child was killed by a falling tree while your child sitting next to him was unhurt, "bad luck" or "randomness" are not sufficient explanations. In Western, scientific societies, people accept that one child happened to be killed, while the other happened not to. The tree just "happened" to fall a certain way.

Blame for misfortune, failure, and non-success is placed on some exterior source. So, for example, if there is a serious accident, the individual typically will not be blamed, nor will he or she feel blame. Rather, the blame will be sought for in the invisible world, outside the person who suffered the accident. This accident will be believed to be caused directly by a spirit but indirectly by one of the person's enemies who has secretly engaged the services of a sorcerer. Hence, the blame is "exteriorized." The individual tends not to look at himself or herself to see what they may have done wrongly or unwisely. Neither will they accept that impersonal causes were to blame.

This raises the question of reconciling two seemingly contradictory belief systems. Under the heading "Public anger" above, I stated that Africans believe that punishment for violating the moral law is meted out by God in this life, not in the afterlife. In other words, punishment comes as a result of people's own actions. Here, we are saying that when Africans experience misfortune, they look outside themselves and blame it on the nefarious work of spirit beings and forces. So which is it? John Mbiti, whom I have already cited, addresses this very contradiction:

---

[70]LeVine 1970:292.

Misfortunes may be interpreted as indicating that the sufferer has broken some moral or ritual conduct against God, the spirits, the elders or other members of his society. This does not contradict the belief that misfortunes are the work of some members, especially the workers of magic, sorcery and witchcraft, against their fellow men. This village logic is quite normal in African thinking. I do not understand it, but I accept it.[71]

Separation anxiety

Tomorrow belongs to the people who prepare for it today.
African proverb[72]

Robert LeVine writes that there are two expressions of personal behavior that are central to understanding differences between Westerners and Africans. One is the Westerners' "desire for intimacy in social relationships, and the relative absence of this desire among Africans." The second is the Westerners' anxiety over physical separation from loved ones. The concerns over such separations manifest themselves in many ways in Western culture. "These tendencies are widespread in Western populations and are exalted in a variety of cultural forms ranging from sentimental literature and films to humanitarian ideologies with their concern about those who are rejected and abandoned."[73] In recent decades such concerns have been extended to animals, and people spend a huge amount of their resources and emotions to their care and protection.

Many of these patterns of behavior seem to be absent among Africans. They appear to find physical separation from loved ones emotionally less upsetting. Sentimental attachments and their residues in longing, weeping, and nostalgia are not conspicuous in African communities. The reaction of Africans to the pet-keeping practices (in the West) is usually one of astonishment.[74]

Tembo observes that African couples and families are often separated for long periods. This happens frequently when the studies of a family member last for years during which time they rarely return home. Tembo writes that this should not be interpreted as due to a lack of love for, or a desire to be with family, but from financial necessity. If there seems to be less "weeping" when a person leaves, or while they are gone, this is most likely because emotions are expressed differently in Africa than in the West.

[71]Mbiti 1989:205.
[72]www.worldofquotes.com,
[73]LeVine 1970:294.
[74]Ibid., 294–295.

Competition

Everyone had better pay attention to his or her peer.
Wolof proverb (Senegal)[75]

African society has many very competitive relationships. There is much competition for scarce resources and the greater the scarcity, the greater the competition. Examples are:

- Co-wives competing for the favor of their husband, to the extent that in at least one language, the word "co-wife" has the equal meaning of "competition."

- Mothers seeking advantages for their children, to get them ahead of the children of co-wives.

- Brothers and cousins competing for the inheritance of property.

- Neighbors competing over land boundaries and blaming each other for damage caused to crops by animals or children.

- Co-workers competing for advancement in plant or office.

- Students competing for very limited academic or employment openings.

- Suitors and their families competing for the most desirous mates by offering greater bride-wealth in the bidding process.

- Verbal dueling, which is part of the competition in language use present in many African cultures.

Many jealousies and hatreds accompany these competitions. Authorities at every level, from the clan to the state, expend a lot of time and effort settling disputes that come to their attention, on the levels of family, lineage, compound, quarter, or at various levels in the modern judicial system, or within the traditional Muslim legal system in some areas. A number of African peoples consider jealousy to be the most corrosive or destructive emotion, or the worst sin, for it divides people who should otherwise form a unified block. Dissension is in many places equated with destruction, and spoken about through the metaphor of poison.

Yet in spite of these competitive pressures and the emotions they create, society decrees that people must maintain peaceful and amicable relations with those around them. This provides for the preservation of order in face-to-face societies where people live in intimate contact. This order also helps

---

[75]Shawyer 2009.

a family or clan present itself as a unified front in the eventuality of attack by another clan or family. If animosity was allowed to be openly manifested it would be very disruptive, if not destructive. Of course there is animosity between members of the same clan or family, even if it is hidden. And people believe they have enemies, including competitors, and that these will secretly take measures to gain an advantage over them.

On an individual level, people seek defense and protection from competitors and enemies and their secret attacks. (People do not admit that they themselves initiate attacks on their enemies, of course.) Such defenses do not identify the perpetrators of harm. Identification is seldom possible and even then of little use. Emphasis is placed on having a good defense and viewing most anyone as a possible enemy or perpetrator. The most common defenses are amulets or talismans (gris-gris, jujus, etc.) that are worn on the bodies of individuals and animals, hung in houses and fruit trees, and placed in garden plots. Most people use these defenses, whether traditionalist, Christian, or Muslim. Only Christians of very strong faith in God refrain from these practices. Muslim clerics preach against the use of black magic, but it is well known that their admonitions are largely disregarded. It is common knowledge in Muslim society that leaders resort to such practices.

This does not imply that people remain passive to assumed attacks. There are many "ritual practitioners," to use a euphemistic label. These include shamans, sorcerers, diviners, mediums, and magicians. These ritual specialists are engaged for offensive as well as defensive purposes. In one predominantly Muslim country, serious attempts to estimate the number of ritual practitioners determined that there was approximately one for every 150 people. This was in addition to non-Muslim practitioners in the population. So in total, several thousand individuals actively performed protective, defensive or offensive magic on behalf of clients.[76] Obviously many customers are required to support such a large number.

Appreciation

Don't praise the legs more than the thighs.
Ibibio proverb (Nigeria)[77]

Africans appreciate receiving expressions of gratitude, as would any people. But expressions of compliments or appreciation are not always easy to recognize or interpret. Different cultures have their own rules or ways of expressing such sentiments. The proper way of expressing them may well contrast widely with customs in the West. In some African cultures compliments and words of praise are only given among close friends. In such

---

[76]Maranz 1993:191.
[77]Clasberry 2010:92.

cultures there is fear of arousing jealousies or a backlash of the evil eye, if the one at the receiving end of the kind words does not have confidence in the one expressing them. The Botswana appreciate compliments; they mark the giver as "respectful and gracious, two qualities most appreciated."[78] But it may be prudent to carefully avoid specifically mentioning what they did, lest others observing the accolade become jealous.

In many African cultures the proper way of showing gratitude is similar to the following example: The way to thank a person is not to give profuse thanks after a favor, but some time later to recount the favor(s) done to a third party in the presence of the one who did the favor. And if someone does that to you, listen quietly, and try to find a way to return the compliment. My interpretation of this way of showing appreciation is especially significant in that it shows the favor is remembered, and acknowledges it in front of peers. This shows more appreciation than does paying someone for their services, after which the favor is forgotten.[79] Implicit in this example is the time factor. Appreciation is best shown some time after receiving a compliment or other circumstance. Returning a favor immediately risks creating a distance between the receiver and the giver. It may be interpreted as a sign that the recipient does not want to maintain the relationship, which is implied in giving and receiving these tokens of friendship over time.

Perhaps even more surprising is the custom of giving a compliment in the form of a request, or even a demand for something, such as saying, "I like your shoes, give me a pair." This can be very off-putting for a Westerner who does not understand this way of giving compliments. He or she takes offense, thinking the person is truly asking that they be given the item in question. A common request is for the shirt or blouse someone is wearing. In such cases, the request should be taken lightly as an indirect compliment (unless of course the recipient immediately takes off his shirt and hands it to the giver—imagine the surprise if this happened!).

Sometimes a request is not a compliment but a literal request for something. Should a child ask for the pen in your pocket, it is not a compliment but a literal request. Determining whether a request is a compliment or a request sometimes can be difficult. In any case, requests should best be treated as Africans do: as part of social interactions, sometimes involving one-upmanship, and often including the art of verbal dueling. They don't get uptight about such things, and neither should the expatriate.

---

[78]Devine and Braganti 1995:18.
[79]Escher 1998.

Generosity

If giving away were to bring us to poverty,
one who shaves would never get his hair back.
Wolof proverb (Senegal)[80]

Generosity is a very important virtue in Africa. A good person is generous. A stingy person is not respected. A foreigner in Africa who wants to be "good" must find answers to two questions: How in practical terms can I be generous? and, How can I be so in ways that are helpful? Too often Westerners, including Western governments and aid agencies, give to individuals or organizations in ways that are detrimental in the long run.[81] The situations addressed below relate to generosity and giving on an individual's level. No attempt is made here to address generosity from the standpoint of an organization or a government.

Asking

Food not liked is still eaten when hungry.
Ibibio proverb (Nigeria)[82]

In Western cultures people do not ordinarily ask for things or for financial assistance from other individuals (asking for assistance from government is a different matter). By contrast, in many African cultures there is no taboo against asking family and friends for whatever may be needed. I have many times been asked for money, my shirt, even my pickup truck. Once someone even asked me for my teenage daughter (and he was serious)! It would probably be rare to find an expat who has spent any time in Africa who has not been asked for money or other things many times. An American tourist who had scarcely arrived in a particular country was so disturbed by this that he asked, "What about all this asking for things and money? I've only been here a few hours and I'm ready to get on the next plane for home."

Expats are uncomfortable and probably annoyed when people ask for money or other things. They normally have several reactions. First, they are unaccustomed to such requests and feel put on the spot. They are in a new situation, have no experience with such demands, and feel pressured to respond immediately. Sometimes the asker is aggressive and insistent, which makes the expat even more uncomfortable.

In the context of generosity, the focus of this section, the expat probably wants to be generous. In such a face-to-face situation, the "asker" presents a challenge. The Westerner is used to giving on his or her own terms. Here,

---

[80]Shawyer 2009:40.
[81]See Corbett and Fikkert 2009, and Schwarz 2007.
[82]Clasberry 2010:106.

the asker wants to set the terms. A major concern is knowing whether or not the asker has a real need or is a con artist. (For example, is the woman along the street with several infants, just "renting" them for the day, which is a common practice? But even when this is the case, there is obvious need, along with a strategy to elicit added sympathy.) Giving small sums to a beggar or person obviously afflicted with leprosy seems reasonable. But if there are many people lined up for a handout, the situation becomes difficult for the clueless newcomer. He or she needs to quickly learn the basic rules of how, when, and to whom to give. First, a Westerner may not realize that mendicants, or beggars, are not necessarily looked down on by society, and may not be in as severe need as they might seem. In some cultures begging is a craft that is often highly ritualized and well developed, intending to play on people's sympathies, or even their sense of humor. Thus, people may have their beggar "clients," just as they develop a patron-client relationship with a vender. They give exclusively to this one mendicant, thus proving themselves to be generous, but ignore the others. They are also careful not to give too much. It is expected that if many people give small amounts to the needy, together they can all help the poor. This stands in contrast to Western systems, where a person, operating individualistically, feels they need to give enough to make a difference on their own. One of the surprising "rules" is to not expect an expression of gratitude for a donation. Muslims believe that if a beggar expresses thanks, it deprives the giver of a reward in the hereafter, as he or she has then already received the reward.

The basic rules in any area are easy to learn so that they need not be a long-term problem. Local people are ready and able to provide advice in this as well as with other areas of understanding the culture. This whole issue is taken up in detail in chapter 3, "Friendship." And as is described there, a key approach to the overall problem of generosity and giving is to find a respected local person to advise you. Advice should be sought for the different circumstances where generosity may be called for, whether dealing with street beggars, casual acquaintances, or friends of equivalent social standing. Local citizens often know certain beggars by name, and know their reputations. They are also careful to ferret out the family histories of people who ask for help, to determine whether there is a genuine need, or whether the person may need to repent of deeds, which have caused their family to isolate them for a time.

Giving gifts

Honor is food.
Yoruba proverb (Nigeria)[83]

Expats often travel to villages. Here the rules for respectful and generous behavior are quite different from those in urban settings. Expats have opportunities to be generous on their own terms as people are less likely to just ask for things. At least this is my experience. Village people often live on the margins of existence so that simple gifts will be greatly appreciated. These would include small amounts of sugar, salt, tea, powdered milk, and other staples, depending on the local diet. In some areas kola nuts are a standard gift that are very well received. However, one needs to be careful in how these gifts are given. One couple handed their hostess a half-kilo of sugar. When her husband heard of it, he was so humiliated that he beat his wife. In his mind the unsolicited gift implied that the visitors did not think his household was capable of properly hosting guests. After seeking advice, the couple would quietly pass a small paper bag with tea, sugar, rice, etc. to a small child and tell them to take it to the kitchen (personal communication, 2014).

Unsolicited "services"

Dust on the feet is better than dust on the behind (from sitting).
Wolof proverb (Senegal)[84]

A common experience in cities is encountering young men offering a "service" for which they expect to be paid, but which the expat invariably does not want. Services include washing and/or guarding your vehicle, cleaning your windshield, carrying your groceries or other bulky items, shining your shoes, and opening your car door, among others. A slightly different situation is when street vendors insist on selling you something. Mostly, these "services" indicate a lack of regular employment and a consequent desperation for finding a means of existence, though it may approach "extortion," as in a guard who threatens to damage a vehicle if he is not paid. Life for the expat is made easier if such "services" are anticipated and the small amounts of local currency usually required are readily at hand so that making change is not an issue. Sometimes the same guard or grocery carrier is always available at a particular locale and a kind of relationship can develop, giving a sense of acquaintanceship rather than mere annoyance.

---

[83]www.gambia.dk.
[84]Shawyer 2009:11.

Sometimes certain services are a way through which poorly paid employees can supplement their income. An administrator demanded that an office courier wash the office vehicles when there was little to do, rather than waiting around. The courier argued that this was not his job, but this made little sense to the American office manager, who did not understand the implications of assigning a menial job to an employee of higher status. Neither did the American understand how employment roles are specialized and multi-tasking by employees is little known and resisted. The courier felt such deep guilt over taking money away from the guard, that he paid the guard to wash the vehicle from his own pocket (personal communication, 2014)!

Men vs. women

With wealth, one wins a woman.
Ugandan proverb[85]

The literature related to African women and expatriate women in Africa, and similar topics, is huge. To begin to do it justice would warrant a separate volume. A very short list of relevant titles could include the following: Arnoldi and Kreamer 1995; Barber 1997; Cummings 1991; McNee 2000; Mikell 1997. The purpose here is to provide a short, introductory discussion of a few helpful points that are relevant to Western women living or working in Africa.

When expats, whether anthropologists or other inquirers of culture, explore local customary life, they are often told by men that African women are unreliable in providing cultural information, except in topics that are specifically part of women's domains. African men think that women are ill informed because they are absent from the discussions of those in positions of authority, or have not been through male initiation rites. Therefore they must be ignorant of the important inner workings of society. To some degree this masculine bias is understandable. Most African societies are patrilocal. There, when women marry they go to live in their husband's compound, surrounded by his male relatives and their wives, to whom the in-marrying woman is not usually related. Although women may be alert to the way their own natal family functioned, they are not accustomed to explain, and may not be immediately conversant, in the way their husband's family works. However, Nigel Barley found women to be helpful, accurate sources of cultural information for at least two reasons.

> Whereas men regarded themselves as the repositories of the ultimate secrets of the universe and had to be cajoled into sharing them with me, women knew that any information

---

[85]Richmond and Gestrin 1998:49.

available to them was unimportant and could quite happily be repeated to an outsider. They often opened up new fields of enquiry for me by alluding in passing to some belief or ceremony I had never heard of, that the men would have been reluctant to mention.[86]

De Jong also found that women even had detailed knowledge of men's affairs. Even though many men believed that spirits would punish society if women learned about ritual secrets, women were frequently able to provide him with details of men's secret societies.[87] And of course when it comes to the affairs of women, men have little knowledge or interest, so women researchers have a great advantage when researching women's and family affairs.

Some expat women working in Africa have found it to be a man's world. When they occupy positions of authority, it is common for some African men to resent them. In such cases it is prudent for a woman to not insist that men respect her rights, authority, or equality, if she wants to build productive relationships. One Western woman describes her experience:

> Working in the accounting office I had a man working under me. I was in a way his boss, supervising some of his work.... He always treated me as if he was my superior....After learning about the social hierarchy (God above man, then in descending order: women, children, animals, and nature) I found a strategy to use when needing men to do something for me. I would say to this man: 'My husband sent me, would you do this or that for me?' This seemed to have a soothing effect and the task would be done very effectively.[88]

Not all Western women have the humility to put smooth relations above what they perceive of as their rights. This example from real life shows that it is more productive to value the project's success rather than trying to change African culture.

Mani points out to what extent Africa, or at least the Kamba region of East Africa, is a man's world. Male dominance is demonstrated even in the way men are served food. At mealtime the best portions of meat are reserved for them. This dominance is also shown in decision-making, where women are thought to be incapable of making important decisions. Decisions which affect the family are the prerogative of men to make. Mani concludes that these patterns of subordination of one gender promotes inequality across the society.[89]

---

[86]Barley 1983:76.
[87]De Jong 2007.
[88] Haibucher 1999a.
[89] Mani 2010.

Westerners may look at traditional male dominance as predominantly negative. They should not do so. In many ways, traditional African women have a great degree of freedom. Beyond performing their required duties with husband and children, they are at liberty to carry on business and other activities outside the home. Many sell products from their gardens in local markets. More and more, development agencies recognize the dynamism and management skills of women. Micro loans to women are part of many successful programs. "In some countries women dominate the markets and the retail trade, and some have become quite wealthy. Those who drive Mercedes-Benz cars are often referred to as 'Mama-Benz.'"[90] On many flights to and from Africa I have traveled with African businesswomen, who are profitably engaged in international trade. Traditional Africa may be a man's world at home, but that is far from being the whole story.

---

[90] Richmond and Gestrin 1998:43.

2

Everyday Africa

Introduction

The best medicine for a person is another person.
Wolof proverb[1]

Africans are social. It would be hard to overemphasize this fact. They believe and practice *inter*dependence, and strongly dislike acting independently. Interdependence means depending on others, being in relationship with wide webs of kinship and friendship. In many African languages there are proverbs which emphasize the importance—even the centrality to life—of relationships with fellow humans. In South Africa the Zulu say, *Umuntu ngumuntu ngabantu.* This means that only through others can a person become complete. Humans cannot live fully except through interacting with their fellows.

At the other extreme of Africa, the Wolof of Senegal express the identical concept: *Nit, nit-ay garabam,* "Man has no other remedy but man." Another Wolof proverb expresses a similar belief, *Ku am nit ñi ñakkoo dara*, "He who has friends lacks nothing."[2]

Theologian David Bosch comments on this philosophy of man as follows:

> There is profound wisdom in [these] proverbs. By participating in the other man's humanity we are both shaped and led to maturity. This is preeminently true of the black man in Africa. For example, I have often noticed that, after a [church] service, the black Christians do not at all appear eager to return to their homes. They linger awhile, almost as though they are unsatisfied, as though they are waiting for more or for something else. The religious service with

---

[1]Shawyer 2009:78.
[2]Sylla 1978:107–108.

43

its emphasis on preaching and one-way communication has not been enough. There still remains the desire to share, to experience fellowship, to reach out to one another.[3]

The topics presented in this chapter at their core involve personal relationships. African everyday customs are centered on people. Western culture could be described as centered on things and technology much more than is the case in Africa. Even the new phenomenon of social media uses "things" as a means to interact with friends and business associates. Instead of direct human-to-human contact, technology acts as a buffer, minimizing the normal give-and-take of personal interaction. In contrast, African societies developed human relationships to an amazing complexity. Although this discussion will not elaborate on the topics, African societies were and are complex in countless ways: involving clans, polygyny, totems, taboos, relations with ancestors, gods and spirits, society in hierarchies, secret societies, and castes in many ethnic groups—the list could be expanded almost ad infinitum. Of course, modern Africans use and rely on technology and machines, for example, in transportation, and more recently in the wide use of cell phones. Still, a case can be made that "technology" has been less important in Africa than in the West, while people and their relationships have been, and still are, of utmost importance.

The Senegalese philosopher Assan Sylla describes the Wolof ethic of life as centered on well-being and living well (*bien vivre*), social peace, and a good religious conscience. It is founded on the dignity of humans, establishing institutions that "assure that its members are more and more interdependent (*solidaire*), horizontally with the living, and vertically with ancestors and descendants." This ethic, and the values it encompasses, is certainly representative of societies across Africa.[4]

Friendliness

There is no one-way friendship
Maasai proverb, Kenya[5]

I have felt welcome wherever I have traveled in Africa. I do remember an exception or two, when I happened upon men illegally engaged in cutting down a forest or other nefarious behavior. After having lived and worked in countries where a North American was not always well received, for example, where people threw rocks at those they did not want to have around, or being stopped by very unpleasant and threatening police, it was most reassuring to feel almost universally welcome.

It is a common sight while driving along rural roads in Africa, to have adults and children wave while looking up from their endeavors, their gaze following your vehicle as it passes. I often wondered what was in their

---

[3]Bosch 2001:96.
[4]Sylla 1978:164.
[5]Bryan 1999.

minds as they did this: Was it friendliness, or curiosity, or wonder at the spectacle, as common as it might be? I always attempted to wave back, but always felt a little hypocritical, knowing that nothing could come of this "friendship."

Nigel Barley, in his perceptive personal chronicle as a foreigner in Africa, describes the reaction of countless visitors:

> It came as a great surprise to me after the officials with whom I had to deal, how friendly and pleasant people were; I had by no means expected this. After the political resentments of West Indians and Indians I had known in England, it struck me as ridiculous that it should be in Africa that people of different races should be able to meet on easy, uncomplicated terms....As an Englishman I was perhaps unreasonably impressed by the fact that complete strangers would greet me and smile at me in the street, apparently without ulterior motive.[6]

For unaccompanied women when out alone, whether in town or traveling, the "friendliness" of some men may be less than sincere. In such circumstances, they may find themselves subject to unwanted attention. Several steps can be taken to minimize the problem. Wearing a ring or wedding band can help. It can be an inexpensive one purchased for just such occasions. If a man asks a single woman about her husband, she can reply that he is traveling or make up an evasive reply, if she would be bothered by telling a fib. If asked if she has a boyfriend, a reply that she already has several husbands and could not deal with another, may well defuse the question with humor. If traveling alone, a woman can search out another woman to travel with or sit next to. She might offer to help look after the children or the baggage of a fellow woman traveler. This can give the appearance of being connected, and not alone. Seeking the advice of respected local women when facing any place, area, or person of doubt, is highly recommended.[7]

Elite society

He who thinks he is leading and has no one following him
is only taking a walk.
Malawian proverb[8]

One commonality found across Africa is the presence of elite society. This is constituted by individuals who have means (political and/or financial),

---

[6]Barley 1984:21–22.
[7]Haibucher 1999a.
[8]www.afritorial.com.

position, and shared values, who are separated from the masses in significant ways. Together they exercise controlling power in their respective countries. Elites are people who have been successful, in whatever realm. Status symbols of the elite include pretentious houses and vehicles, jewelry, the type of cloth and the amount of embroidery on the clothing of both men and women. They often give the impression of pretentiousness. They comprise high society, often live ostentatiously, travel internationally, and congregate together in nightclubs and other venues that common folk cannot afford. Their power is often described as advancing personal interests rather than those that benefit national interests. They do have a positive influence in that elites from different ethnic groups socialize together, often marrying across linguistic and "tribal" boundaries. Yet in spite of their often-humble village origins, "many African elites in government and elsewhere continue to trivialize the indigenous cultures that gave them birth and consider them retrogressive and irrelevant in today's world."[9]

Certainly elite society is, and historically has been, a common feature of cultures almost everywhere. Royalty was not limited to Europe: African kingdoms had their own elite families or clans. The super-rich, celebrities, and sports stars in Western societies are "elites," with some of the same characteristics as elites in Africa but also with fundamental differences in their roles in society. The reason for focusing on them in the context of Africa is that they have preponderant influence and power in many countries. Their position in African society is more akin to that of royalty in pre-democratic times, whereas elites in the West exercise influence more indirectly. This is done through expressing opinions publicly, financing political action and lobbying, supporting particular candidates for office, and other such indirect activities. Western elites also tend to hold their positions relatively short-term. Politicians come and go, and even rise from "nowhere." Titans of business disappear after retirement. Celebrities pass like comets. In contrast, African elites tend to remain in self-perpetuating power, passing their positions and power to their heirs or others of the same restricted class.

As "elites" are a universal phenomenon there has been much scholarly study of them worldwide, that has given rise to a very extensive literature. This stems from their important, even preponderant, role in how countries and the world are run. The influence of elites extends into politics, business, economic development (or non-development), from international relations down to local politics—in short, most areas of national and international affairs. Many events and policies across the continent and within individual countries cannot be adequately understood without giving due attention to the role of elites in society.

Overall, elites are blamed for many of the ills so prevalent across the continent. Many studies examine the historical roots of these ills, including the

---

[9]Maathai 2009:46.

continuing negative heritage of colonialism, unjust international markets, and many other factors. These are not discussed here, as the purpose of this section is not historical analysis, but an overview of the current situation. Here is a sampling from the extensive literature regarding elites:

- "Viewed from a comparative perspective, the primary reason that African elites seek to control land is that they seek power, and in African customary land tenure systems, land is linked to power."[10]

- Elites are engaged in a "politics of the belly" (a much-used metaphor originating in French from Cameroon, borrowed originally by Jean-François Bayart). It refers to "a form of governance that arose across Africa...(It is) characterized by...the elite in control of the private and public spheres, actors on both sides us(ing) their status to strengthen their economic and political power."[11]

- Although there has been a widespread move toward democracy across much of Africa in recent years, ruling elites maintain a "continued ability...to manipulate the democratization process for personal gain at the expense of the welfare of their respective political systems (through) a process whereby newly installed multiparty systems merely allow rotating and competing portions of ruling elites to exploit the vast majority of Africa's largely rural populations."[12]

- One dimension of the struggle for power by the elites would be unexpected by most Westerners. Reviewing a book dealing with African elites, the knowledgeable Donal Cruise O'Brien writes that their "struggle crucially involves a quest for 'mastery of the invisible,' with sorcery seen by the political actors as indispensable to the conquest and use of power."[13]

The discussion above may seem largely to put elites in a negative light, with their quests for power and their greed seeming to be dominant characteristics. As will be seen in the following section, elites are under a lot of external pressure, which certainly allows for some sympathy and mitigates the negativity. Many governments and institutions are unstable, rendering life unpredictable. Rivalries between ethnic groups abound in many countries.

[10]Rose 2002:206.
[11]Wikipedia, "Politics of the Belly," accessed Jan. 27, 2014.
[12]Schraeder 1994:70.
[13]Cruise O'Brien 1989:528–529.

Kin put extreme pressure on those with means or access to means. Even those in high positions can never meet all the expectations of those who depend on them in the spoils system that exists in many countries. These may be extenuating circumstances, but at the least, the behavior of elites is too often a betrayal of African ideals.

Peter Geschiere points out that traditionally, where society was organized into kingdoms, wealth was the exclusive prerogative of the nobility, or traditional elite, a system that assumed ritual control over wealth. However, the elite were held responsible to use their power, status, and wealth for the benefit of their subjects. If they did not, they would be held accountable by God, or the spiritual powers who enthroned them. Thus, as non-elite individuals gained access to wealth and power, the populace assumed that they had somehow manipulated the system for their own benefit, at the expense of others. To the extent that they indulged in conspicuous consumption, hoarding of resources, or investing their wealth outside the homeland, they were perceived to have immorally or deceitfully acquired wealth, and were mistrusted or even ostracized. In modern Africa, the new elite stand in contrast to traditional idioms of wealth, both in the way they use their wealth and the way they are assumed to have acquired it.[14]

Clientelism and dependency

The influential are those who get the most of what there is to get.[15]
Ugandan proverb[16]

A type of interpersonal relationship exists in Africa that is different in practice from relationships in the West.[17] Westerners traveling or working in Africa bump into it in many situations. Typically, they don't understand what is going on and don't know how to respond to it.

Upon arriving in Africa and trying to be friendly and make friends, sooner or later many of these new African "acquaintances" will try to fit Westerners into roles the Westerners don't understand. (Note that the Africans being discussed here are not government officials or business contacts. What are being discussed are clerks, peddlers, neighbors, domestic workers, and others whom the expatriate encounters in day-to-day life.) These Africans are attempting to draw expats into their system of relating to people. Africans have no way to know that the Westerners don't understand

---

[14]Geschiere 1997.

[15]Lasswell 1958:13.

[16]www.allgreatquotes.com.

[17]Although sociologists accept that "clientelism" exists in Western democracies, as in the relationship between voters and politicians, such clientelism operates very differently from that described here.

it. The Africans are on their home turf and don't (and shouldn't have to) understand that the foreigner has a very different way of relating to people. It is up to the Westerner to understand the system and how to relate to it.

The system in focus is known as clientelism.[18] In various forms it is found in much of the world, but it has particular characteristics in Africa.[19] It is "the ubiquitous presence at every level of African life of the exchange of gifts, favours and services, of patronage and courtier practices."[20] Basically it is a system where people with economic means enter into informal, long-term relationships with people who have less access to power, wealth, and influence. "Less access" is relative as there is a hierarchy of clients and patrons. The patron of one client will be the client of one above him, from lowest to highest members of society. Patrons and clients enter into a relationship for purposes that both see as beneficial. The type of relationship practiced in clientelism "is clearly the rule rather than the exception in most of Africa."[21] Some real-life examples will help explain the situations and relationships involved.

A man I slightly knew started to pay me near-daily visits. I was new to the country and did not understand why he would do so. For me, he was wasting my time. Finally after maybe a couple of weeks, and to my increasing exasperation, he told me he wanted to be my client. I would be his patron and take charge of him. He thought he was honoring me but I was not looking for such honor.

Implicit in his "offer" was the understanding that if I accepted him as my client, I would take responsibility for him and his family, including financial support, assisting with the educational expenses of his children, finding employment, meeting health needs such as providing money for filling prescriptions, etc. There were also implicit responsibilities for him as client, as patron-client relationships are by definition two-way. Each party receives what it needs from the other. So my friend would frequently come to my house. He would also be "loyal" and vote for me if I ran for public office (if I were a national) or needed public or moral support. He would encourage his friends to do likewise.

I have been to the houses of "big men" who have wealth and influence. Their courtyards have many men sitting around, and coming and going. Some are just hanging out opportunistically; some are seeking an audience so that they can present their need of the moment. In societies where this pattern of behavior exists—and there are many in Africa—such attention by clients gives prestige to the big man, indicating his importance and

---

[18]Other terms that basically refer to the same political-economic system are patron-client, prebendal, clientage, and patrimonial.

[19]Brinkerhoff and Goldsmith 2004.

[20]Walle 2003:311–312.

[21]Lemarchand 1972:69.

following. Note that patrons do not normally visit clients, except for funerals and weddings. Visiting is one-way.

Naturally, for the Westerner there is no attraction to accepting an invitation to become part of this system. What a "client" could offer a Westerner is not what he values or wants. The "benefit" of having a constant flow of visitors and supplicants would be considered an unwelcome intrusion on one's privacy and time. Becoming a "big man" in his home culture might be appealing, but it would have a totally different definition from that of an African clientelistic setting. So when Africans try to pull Westerners into their system there is a total misfit. Any benefits would be entirely one-way in the eyes of the Westerner: financial resources flowing from the Westerner to his client. Such a relationship would involve benevolence, not true clientelism.

A very different real-life example of the implications of clientelism was a high-level African who was named to the board of an international nonprofit organization, an NGO with head offices in the USA. He served for a total of six years, attending semi-annual meetings. All board members served without remuneration, as required by law. Upon his retirement in his home country, he requested a pension from the NGO. When he was informed that his service did not warrant a pension, as was the case with all board members, he became very bitter and critical of this "unfair" organization. I believe that in his mind he had been a faithful client of the organization for several years, which therefore obligated it to take care of him long-term.

An employee in one African country suffered a brain tumor. His medical expenses were covered by health insurance for some time. The insurance finally ran out as he was hospitalized for a very long period. The organization continued to pay his medical bills and salary for many months beyond the legal requirements, but when he moved to his home village to be with his family, it stopped supporting him. He became very bitter that the payments stopped. He spread the word that the organization was unjust, unreliable, and uncaring, that it treated its employees very badly. This critical behavior was also typical of clientelism: loyalty to the patron continues only as long as the patron-client relationship remains intact.

An expat researcher in agriculture had a young man assigned to him as an intern by a government ministry. The intern was a vocational high school student already in his twenties. The researcher saw that he was honest and capable, and took him under his wing. The researcher understood the patron-client mindset that was part of the young man's culture and tried to educate him to think and act independently. He taught him various agricultural methods: how to graft fruit trees, establish a tree nursery, etc. He pointed out business opportunities. He explained about entrepreneurship and taking initiative and that the system wasn't going to help him so he needed to do what he could to get things going on his own. The intern often expressed his appreciation for the training but did not seem to absorb much of it even though the training continued many months.

Then one day after the researcher told the intern that he was going on home leave, the intern came into the lab beaming,

> with his face shining like he had gotten a revelation. He said he now understood how it could work out in the future. So I said, "Good, how?" He said, *"Vous pouvez me prendre en charge"* (you can take me in your charge). He was in a country where life is very difficult and discouraging, where it takes bribes even to get beyond primary school, to pass exams, to receive a diploma that has been earned, to obtain a paying job....Consequently, he just could not think beyond being connected with someone, with having a sponsor (personal communication, 2008).

The significance to this discussion is that although this was an intelligent young man, in spite of the training in taking initiative that he had received and the opportunities that had been offered to him, in the end he could not think beyond a patron-client relationship. He did not believe he had the resources to take charge of his own life, so his only reliable course of action was to be dependent on a patron.

A different kind of encounter, that could be labeled opportunistic or attempted clientelism, is frequently experienced by foreigners in Africa. It is different from those described above in that the hopeful "client" is unknown to the foreigner. Typically, an African stops you on the street or rings the bell at your residence. This petitioner usually asks for money or sometimes for employment. He may have a prescription for medicine in his hand, or he may describe the plight of himself or his family, often in pathetic detail. The Westerner doesn't know what to do. He doesn't know if the need is genuine or not. In the end he may give the person some money, but is not content, not knowing whether he has really been helpful or has merely been duped. What puts this in the category of clientelism is that the petitioner will, if possible, seek a long-term relationship with you as his patron.

All the examples above give an idea of how clientelism affects foreigners in Africa. Africans view clientelism very differently. For Africans with limited means, who live in a society where opportunities are few, clientelism offers hope and the possibility of gaining access to resources beyond their reach. Even for Africans with some means, clientelism offers increased opportunities.

The hope of both patron and client is that the relationship will be enduring. But in practice, the loyalty of the client depends upon a continued flow of resources to him. With decreased benefits, the client will look for another patron. Hence, these relationships are often unstable. This has been the case in countless African countries where economic conditions have deteriorated, with the result that patrons have fewer resources to share with clients. In these situations, the clients look for other patrons who can supply them with goods and services that they lack. Note that the local terminology for clients and patrons can differ from place to place. The system may not be known at all by the terms used here, even if it is basically the same.

Two tables are presented below. The first contrasts the ways essential services are made available in Africa and in Western societies. The second table contrasts some of the differences between the organization of African clientelistic societies and Western societies.

Table 2.1 Service Providers in Africa and Western Societies

Service	Provider in Africa	Provider in Western Societies
Money or loans	Sponsor's friends and family, through personal relationships*	Banks or other lending agencies
Credit	Sponsor, often as an "advance"	Credit cards, banks, loan agencies
Charity: gifts of goods and services	Sponsor, personally to his clients	Government, religious and charitable organizations, on impersonal basis
Employment	Sponsor employs kin or clients. The relationship of the employee is frequently more important than qualifications. Nepotism is the norm.	Education, experience, and proficiency provide the bases for employment, although contacts open doors.
Insurance	No legal contract. Sponsor, family, and friends are the only possible sources of help.	Is purchased formally through binding contracts.
Access of client to sponsor, or employee to employer	Sponsor has personal relationship, client calls on sponsor at his home.	An employee is expected to handle personal matters outside of the business environment.
Attendance at ceremonies, weddings, funerals, and special events	Sponsor, in personal relationship	Personal matters are not brought to the workplace, although an employer may take an employee to lunch on special occasions.
Vehicle use, transportation, shipping, moving house	Sponsor, in personal relationship	Employee's own vehicle, car rental, or commercial movers; occasionally friends

*Although "patron" is the correct technical term, the word "sponsor" will be used here, as in modern English a patron usually refers to a wealthy supporter of the arts.

Table 2.2 Clientelistic and Western Societies Contrasted

Clientelistic Society in Africa	Western Society
Power	
Power is derived from giving out resources (money, jobs, entrance to education, etc.).	Power is derived from the expressed will of a majority of the population; governing by consent.
Power is personalized through dominant persons.	Power is institutionalized, e.g., through political parties.
Power may be "legitimate" (because it is accepted by the people) but also illegal (often in spite of laws that are not enforced).	Power is legitimized through the rule of law.
Public resources	
Office holders are expected to distribute to clients the public resources to which they have access.	Office holders, as temporary custodians, have no direct ownership of public resources.
Civil society	
Society and political parties are organized vertically along ethnic, religious, or regional lines.	Society is basically organized horizontally without regard to ethnic, religious, or regional differences.
Civil society (organizations) is largely co-opted by ruling elites and becomes subservient to those ruling them.	Civil society, such as unions and trade associations, serves as an independent counter-force to the state.
Civil society is weak to negligible, allowing government to act with little restraint on those who control the levers of power.	Civil society is strong, serving as a counter-balance to government power, and is essential to the promotion of the common good/weal.

Clientelistic Society in Africa	Western Society
Politics	
Politicians, bureaucrats, and military chiefs "serve" their clients (kin, communities, region, religion) but do not serve the state or population at large.	Politicians and public employees are "public servants" of the state and the population at large.
Politics is informal, based on vertically organized individual networks, and men of power who cling to office.	Politics is institutionalized, based on interests, ideology, and regional interests, with individual leaders temporarily holding office.
The higher the office as "Big Men," the greater the demand that they distribute resources directly.	Politicians serve their constituencies, but through legal mechanisms negotiated with other politicians.
Government	
Weak government institutions allow favoritism.	The state is at least theoretically neutral in regard to those who are eligible for resources.
Bureaucracy is arbitrary and personalized.	Bureaucracy serves those who meet legal criteria.
Government has few resources to distribute and therefore restricts distribution to those most loyal.	Government has relatively ample resources so that they can be widely disbursed.
Government is personalized, prone to favoritism, ineffectual, so is largely an "empty shell"	Government is institutionalized, professionally competent, legitimized by nation-wide vote.

Clientelistic Society in Africa	Western Society
Economic development	
Weak government favors political elites who control and distribute resources to clients; others are left out.	Strong government allows resources to be allocated for the common good, benefiting all.
Clients demand immediate returns, which preclude long-term investments for the good of all.	Development requires long-term investment with delayed but increased returns.

*Chabal and Daloz 1999:14.

Note that some of the behaviors of Western society in real life are often carried out in ways that fall far short of the ideals of democratic practice.

Some of the common effects on society that clientelism engenders are the following:

- Politicians who attempt to build electoral support in order to gain access to state resources consistently use clientelism as their main tool. It thus becomes the politics of competition for power and resources—"politics that are obsessed with the spoils of political victory."[22] It is common where peasant or migrant populations are otherwise excluded from the resources of the state.

- Clientelism enables the elite, "propertied classes to legitimize their political dominance."[23] They may be elected democratically but beneath the surface, the distribution of state resources trumps other considerations.

- "What is striking about many African countries is how little trickles down to the worse off through the patronage network and how much sticks to a few hands at the top."[24]

- "The patron has disproportionate power and thus enjoys wide latitude about how to distribute the assets under his control."[25]

- "Several sub-Saharan African countries have been ruined by criminal dictators...who shifted much of the national

[22]Szeftel 2000:247.
[23]Ibid., 435.
[24]Walle 2003:312.
[25]Brinkerhoff and Goldsmith 2004:165.

wealth to their own foreign bank accounts.... In these countries children die of malnutrition because of past corruption."[26]

- "Such views are, if anything, held even more strongly on the African continent than abroad. It is difficult to find (or even imagine) any African reformers or activists who do not identify corruption as a major cause of crisis and abuse of human rights or who do not demand action to curb it."[27]

- Some presidents were formerly dictators, who used their authority, power, and wealth to pose as legitimate candidates and run successful campaigns under a veneer of democratic process. They built extensive networks, client relationships, etc., which enabled them to become big men. Their clients and members of their networks are sure to vote for them, whatever were the means they used to attain prominence and resources, rather than for someone who is unknown, or a rival who supports a different network. Voters may ask, "What does a candidate have to share? Even if he might have resources, we are not part of his network and we don't know who is. We want to know how we would gain access to them? None of our relatives have connections to him, so we will support the big man who has more to offer us, on a personal or family or clan level."

- It is not unusual to see a large house, perhaps what looks like a mansion, in an otherwise poor African village. A Westerner may be surprised to discover that villagers appreciate this even though they may live in mud houses. Such a house and the big man who is sometimes resident, raise the prestige of their village, and give them access to resources otherwise beyond their means, or opportunities for help in time of need: sickness, family celebrations, naming ceremonies, deaths, etc.

- "Individuals might prefer an alternative to clientelism, but they support the status quo as a safety-first strategy."[28] In short, the clientelist system inexorably implies the existence of a small ruling class capable of obtaining and controlling the resources produced by the masses;

---

[26]Szeftel 2000:428, citing *The Times*, London, Feb. 15, 1999.
[27]Ibid.
[28]Brinkerhoff and Goldsmith 2004:163.

> it is inherently hierarchic, exploitative, and corrupt....
> It embodies (the) self-interested search (of the patron)
> for financial aggrandizement. Thus, inasmuch as patron/
> client politics rests on the unequal sharing and acquisition
> of material rewards and payoffs, it is embedded in
> unlawful and illicit practices. This, in turn, stifles the
> civic culture, corrupts public life, and engenders a
> pervasive political cynicism. As clientelism displaces any
> notion of the common good and functions as a means
> of enrichment for the...ruling class, politics inevitably
> becomes a struggle between competing factions and
> clans over scarce resources.[29]

The list of the negative consequences of clientelism listed above is long, and these are but a sampling from the extensive literature available. Still, even outside observers find redeeming qualities in the system. If individual autonomy were a viable option, clients might prefer a different system, but if they don't see any options, it is good to examine the advantages the patron-client system offers. What are referred to here are benefits that the system provides to society. Some benefits attributed to it include social stability, a significant—if very uneven and unjust—distribution of the resources of the state, which in the absence of clientelism would be even fewer. Patron-client arrangements reduce social conflicts between clients, allows them to participate in national life to some degree, and provide a functioning political order, which is better than open, hostile conflict or civil war. For clients who are part of an organized body, such as a religious order, there is strength and power in membership in such a close-knit group.

Westerners react negatively to the patron-client system. They place a high value on the ideals of equality and equal opportunity for all citizens. When they see that elites are able to acquire for themselves a disproportionate amount of the resources of the state, they are offended or even disgusted. Certainly unfairness exists in Western countries too, but at least people have a strong voice in selecting leaders who are responsive to the population as a whole. They think Africans need an impersonal system of laws that are enforced justly, and bureaucrats that do not give special treatment in exchange for bribes, or to those with whom they have personal relationships. Part of the resistance of Westerners to becoming patrons is that they react negatively to the idea of participating in a society that is basically built on institutionalized inequality.[30]

Americans and other Westerners idealize personal independence. In many ways Africans idealize interdependence. While they may not idealize

---

[29]Fatton 1986:64.
[30]Hill 1996:4.

dependence, many see it as their only hope for acquiring needed resources. It is easy to see in light of this discussion that independence without resources or justice in society, does not lead to progress or prosperity.

Is dependency inherently bad? It is a most natural response to certain conditions. Americans, for instance, have had the luxury of idealizing independence. For them, government was stable, laws were clear and applied to all citizens, opportunity for advancement existed for anyone with ambition, ideas, and drive. In sum, individuals could consider themselves to be "independent" because basic legal, social, and economic conditions provided an environment that was favorable to the individual. Without these and other factors, attempts to be independent would be imprudent. Where laws are arbitrarily applied, non-existent, or subject to the whims of those in power, and where economic resources and social advancement are available and open only to those with authority and control of resources, dependency is the prudent route to a better life. In such an environment, whom you know and which network you belong to, are all-important. If you cannot depend on the justice and evenhandedness of the "system," you must depend on people with means, resources, and power. Getting ahead is a matter of having connections, which means depending on others.

Dress

Eat whatever you like but wear clothes that please others
Wolof proverb[31]

I once asked a highly placed African how I should dress when going to a government office. He recommended that I always dress to the standard the official himself used, which often meant a full suit and tie, for a man. He said that in Africa people dress for others, whereas in America they dress according to their personal tastes. My experience and further reading confirms his advice. To dress too casually in African eyes is taken as showing a lack of respect for the person being visited. Dressing conservatively until being sure of the appropriateness of informality is the best rule. Africans may show up in full traditional dress, whether in an office or at a social event. That does not mean that the same sort of dress for a foreigner would be appropriate or be appreciated by the local people present.

Most Africans are offended when a foreigner comes to an official context dressed in traditional African style. For one thing, the foreigner probably does not understand the rules involved and will likely appear a little foolish. I knew a foreigner who often wore African clothing which was entirely out of place in the environments in which he operated. He chose a style of dress worn by poor people which made him look entirely out of

---

[31]Shawyer 2009:22.

place in government offices. A Westerner may intend to communicate solidarity with Africans by dressing in local fashion, but they may perceive it as patronizing, or even insulting, as if the Westerner considered all Africans to be poor.

In village situations, local dress may be both appreciated and a way to be less obviously an outsider. The foreigner in such environments is well advised to ask his or her host how a Westerner should dress. I once went to a major religious celebration dressed in a very traditional style. I had obtained the advice of friends beforehand and had ordered a traditional outfit from a tailor. During the celebration I received many compliments from complete strangers, telling me they appreciated the way I was dressed.

Somewhat different rules apply to women. Dress is one domain in which women can express their tastes for color, fashion, and style. Thus, they are often much more at liberty to follow normal local dress codes, but again, it is best to ask local people of respect and approximate economic and social standing as to how best to dress in different business and social situations.

Clothes often communicate unspoken messages that foreigners are totally unaware of. I knew of a Westerner who went to an audience with a minister of state, "under-dressed." Although the foreigner never said anything wrong, the minister felt disrespected by the informal dress. It was as if the foreigner, through his choice of dress, said, "This is all I think you are worth."

In some African countries people wear untailored ensembles that Westerners think look like pajamas. On the other hand, Africans may think the informal, untailored, unironed clothing of Westerners seem like nightwear. In many African cultures, polished shoes are also part of dressing correctly.

Some Westerners have limited budgets and go to the market and purchase economical cloth from which to make outfits for either men or women. This is appropriate for wear at home, but in public people will not respect a person who appears to be dressed beneath his or her status. At the least the Westerner will be seen as strange, or cheap, or even insulting. Westerners may think no one will notice the cost of the cloth, but Africans are very knowledgeable about the cost and quality of cloth. In general, clothing is important to Africans, and they often spend what seems to a foreigner to be an inordinate amount of family income on it. African women frequently complain of the crushing financial burden they experience in dressing adequately for weddings, religious ceremonies, and other occasions, yet they continue to feel compelled to meet the expectations of their peers, who themselves express the same complaints. A Westerner may attempt to set an example of humble counter-extravagance by wearing clothing that is seen as beneath her or his dignity, but the "lesson" will almost doubtlessly be lost on African observers.

For African Christians, people wear their best as part of showing respect for God. Just as the norm is to dress for others, so it applies to dressing to honor God. This might seem nonsensical to unbelieving Westerners, but Christians and followers of many religions, believe they honor God and show their devotion through their religious attire, their architecture, art, and other symbolisms.

Concrete vs. abstract thought

You learn how to cut down trees by cutting them down.
Bateke proverb[32]

African education does not place as high a value on abstract theories as does Western-based education.[33] The distinction between abstract theory and concrete application has nothing to do with intelligence; it relates merely to ways in which information is analyzed. For example, when working on worldview issues I arrived at abstract definitions and tried them out on several Africans who had had limited formal, Western education. They seemed so far removed from their way of expressing their thoughts that I received few comments. However, the same individuals freely commented on the same topics when expressed in specific terms. One man was an exception. He was comfortable with theoretical abstract formulations.

A linguist devised an orthography for an African language in which the sound system was abstractly organized. Speakers of the language rejected it, saying they wanted an orthography that reflected the way their language sounded. The linguist was frustrated, as he had worked long hours to figure out how to present in a simplified way the complexities of the language. The problem was not that they did not understand abstractions. They were well aware of their language, evidenced by complex word-play and poetry in which words were chosen specifically to take advantage of intricacies of the language. They knew beginning readers would struggle to apply the many layers of complexity found in the linguist's scheme.

LeVine believes the tendency for Africans to think in concrete terms ties in with two other aspects of African behavior already discussed: (a) the importance of material exchanges in maintaining relationships, and (b) the seeming low level of emotional content in many relationships.[34] As to the first, one can imagine that where there has been a history of living on the margins of survival—whether from endemic disease, the consequences of slave-raiding, crops with low caloric yield, or other causes—"friendship" that did not respond to the needs of others would be rather useless, so that

---

[32]www.afritorial.com.
[33]LeVine 1970:296ff.
[34]Ibid., 296.

sharing became an essential ingredient of friendship. For the second tendency, given the widespread concept of African gregariousness and extroversion, the perception may follow that, typical of extroverts, friendships are pursued widely, perhaps at the cost of focusing on a few that are intimate and deep.

LeVine's characterization of African friendship as low in emotional content is at best problematic, and certainly debatable. One expat reviewer of this text, who lived in Africa for many years, had this to say:

> I really do not think this is an accurate portrayal of African friendships (writing of LeVine), and my African friends find it objectionable. I have found deeper caring and more intimate sharing from Africans than from most Americans, who I find hold people at arm's-length. It is especially deep between age-mates (personal communication, 2014).

Westerners may read in literature that African friendships are typically wide but not deep or intimate, but they should consider at least three perspectives. First, Western authors have looked at African culture from the outside, and it is extremely difficult for outsiders to judge emotions and other subjective qualities. Second, there are types of friendship in Africa that are practically unknown in the West, except from literature, reflecting European interactions with some Amerind tribes. Otherwise it is currently only found in gangs and other extremely tight-knit organizations. Examples come from bonds between age-mates, and the "blood compact," elsewhere known as "blood brother" relationships. Such a friendship is described in the historical novel *Sahwira*.[35] In it, two boys living in pre-Independent Zimbabwe, one African and the other white, prick their fingers and exchange each other's blood. This makes them *sahwira*, a Shona word for blood brothers, who are closer than brothers, forever bound together, vowing that nothing will ever come between them. Such blood covenants have been attested in several African countries. A third consideration is that even in the West deep friendships are the exception, especially between men.

Decision-making

One mind is not enough.
Wolof proverb, Senegal[36]

African decision-making traditionally ranged from autocratic, to democratic, though the term "democratic" is not intended to imply that it was determined by a majority vote. That is, the African way of arriving at

---

[35]Marsden and Matzigkeit 2009:187.
[36]Shawyer 2009:96.

decisions is to have a gathering, usually men, thoroughly discuss an issue, allowing participants to raise any issue on their minds. The process can be slow, as it may take time to convince dissenters to agree with a developing consensus. During the discussion process people involved are often called on to give their perspective on a problem, but open confrontations are avoided as they too easily lead to personal attacks, whether intended or not. In extreme cases it may be taboo to directly say, "You are wrong" or "That is not true," but where more open conversation is permitted, discussions can get very emotional. Difficult points may need to be restated repeatedly if necessary. There is a strong belief that discussion is the best way to handle disputes. When a dispute continues, Africans try to propose alternatives that take into consideration dissident opinions.

Nelson Mandela is quoted as saying, "Democracy meant all men were to be heard, and decision was taken together as a people. Majority rule was a foreign notion. A minority was not to be crushed by a majority."[37] There is a potential downside to consensus building. From an early age children learn to please their superiors by giving them the answers they want to hear. This too often means that subordinates say what they think will please their superiors, such as teachers, elders, and employers. Employees assume that it is in their best interest to not express ideas that may not be well received by the boss.[38]

Time

The clock did not invent man.
Give this thought. It is deeply philosophical.[39]

Time is a universal experience, and humans universally find it necessary to measure it or divide it up. Everyone has a way of talking about years, months, or days, but beyond these units, different cultures treat time in many varied ways. Scholars have come up with many terms to describe the differences, such as solar, lunar, linear, circular, monochronic, polychronic, past-oriented, future-oriented, etc. This brief discussion will look at a few basic differences between the use of time in Africa and the West.

The attitude of many Americans to time can be summarized as "impatient time," to coin a phrase. They move at a rapid pace; everything about their business lives is hurried. Wanting quick answers, and quick solutions, they are not used to waiting long periods of time for decisions and become anxious when decisions are not made promptly.[40]

---

[37]Mandela 1994:18.
[38]Richmond and Gestrin 1998.
[39]Enahoro 1996:65.
[40]Hall and Hall 1990:141.

Punctuality

Always being in a hurry does not prevent death,
neither does going slowly prevent living.
Ibo proverb[41]

Hurry, hurry has no blessings.
Swahili proverb[42]

One of the greatest differences in the use of time is reflected in the need for or relative disregard for punctuality. Westerners tend to value punctuality very highly. Some have said that Westerners are slaves to the clock. They plan their days down to the minute, so as not to "waste time," but as a result any delays are disruptive to them. They expect that appointments will be adhered to on time. If someone is even five minutes late, he or she will apologize for holding up the others or the meeting. If they expect to be more than ten or fifteen minutes late they are expected to notify the other party. This is especially true now that so many people have cell phones.

In Africa, punctuality is much less of an issue. In many cities, a majority does not own vehicles and public transportation can be problematic, so people are willing to forgive someone who is late. Even where an attendee owns a vehicle or public transportation is reliable, old patterns of time usage seem to persist. Also, Africans give relationships priority over time, so that if a visitor or a family need delays someone, others understand, for they would have done the same in like circumstances. A Westerner should not be surprised if an African who arrives late does not apologize or give an excuse for being late. Other Africans who are present understand and do not expect an explanation. A foreigner should never become visibly upset at time delays in Africa. To be so does not help or change the situation and will actually diminish the respect Africans have for the impatient Westerner.

A missionary constantly chided her house-help for being late, even during the rainy season. Finally, in exasperation the African girl told her that when it rains people stop what they are doing and get out of the rain. She then assured her employer that she always stayed longer on days when it rained, making sure that all her work was done. This helped the Westerner realize that employment was not regulated by the clock, but by the work that needed to be done. In America, employees are expected to take adverse conditions into account, and leave home earlier than usual if need be, in order to arrive exactly on time. This may not be feasible when Africans have many other people to consider before they can leave home. Thus, a Westerner may be seen as rude, inconsiderate, or unconcerned about their employees if they pressurize employees to be on time.

---

[41]www.afritorial.com.
[42]Ibid.

Past vs. future

Once you finally get smart and go an hour late to a village function, it turns out to be the first time in living memory that anything happened on time.[43]

People in some cultures seem to look back and idealize the past, while in other cultures people are future-oriented. Economic progress is often thought to be linked to future-oriented people, who believe that the future holds increased possibilities for their betterment. Those who idealize the past, especially older, rural Africans, may resist change. For example, farmers may not want to try new crops or farming methods. Their resistance to new ideas may be founded on experience, but it may often involve a desire for continuity with the past, or a concern that experimenting with new things will alienate their ancestors. Frequently it is young technocrats or agricultural agents, who have theoretical or school-based ideas but lack experience, who advocate for changes. For them, change may symbolize entry into the modern world they learned about in school. But village elders may be worried that new, untested ideas, crops, or methods, risk the survival of their families, so they take a conservative approach.

Americans have generally been a people who are optimistic about the future and are open to new ideas. Their attitudes have been molded through their history. New developments, inventions, and technologies have made their lives much richer and more comfortable than the life their forbears had, which they classify as progress. This process has involved many more factors than just being future-oriented. Personal freedoms, the rule of law, good governance, and many other factors have led to progress and justify being future-oriented. Westerners are only now beginning to recognize the negative effects that reckless development has had on their environment, leading some to idealize the "wisdom of tribal knowledge," but they still measure progress in terms of technological innovation and convenience.

Monochronic vs. polychronic

If you want to go quickly, go alone. If you want to go far, go together.
African proverb[44]

The terms *monochronic* and *polychronic* are used to describe a person's preference of doing one or many things at a time. Westerners have been thought to favor doing one thing at a time and then moving on to the next thing. In contrast, Africans have generally been thought to prefer polychronic use of time, especially in the sense that they don't get upset

---

[43]Burmeister 1995:14.
[44]www.afritorial.com.

when the business at hand is interrupted by other people, or attendees at a meeting keep coming and going.[45]

But "monochronic" refers to other measures as well. Europeans prefer that people stand in single file, and that usually in a straight line, and that each person wait their turn. Likewise, they want rows in a field to be even and neat, and consider a field with many crops growing in it at once to be messy. They do not like to hear multiple songs playing at the same time, and want rituals, like those performed at weddings or baptisms, to keep events in the same order. They have invented protocols, like Roberts Rules of Order, to keep a committee focused on one agenda at a time, and are not comfortable moving on to another item until one has been resolved, or at least orderly tabled. They do not think that money from one account should be used to pay off another, they want maintenance performed at regular intervals, and get concerned when children do not reach developmental stages at a prescribed time.

Africans tend to cluster around a bank window instead, each trying to get the attention of the teller. They are not concerned that rows be evenly spaced or precisely straight, plant several crops together, and seed fields according to their fertility, or broadcast crops into standing stubble. While Africans also value ritual, they are not as concerned about the timing, or order of events, as long as they are all performed correctly. They readily mix accounts, reasoning that it is foolish to leave one bill unpaid if there is money available elsewhere. They reason that children develop at their own rate, learn when they are ready, and try to meet people where they are at, rather than insisting that everyone follow the same rigid outline or line of progress.

Public sounds

Arguments between ants are settled underground.
Ibibio proverb Nigeria[46]

African peoples and cultures have been described as "exuberant." One of the ways this is expressed is in the public "noise" common to communities, especially in more populated sections of cities. A recent arrival in Africa described it this way:

> The amount of noise at night is something that I am not used to. Last night, for example, there were at least two, possibly three, parties or whatever, going on in the vicinity. The drums, guitars and singing were hard to ignore. From my Western perspective this kind of noise when I want to sleep

---

[45]Foster 2002:211.
[46]Clasberry 2010:115.

is a breach of my personal rights! However, here in Africa celebrations, it seems, take place outside and neighbors just have to accept it.

Conflict with Westerners over all-night events was an issue even during colonial history. The prohibition by French authorities of all-night events was one of the major conflicts that Amadou Bamba, an early leader of the Senegalese resistance, had with the French colonialists. Africans believed that the prohibition of all-night events was destructive to their culture. To the French, such events contributed to loss of production by workers who were too tired to work or did not show up for work.

> The French had totally alien ideas about education, about the use of time (no traditional days or nights of celebration, ritual or dancing, as work output would be diminished), enforced labor (to take people when and where the colonizer pleased), and so on. In sum, much of what the Senegambians held most dear was being destroyed. The shame was felt profoundly.[47]

Even today, not only are there night noises, but Africans seem to enjoy events that continue late into the night, and use "all night" as a metaphor for a successful party, or a really good time. Many social gatherings—both religious and purely social—continue through the night.

In communities dominated by Muslims, the calls from countless mosque loudspeakers, exhorting the faithful to prayers and other religious duties, are most noticeable. I was surprised when an African Muslim businessman complained to me, "We know when to pray and don't need reminding from the loudspeakers." The calls, and sometimes harangues, begin before daylight and don't end until late in the evening. Some branches of Islam also organize all-night chants on anniversaries of the deaths of their leaders, as well as on certain weekdays. Hence, in many Muslim communities in Africa, "noisy nights" are a common phenomenon.

Horns blare in many cities. Traffic police blow their whistles incessantly in their efforts to direct traffic and to stop vehicles. Music, essentially drumming to foreigners' ears, continues to all hours of the night. In fact, a quiet night in an African city may constitute an ominous sign. One evening during a stay in Bangui, an old man told me to listen. "Do you hear how quiet the city is?" I then noticed how very quiet it was. He said, "When an African city is quiet at night, it is a bad sign. Normally an African city is full of sounds. When it is quiet, something is wrong." Some time later there was an attempted coup in the country.

A Nigerian journalist expresses, with much-needed humor, the differences in attitudes in relation to noise.

---

[47]Maranz 1993:205.

No noise is ever quite like the Nigerian noise. If you were a good student of noise, you would soon find out that the solid, compelling monotony of Nigerian noise is something exciting and companionable: and after a while, that you really begin to miss this regularised, unabated noise, such as when you are temporarily abroad for instance.

A successful European buys a house in the country and spends the greater part of his life seeking solitude and quiet. He climbs mountains and joins a country club distinguished for its silent fun: where members do not speak to one another unless it is absolutely essential, such as when a brooding club-mate is on fire and hasn't noticed it.

In Nigeria you are regarded with suspicion if you seek solitude, climb mountains and have a house in the country.[48]

Part of the reason that "noise" is so noticeable to expatriates in Africa can be attributed to the fact that Africans spend more time outside their houses than the average Westerner. This is partly due to the tropical climate. Not only are temperatures warmer, allowing people to be outside more of the time, but most houses are not insulated, the windows are small, and the walls absorb heat until they become intolerable, especially during daylight hours. So people prefer to be outside until the evening gets chilly. In many villages in especially hot areas, people sleep outside their houses, often on roofs. Many people also prefer to dance and sing at night, especially moonlit nights, because it is cool enough to exert oneself without sweating, yet it is light enough to see.

Lodging

A small house will hold a hundred friends.
African proverb[49]

Many more people sleep under one roof in Africa than in the West. Westerners typically underestimate the population of a village when basing their estimates on the number of houses found there. At night many single people will unroll a simple mat and sleep on the floor, practically wall-to-wall. Men and women will be in separate rooms, so trying to guess the total population by counting only men, or women, can lead to erroneous estimates.

These common sleeping arrangements have an interesting effect. Because people go to bed at different times, some will be sleeping while

[48]Maranz 1993:205.
[49]www.dshenai.wordpress.com.

others are conversing or otherwise carrying on normal life. This means that people must develop a high tolerance for noise and light, since those still awake make little or no attempt to speak in a lower voice or otherwise take into account those wanting to sleep. The ability to sleep in spite of noise and commotion meant that when I took an assistant on field trips, and needed to wake him early in the morning, I had to shout, shake, or use almost violent means to awaken him.

Sharing and hospitality

However little food we have, we'll share it even if it's only one locust.
Malagasy proverb[50]

This discussion applies mostly to field workers and others involved in visiting or living in villages. Village poverty in Africa is endemic. Part of the reason is poor land, a lack of machinery and fertilizer to increase productivity, poor infrastructure like roads, and many other commonly understood factors. Yet there is another widespread factor that is less obvious to a casual observer. This could be called "coerced generosity." It stifles any ambition a person may have to "get ahead." For example, if a farmer bought fertilizer and equipment that could increase production which would lead to greater income, health, and overall well-being, others would insist that he share his bounty with them, and criticize him mercilessly if he did not. So people lose any incentive to improve their lot, and unless everyone improves their output together, they all remain in poverty. In effect what happens is the opposite of what the system purports to bring about: through forced sharing, people end up sharing their poverty rather than sharing their wealth.

A real-life example of how sharing leads to continuing poverty comes from an expat development worker in a sub-Saharan country.

> A development demonstration project in this country had established that the use of fertilizer consistently increased millet yields by 400 percent. The greater yields were entirely due to the use of fertilizer because the same farming methods were used in the project as were typical of the area. Farmers in the area were well aware of the project and the results that it made clear.
>
> In the project area, given the normal low rainfall and poor soil, the millet harvest was so little that the typical family ran out of millet, the basic staple, during the dry season. Had the farmers used fertilizer, their food would have lasted until the next harvest, with even a surplus to sell.

---

[50]afritorial.com.

Although many farmers did not have the cash to buy fertilizer, some did. In spite of the ability of some to buy fertilizer, none did so. The development worker concluded that the reason for this seeming illogical behavior was in fact quite logical. When some farmers had grain while others had run out, those with grain were obligated to share with those who did not. Because there were many more without grain than with it, those with it quickly exhausted their surplus. So there was no financial or even dietary reward from expending money and effort to raise more food. Thus farmers with the possibility of getting ahead seemed to decide that it was easier to stay 'the same poor' as the other households in the village (personal communication, 2000).

One more example comes from a different African country. Sharing in this culture goes to the extreme, by Western standards. While Westerners consider sharing to be admirable, they expect to keep a significant amount for themselves. Not here: sharing means giving up whatever is involved. "In Congolese French *partage-moi ça* (literally: share me that) is barely distinguishable from *donne-moi ça* (give me that)."[51] One of the consequences is rural exodus. Individuals who want to get ahead are forced to leave their home area. They cannot achieve material success when sharing becomes a leveling mechanism where no one can accumulate even a reasonable amount if it is more than everyone else has. Hard work is not worth the effort when the fruits must be given to others. In the city, where people live in ethnically mixed communities, far from kin, individuals have the freedom to pursue their goals.

It is not only villagers who experience coerced generosity. Wealthier urban Africans may also feel that they are victims of an antiquated practice that they are obligated to follow. These men are not seeking clients to enlarge their political base. As kinship relations are so highly valued, even wealthier individuals who do not aspire to public office often find needy kin come to town to live with them and take advantage of obligatory hospitality. Importunate claimants to the obligations of kinship may arrive at the house of a wealthier kin, expecting to be lodged, fed, and provided for. Their visits may be prolonged until a crisis develops or the host takes action. They may ask for money, health care, and make limitless demands. In these cases, the hosts may see themselves as victims, with such a drain on their resources that it is difficult to provide for their own family needs, let alone the intrusions into their privacy and the inconveniences involved.[52]

---

[51]Phillips 1999:4.
[52]LeVine 1970:301.

Hospitality

A man is not a turtle; he doesn't travel with his house on his back.
Cameroonian proverb[53]

If someone comes to your house near mealtime, you should not ask if the person has eaten or not, or even if they would like a drink of water or other beverage. (Asking them to choose between the beverages available may be acceptable.) Rather, the hostess should just set food and drink before the person, or if the family or group is ready to eat, to tell (not just "invite") them to come eat. In many African cultures it would shame the person if he was forced to admit he had not eaten, or that he was hungry. This hospitality avoids embarrassing a guest. Even if a person drops in on a family for a short, friendly visit, they may find, when they prepare to leave, that the family has prepared tea, or a treat for them, and perhaps may have even started cooking a meal. It is then almost obligatory to stay and eat.

Meal etiquette

A united family eats from the same plate.
Baganda proverb[54]

African hospitality is proverbial. Foreigners are often invited to eat with African friends at their homes. Knowing the basic rules is very important. Many of the traditional and modern practices are common across the continent, so once learned, they are generally applicable wherever the foreigner travels or lives. But there are also regional differences that need to be learned.

One of the rules all travel guides or accounts include is, Wait to be seated or shown where to sit. Urban Africans often eat at a table, but very many follow the traditional, communal way of eating, gathered around a bowl of food that is placed on a mat on the floor. Before eating, a bowl of clean water will be passed around, with a cloth towel being provided to dry the hands, or a person may pour water over the diners' hands. After the meal, clean water is also offered to wash the hands again, as their hands have become sticky from handling food. The meal is often served dry, since water needlessly fills the stomach. Instead, fresh drinking water may be passed around once people have eaten.

Africans typically eat with their hands. This can be very off-putting to a Westerner, both because they spill food, and because they have been told by their parents not to eat with their hands. Africans are conscious of this

---

[53]Devine and Braganti 1995.
[54]www.allgreatquotes.com.

and usually will gladly furnish an article of silverware, which is invariably a spoon. I have been in villages, invited to join my host family, when I have been asked if I would prefer to use a spoon. On more than one occasion, after the host ascertained my preference, he would say to his wife, "Don't we have a spoon someplace?" And after a search, one was found. This usually provided a good laugh as everyone saw humor in the situation.

Why do many people prefer to eat with their hands? One anonymous blogger wrote: "Non Africans, especially Europeans, usually ask me why the Africans use bare-hands when eating. In response I often joke by telling them that if you want to feel the true taste of a dish use your hand."[55] Some Asians expressed it this way: "People feel more comfortable eating with their hands....It is the way how we feel satisfied eating food....It's my cultural practice and I was taught to eat with my hand."[56]

A few general customs of African meal etiquette are:

- Wait to be told where to sit or squat. You may need to remove your shoes.

- Do not refuse to eat. If you are not hungry, eat a little to be polite and give an excuse for not eating more, such as that you just ate.

- Men eat first, with women and children eating separately. People do not eat alone, although if the man of the house works late, a bowl or plate of food will be reserved for him.

- Begin eating only after the host has begun.

- Eat with the right hand only, as the left hand is considered to be unclean.

- The bowl that has been placed on a mat on the floor (or in urban settings, sometimes the bowl is placed on a table, with chairs placed around it), usually has the staple on the bottom. The staple often has little taste, so fish, meat, or vegetables, often prepared as a sauce, are placed in the middle. It is the job of the host to distribute the choice pieces from the middle.

- Each person eats only from his or her imaginary "slice" of the staple, or accompanying food. Think of a circular pie or cake, cut into wedges coming to a point in the

---

[55]www.blogspot.com.
[56] www.mbhs.edu.

middle. This is a great system when visitors or others may join the meal. The system stays the same; with the slices just becoming narrower as more people crowd around the bowl.

- Conversation is usually limited, sometimes to the point of silence, but the guest can just adapt to the particular behavior being followed by the hosts.

3

Use of Resources

The giving, borrowing, and loaning of money and material goods demonstrate solidarity, generosity, and acceptance by society. In this chapter *solidarity* means "mutual economic and social support, hospitableness, putting group interest ahead of individual interest to the extent of showing a definite bias against individuality, and active particpation in society." In a word, it means interdependence rather than independence. It also means living in community rather than living in social or spatial isolation. These are some of the highest values in African cultures, essential to each person. In contrast, persons who refuse to share, give, and loan of their resources demonstrate a refusal to be integral members of society. Such persons are considered to be selfish, egoistical, and disdainful of friends, relatives, and even of those outside their immediate social circle.

Africans are basically content to be part of this sharing of resources. They consider this way of life to be superior to what they understand to be the Western way: individualistic and independent, with an overdeveloped sence of individual ownership. (Sometimes Africans complain of the burden of the system but end up strongly defending it, overall. They are not happy with those who abuse their generosity, but they put up with them. People are more important than possessions. This is part of being generous.) The African attitude toward things at this level of the economy has much to commend it for the way those who have resources share them with those who do not have them. This often strikingly contrasts with a typical Western attitude that tends to emphasize personal possessions and personal rights above responsibility to others.

Although the often relaxed attitude toward things has much to say for it, there are probably linkages between this attitude and a lack of accountability—seen in the way many people view resources. If things are unimportant, then making an issue of having them or of a way of obtaining them shows that the critic is unduly concerned about trifling matters. In this context, those individuals for whom things are important are able to avoid scrutiny of their unscrupulous behavior. Another consequence of devaluing things is that for some people ambition is undermined. Such people are quite content to live very simply or even off the generosity of others.

Following are twenty-four observations (numbered 1–24) about the use of resources in African culture. In some cases, an observation is made about Western culture in contrast. This is indicated with a W. See for example observation 7 and 7W.

General practices

1. The financial need that occurs first has first claim on the available resources.

The treasurer for a collective fund is allowed to dip into the common kitty in case of urgent need, such as to pay a personal bill. The following incident happened with three of my friends and is typical of many similar accounts I have known.

Three single men were renting an apartment together, sharing the cost of utilities. One of the three, Mr. Ekwa, was designated to collect agreed-upon amounts from the others each month and to pay the electric bill. Just before the due date on one occasion, Mr. Ekwa had a personal bill that had to be paid before the due date of the electric bill, so he used the money he had collected from the others to pay it. He did this knowing he was owed money by a friend who had said he would pay him before the electric bill was due. Well, the friend did not pay Mr. Ekwa, the electric bill was not paid, and the electricity was cut off. To get the electrical service restored, the bill plus a fine would have to be paid. The apartment mates did not consider Mr. Ekwa as irresponsible or dishonest, although they grumbled about having to pass some evenings in an apartment lighted by candles. Readers of the first edition note that this kind of behavior does happen, but it is not considered acceptable, and that relationships have been broken over this kind of situation.

They cut off the electricity because Ekwa didn't pay the bill.
(Observation 1)

A friend of mine tells how he met a man on the street, a perfect stranger, who asked him for money. My friend said he did not have anything extra; everything he had was already budgeted. The man replied, "But you won't need to pay your bill bills right away, and mine is due tomorrow." He was trying to make the point that his financial need had priority because his need was more immediate.

An employee was being paid a generous salary, about double what he could expect given his education and training. In addition, he had recently received some additional money by doing some outside work. Just before a big religious holiday, he came to me asking for money to buy medicines. He said he was sick and badly needed the medicine. I suggested that he go to his employer for money for the medicines. He replied, "But I already did

and he gave me the money for them, but I spent it on holiday preparations."
I gave him the money.

He had had enough money in his pocket to finance all his expected
needs for the holiday celebrations. But then he made a choice to buy a
larger, more prestigious sheep for the sacrifice/barbeque than the modest
one he had originally thought to buy. He knew he was ill and needed the
medicines, but the money was spent on a bigger animal. This was obviously
not spending money that belonged to someone else, but the same principle
was followed—the first need that came along received the resources.

This principle sometimes works out another way. A national organization that had been established by a nongovernmental organization (NGO)
put in a request for funds for a printing press. The NGO headquarters in
the U.S. provided the money, about thirty-five thousand U.S. dollars. After
the money was received by the African organization, they decided they
did not want to use the funds for a printing press, but for something more
urgent. The NGO said it was not possible, the funds could only be spent for
the duly planned project. The leaders of the African organization were so
upset they gave the entire sum back. They believed it was an affront to their
organization, that the foreigners were trying to exercise undue control, and
that there was a lack of confidence in them that would make it difficult to
continue their relationship. Although there were other complicating factors
involved in this transaction, a major ingredient was that the Africans believed that the immediate need they had should take precedence over other
considerations.

In these examples the point being made is that the shortage of funds did
not arise because costs went up or that insufficient funds were available,
but that there was a deliberate choice or desire to use earmarked funds to
cover immediate needs, thereby jeopardizing the funding of known and
planned-for future needs. This point overlaps with questions of budgeting,
overspending, and changing designations, all to be discussed in later sections. The unique factor here is that the funds were available for the budgeted expenditures, but were actually, or planned to be, spent elsewhere.

2. Resources are to be used, not hoarded.

It is a general rule that people expect that money and commodities will be
used or spent as soon as they are available. If the possessor does not have
immediate need to spend or use a resource, relatives and friends certainly
do. To have resources and not use them is hoarding, which is considered to
be unsocial.

Although it is a general rule that resources are to be used immediately,
it does not mean that people have no way of putting away money for future
needs, or that there is no way to do so without incurring the disfavor of others. One widely used form of accumulating savings for particular needs is

the *tontine*, the term used in Francophone and some Anglophone countries. It is also used in the Caribbean and among communities of the African diaspora. Many ethnic groups also have their own words and customized practices for this very old savings system. Across Africa these savings clubs are very common both in cities and in areas. They take different forms, but the basic operation involves each member of the *tontine* depositing a set amount each week with the treasurer. At the end of a predetermined period of time, or when a set amount is accumulated, one or more distributions are made. Sometimes a lottery is used to award the kitty to one lucky person; other times the *tontine* takes the form of a *tour* (from the French, *tour de rôle*), in which at the end of a specified period, each member receives back the sum of the weekly deposits he or she made. This is usually just before a major holiday, when members want to buy new clothes, or in a village, when the village will buy a beef that all members will share. *Tontines* are also used by villages or city neighborhoods, or associations, to save for many kinds of major expenditures, such as building houses, paying debts, celebrating marriages, making pilgrimages to Mecca, constructing churches or mosques, and paying for funerals.[1]

As is to be expected, there are many African ways of "budgeting." People of some ethnic groups are known to be good at budgeting and otherwise handling finances in ways that lead to prosperity. Another example of using what is on hand concerns a medical doctor in Chad who was in charge of a hospital there. He had grown up in the area as the son of missionaries. He understood the local culture and used the resources of the hospital in culturally relevant ways. When the hospital had gasoline available for its ambulance and other vehicles and the local government vehicle pool had run out, government vehicles could get gasoline from the hospital. When the hospital supply of gasoline ran out, its vehicles could go to the government vehicle pool for gasoline. When neither the hospital nor the local government had gasoline, the ambulance and other hospital vehicles could not move, and services had to be curtailed. Gasoline is just one example of the way the hospital shared resources. The hospital was greatly appreciated and made a big impact on the community in ways beyond its valuable medical services. It fit right in with the values of the community, of resources, and also of sharing deprivation.

3. Money is to be spent before friends or relatives ask to "borrow" it.

Of course people do not always spend all their money as soon as they receive it. However, a major factor in people's use of money is the expectation that friends and relatives will ask to " borrow" from them. This is doubly true as people are keenly aware of each other's business. Almost always if someone

---

[1]There is an abundance of literature on *tontines*. See, for example, Nzemen 1993.

receives money, those people who are socially close will know it. Yet certain monies must be reserved for essential expenditures, like food and shelter. Short-term reserves for essentials are allowed within the system, but even then the expenditures need to be made without delay. If this is not done, the cash will appear to be available for borrowing.

One Western friend encouraged some of his close African friends to consider well ahead of payday what they really wanted their money to go for. This would enable them to avoid making impulsive purchases that were of no long-range benefit to them just to keep it from being borrowed. This advice was given in response to their complaints that people permanently borrowed their money, when they had any. Consequently, on those infrequent occasions when they were able to earn money, they often made wasteful or ill-considered expenditures just to keep friends from borrowing it.

4. If something is not being actively used, it is considered to be "available."

Many people like to think that if something is not in active or current use, it is "surplus." If they do not have one, or have less, then the owner should give it or some of it, to the one who has none or less. This can apply to anything from personal possessions, money, supplies, buildings, land, and equipment. If the owner of the resource is perceived indeed to have this resource available, in terms decided by the one who wants it, yet does not accept or yield to a request for it, he or she will be criticized and be considered selfish, ungenerous, not a friend, or worse.

Several African friends have mentioned how Westerners living in African communities leave things in their yards, like children's bicycles. The bikes may lie in one spot for days or weeks, sometimes getting rusty. To many Africans this is selfish, ungenerous, and inconsiderate of people who do not have such possessions and could profit from using them.

"You're not using it and I need to go visit a friend."
(Observation 4)

In the words of another African friend:

> Everything that is not in actual use is seen as being "available." Consequently, if relatives or friends consider that they have immediate need of a thing, they believe they are entitled to take possession of it. Thus, the real Africans, ones who do not have a "double culture" that is, who have not been overly influenced by Western ideas, and who have not been alienated from African ideals are subject to this custom.

> In our traditional conception of things…if someone has goods or assets of whatever nature, if that person refuses to hand them over to a petitioner, the latter will judge the owner to be an egoist and insensitive to the needs of others. From this it follows that the notion of "surplus" cannot be separated from that of "selfishness." Indeed, people tend to think that those who have many goods are usually egoists. Their thinking starts with the concept that the African "family" is excessively inclusive and elastic. In this thinking, there certainly must be many in the family who are needy and deprived, and therefore, if they fulfilled their family obligations, they wouldn't have accumulated so many goods. If they have accumulated so much, it is because they have chosen to close their eyes to needs and to remain deaf to the implicit or explicit requests of others (personal communication, 1998).

It is not hard to guess that ways are often found to get around this rule. Africans are generous, but they do not always take kindly to their things walking off in the hands of others. Three of the many strategies followed to avoid losing personal property are: (1) hiding prized possessions, such as in a locked box or wardrobe; (2) purchasing cattle in a rural area and consigning them to cattle herders who get half the offspring as payment for caring for them; and (3) putting available resources into fixed assets such as buildings. These are often under construction for many years. Money is put into them piecemeal whenever it is available, to keep it from being borrowed. Thus, one of the most common sights in Africa are partially built houses—frames of concrete with protruding rebar, looking like large animals lying on their backs, hairy feet pointing to the sky. Readers of the first edition have pointed out, however, that this "borrowing" of things not being used, is far from universal behavior in Africa and may even be seen as rude or a sign of a bad character.

5. Africans are very sensitive and alert to the needs of others and are quite ready to share their resources.

This observation rather summarizes African attitudes toward the use of resources. In some ways it provides the key insight into African financial practices.

An African explained this in helpful detail:

> People are very observant of others and attentive to their situations. Consequently, all the needy people in a neighborhood are known. In traditional villages it is the custom for women to begin to pound millet in their mortars at dawn. There is a hidden reason behind this schedule. If the women note that a neighbor is not pounding millet they will send a delegation to discreetly investigate. If it is because their neighbor's granary is empty, they will unobtrusively send grain over to the neighbor without exposing the problem to the whole village.

> Today, this custom of looking out for the welfare of others in the community is breaking down. This stems from a variety of factors. African societies are moving more into money-based economies. Economic conditions in general have deteriorated in recent decades. Urban people must purchase all the food they consume; they do not grow it as in the past. A majority of people find it more difficult to adequately meet the family minimum needs, so they have less capacity to help others. And as in the industrialized world, there is a greater tendency toward consumption as a way of

life, so the sacrosanct requirement of hospitality becomes more difficult to uphold.

Besides the economic factors, there is an increasing breakdown of social cohesion. Some people take advantage of African solidarity and sensitivity to the needs of others. These individuals have lost the former shame of being needy. They openly make it known that they are destitute, whether real or feigned, with the intent of attracting the pity and compassion of others to glean some resources. They wander the streets—in both business and residential areas—looking for easy aid as they approach all who pass by. In urban settings, especially, this makes it virtually impossible for the African as well as the Westerner to tell who is needy and who pretends to be (personal communication, 1998).

However, in the modern city, African solidarity and sense of community continue to live on, even if diminished from earlier times.

Further illustration of African sharing comes from an African friend:

Not far from where I live there is a woman of about forty years of age who "operates" in front of some shops. If you buy something in one of these small shops, the woman will approach you and open her hand to show you ninety francs. She then says, "I came to buy some soap, but I don't quite have enough. Could you give me ten francs?" She has done this for a long time and everyone in the neighborhood, who the first time fell for the ruse, have long since understood what she is doing and that she has some mental deficiencies. Yet people continue to give her ten francs, while they tell each other, "What a droll woman that is, forever haunting the same spot, with a phony story known to everyone."

Everyone knows the story but they continue to give her what she asks for. This leads us to say that African generosity and sociability have a negative side. They tolerate certain behavior to the point of making it acceptable. This excessive indulgence may be seen as fostering laziness and idleness.

If these customs persist, it is because Africans cannot close themselves off from others. They prefer to take risks in allowing themselves to be deceived, rather than risk failing to help someone who is in real need. The phony poor take advantage of this characteristic behavior of Africans.

How to separate the wheat from the weeds? How to make the distinction between those who merit help and those who should be bypassed? These are complex questions that Africans find difficult to answer. Therefore, besides the high values of solidarity and sociability, which are tangible, there is also the intangible fear of being excluded from society, of behaving in a way that will bring criticism and rejection. As is often said, "Man is nothing without men. He lives in their hands and dies in their hands." (personal communication, 1997).

So although in the main, ideals of African traditional culture live on, many are changing under the pressures of modernity. But the old system idealized looking out for your neighbor so he or she did not have to beg or even ask. People are becoming motivated to seek results, not just to keep the old values that are losing force and adherents. Now more and more Africans, it would seem, are not waiting for help to come to them from sensitive Africans, but they are going out and asking for help. That is only natural as very few resources will come to them in an increasingly impersonal world.

6. The fact that most people are overextended financially produces profound effects on society.

One Western friend and long-term volunteer in Africa commented on people's reactions to widespread poverty and personal debt in these terms:

Many people are drowning in debt. When any one person starts to get out of the muck, he is grabbed onto and pulled back under. No one gets ahead. The society cannot build equity. Wealth is redistributed, not for the good of society, but for the good of whoever has power, influence, or authority over the individual trying to get ahead. These may be in the family or in government (personal communication, 1996).

Although this discussion of effects goes beyond an examination of facts and into the realm of psychology, it is reasonable to conclude that a great many, if not most, people have double worries of how to meet current expenditures and how to repay overdue obligations. African friends have assured me that this is quite true. The level of individual worry is very high. There are widespread anxieties over the basic food supply, employment, health in general and AIDS in particular, government instabilities, education for children or self, increase in thievery in many urban areas, and others. Any one of these problems would cause any people to worry, but since in Africa they loom over the populace en masse, the validity of the statement seems quite obvious.

One of the effects is that friendships are often strained or even broken. When one owes money to another and cannot or will not pay, they begin to avoid each other and in other ways to cool their relationship. Another effect is that though Africans do not spend to the limits of their credit cards as do Westerners, they borrow to the limit from friends. So when an emergency arises they have fewer options than they would otherwise have. The resultant effect is that the quest for expanded financial networks, visiting potential patrons, and worrying about finances saps energy and diminishes the ability to do more productive work. Individuals and society in general are held back because spending is largely limited to meeting immediate needs, rather than to creating any savings with a surplus being invested into job-creating businesses. Further financial pressures engender a constant temptation to cut corners by dipping into funds under the person's control, and otherwise to act unethically.

The average American is overextended also, but for him the solutions are quite different from those available to an African. Americans meet their financial challenges by becoming a two-salary family, with both husband and wife working; or they take second jobs, sometimes called moonlighting. And as has already been discussed, they seek more credit. In other words, they seek impersonal solutions. Africans in general have only personal solutions available—help from friends or kin. As a result, in Africa expatriates are often approached by strangers or neighbors, who ask for assistance, whether financial or material. This often leads them to the wrong conclusion, that Africans prefer to ask rather than to work. Part of the problem in Africa is that there may not be any governmental or private agencies to whom people in need can go, as is expected in the West.

The social use of resources

7. Being involved financially and materially with friends and relatives is a very important element of social interaction.

Basically the only Africans who are not involved materially with friends and kin are either those who have been socially ostracized or those who by virtue of their wealth, position, or modern education have been enabled to distance themselves from their fellow men. Not that this is always the case. In fact, many wealthy people will do projects in the village to help the local people.

People are not under obligation to help those who are outside their social circle, an African explained to me. Refusing them should not ordinarily be a problem. The real difficulty comes with Africans when they refuse to help someone who considers them to be a real friend and part of their social circle. "Social circle" would usually include family, close kin, sometimes all others of the same ethnic group or clan, and close friends who are nonkin.

The situation is different in several ways for Westerners:

1. They have egalitarian ideals and come from prosperous countries so they are surprised, even shocked, in some countries at the obvious and widespread needs they see all around them.

2. They are not used to being directly confronted by needy people, as they ordinarily give to charitable organizations whose personnel deal directly with those in need.

3. They feel unease, regret, or perhaps even some subconscious guilt, for the basic needs they see in Africa, especially if they are pained about the colonial era in Africa, and more recently, distressed by the harm done by policies of the Cold War.

4. The needs seem so overwhelming they have a sense of futility in trying to provide help. Even if they gave away all they possess, it would not make a dent in the need.

5. They know there are cheats who pretend to be needy when they are not; they cannot tell one from the other, and they do not want to give to cheats.

6. For Africans it may be easy to define their social circles and therefore to be able to limit their obligations, but how do Westerners define theirs when they are resident foreigners who have no blood ties, no ethnic connections, and are otherwise typically isolated (even if physically present) from African society? Mostly, the foreigners' circles are composed of other foreigners, so those with needs are all outside their circles. Even when Westerners are part of an African social circle, it may well be composed of Africans who are at least relatively well off.

7. When Westerners are part of African social circles that include the unemployed and other kinds of needy people, it is difficult, if not very improbable, for them to maintain balanced, reciprocal relationships within such circles. They remain largely social outsiders even when they appear to be insiders.

So for Westerners, being hard on outsiders and open to providing help to those who are inside the social circle does not much solve their problem vis-à-vis determining whom to help and whom to refuse. This is a constant problem for those Westerners who are in Africa and who have charitable ideals and would like to contribute to meeting needs of some of the people they encounter in their daily lives.

7W. Westerners distrust friendships that regularly include financial or material exchanges.

Westerners are not unwilling to share their resources with friends—they frequently even share them with unknown people who are in need—but they believe the only way they can know if a friend is true or not, is to remove material considerations from their association. This attitude comes from at least three sources. One is that they have experienced or have heard about many friendships, or even marriages, that lasted only as long as the resources. When the resources were gone, so was the friend or even spouse.

Second is the basic Western worldview tendency to dichotomize many concepts, that is, to separate them into two opposing categories. So life is divided into the sacred or the secular, objects for many purposes are either clean or dirty, actions are legal or illegal. In such thinking friendship is a different category from business associate. In the latter, financial or material considerations are not only admitted, but understood as the essential basis for establishing the relationship. To the Westerner it is clear what is expected in each category, even if there may be considerable overlap, as when business associates develop personal friendships.

> Westerners, especially Americans, tend to think of a friend as someone whose company they enjoy. A friend can be asked for a favor or for help if necessary, but it is considered poor form to cultivate a friendship primarily for what can be gained from that person or his or her position.[2]

A third source of mistrust of mixing finances with friendship comes from the observation that many friendships have been wrecked over the issue of money. People know of good friends who became estranged because of misunderstandings regarding a loan, or other material exchange. Therefore, to preserve a friendship and avoid such misunderstandings, they consider it best to leave money out of the friendship. This is true to the extent that there is an American adage that explains this: "If you want to make an enemy of family or friends, loan them money." This even suggests a strategy for getting rid of an unwanted friend—just loan him money, and the result will be practically automatic.

8. Africans assist their friends who are in financial need as a form of investment for those future times when they themselves might have needs. This arrangement constitutes a virtual banking or savings system.

Another slant on the social use of resources is the rejection of personal budgeting of finances. This stems from the realization that "If I budget my

---

[2]Nydell 1996:25.

money, and thereby always have funds available to meet my current needs, my friends will know it and will ask to borrow money from me. I will not be able to refuse, so I will be worse off by attempting to live within my means. So it is better for me to continue to be part of the system. I will assist my friends when they have needs, and when I run out of money they will assist me." One day I was talking in detail about this with an African friend from eastern Africa, explaining the Western viewpoint. He was very content with the African way, totally convinced that it was an excellent system.

Of course people do not assist others only because they may need help in the future. Helping others has high value in the culture, but it is difficult for an outsider to locate the boundary between generosity and self-interest. An African friend told me that some persons help others as a way of demonstrating that they have financial means. The mixing of motives is not limited to Africa. It is very basically human. Certainly also in the West, much philanthropy has this motivation.

Further reason most people would rather share, using virtual banks rather than brick-and-mortar banks, is that the latter's services do not meet the needs of small savers. Banks are basically institutions that cater to the elite members of society. Some of the problematic characteristics of banks in many countries are: charges are high and often even arbitrary, accounts are sometimes "lost," banks too frequently fail and go out of business with small depositors losing all their savings, there is no deposit insurance, and bank employees rather regularly go on strike.

9. The financial implications of friendship and solidarity go beyond immediate friends to include secondary relationships.

A Westerner finds it hard enough to be asked personally for help from African friends and acquaintances, but it is even more difficult to accept requests when help is asked for a third party who is completely unknown to the Westerner. These indirect social interactions can be called *secondary* relationships.

There is no way to evaluate the validity of such requests, or to size up the petitioner. The African way is to trust the friend who is making the request. To question the validity of the need is to question the integrity of the African friend. Westerners are accustomed to making value judgments for themselves. An African friend explained: if my friend asks for help or for a loan because he was asked by one of his relatives or friends for help, even though that person is unknown to me, society dictates that if I have the means, I should provide the help, whether or not my friend will be able to repay me. Africans tend to idealize interdependence. In the past, Westerners too depended much more on the help of neighbors than they do today. Today Westerners tend to idealize material independence. As a result, modern Westerners tend to not understand, and misinterpret, behavior that assumes kin and neighbors will be involved materially in their lives.

10. **Not all Africans follow the normal and accepted financial principles of the sharing that society dictates, but people who do not do so pay a very heavy social price: they are shunned and marginalized by friends and relatives.**

Traditionally in Africa, social infractions were punished by the council of elders with the sanction of shunning, also called social quarantine. It was a very severe punishment, and people usually would conform to village mores rather than be condemned in this way. Shunned people continued to be present in the society, but practically as nonparticipants, except for eating. Food was an inalienable right, even for pariahs and the mentally ill. It was just short of the ultimate African punishment, banishment or expulsion from society.

The African philosopher Assane Sylla describes this social sanction:

> When a troublemaker persists in his bad behavior...if he stubbornly continues, he is punished by being put in psycho-social quarantine. The whole village or the social group he belongs to will stop all conversation and other normal relations with him, including a refusal to carry on any business. The person so condemned is left to exist in total social isolation, living with a strong sense of disapproval, of enmity and of disdain. In Wolof society, to lose the esteem of one's friends, of lifelong companions, of one's age-grade, is to lose the place in life that cannot be found elsewhere. It is worse than being in prison.

> Every person is sensitive to the possibility of losing the esteem of and interaction with others, as it is the sympathy of friends and the multitude of family relationships that are essential to personal well-being and growth. In such a strongly integrated society, the social pressures on the individual to conform are extremely powerful. And omnipresent. The outsider can guess the effects on behavior and on the kind of arguments that are used to justify personal acts and decisions. It is not rare, for example, to see someone spending a fortune for a family celebration, becoming financially ruined in the process, to hear him declare, *nakka ci pexe?*—'What can I do? I can't betray the expectations of everyone who has their eyes on me, looking to see what I will do....' And then adding, *alal fajul dee gàcce lay fac,* 'Money won't keep death

away, but it will keep shame away' (that is, it will enable a
person to meet his obligations).[3]

In cities the threat of being shunned is less serious than it is in traditional, rural society. This is especially true for those with good, steady jobs.
Still, the pressures to conform socially to the accepted mores continue, even
if some individuals take chances at living independently. For most, even
if they would like to be free, the fear of needing favors and support in the
future keeps them from straying far from the system.

However, I have known some city-dwelling Africans who risked independence. They tired of continually hosting a houseful of relatives from
their rural village, who required entertainment, food, a place to sleep, and
probably even pocket money. They got out of their obligations by moving
into a house or apartment so small that there was no room for visitors. This
is not acceptable practice and results in hard feelings, criticism, and aliena-
tion. In other cities it is common for city residents to accuse the relatives
that are imposing on them of witchcraft. Because denunciations of witchcraft are the only bases possible for denying someone hospitality, it is difficult to accept the sincerity of accusations made under these circumstances.

**11. Many people buy meals at canteens set up on many street corners,
outside of factory gates, and at other convenient locations.**

The spirit of sharing resources extends to eating patterns. Working men
and women do not carry lunches from home to the workplace in order to
economize on food costs. Neither do single men make breakfast or other
meals at their places of lodging. They typically have coffee with milk and
bread spread with mayonnaise, but at one of the convenient canteens found
throughout a city. It is of course more expensive to purchase breakfast in
this way than it would be to fix it at home.

Again, the reasons for this behavior are complex: (1) people don't want
to eat alone, preferring to eat with friends; (2) the profit margins at these
coffee and meal canteens are moderate, and the daily savings in doing it
yourself would not be great; (3) there is the sentiment that those men and
women who operate coffee and meal stands also need to make a living,
which becomes an unspoken, "I am showing solidarity with them and helping them, while it is much more convenient and less hassle for me while I do
so"; (4) the idea of a bag lunch, that is, a cold meal, is unknown and would
not be attractive if suggested; and (5) a goal of economizing in order to save
(put away) money is unrealistic. So there is little incentive to follow future
preference (cf. observation 51W). If one manages to accumulate a surplus,
others will be sure to have immediate needs that require those resources.

Businesses in African cities come in a kaleidoscope of sellers from peddlers carrying a few items along the street to large department stores. The

---

[3]Sylla 1978:155–156.

sellers and their clientele reflect social and economic status. Clients patron-
ize businesses that correspond to their station in life and economic means.
Many business people operating at the lower levels aspire to higher levels
for greater profitability and prestige. In West Africa the levels are as follows, from lowest to highest:

Table 3.1 Hierarchy of Businesses in Africa

English	French	Location and type of business
street vendor	*colporteur*	sells along city streets, carries merchandise on his person
table vendor	*commerçant tablier*	sells along city streets, merchandise is sold from a table or cart
canteen	*cantine*	sells food or drink from a very simply installed, open-air, fixed location along a street
shack	*baraque*	operates a store of limited stock or a restaurant from a rustic building
store/shop	*boutique*	is a store or shop with adequate stock of goods, decently appointed
department store	*magasin*	is a large, well-appointed store or shop, specialized or not

Not only are there classes of business enterprises, their clients tend to
come from different classes. On one occasion, I took a neighbor girl to a
hospital and waited many hours for her to be taken care of. Her brother
had accompanied us and we waited together. After a while I needed some
caffeine and suggested we go outside the gates and have coffee. We picked
out one of the many canteens and sat down on the crude bench in front of
the table where customers were served. My friend looked at me in great surprise. He said, "It must be because you're an American; a Frenchman would
never be seen having coffee like this." Neither would an African get out of
his Mercedes and have coffee at such a place.

12. Africans readily share space and things but are possessive of knowledge.

12W. Westerners readily share their knowledge but are possessive of things and space.

This chapter has already given many examples of Africans' willingness to share their resources with kin and friends. See, for example, observations 5 and 8. The high value put on sharing is part of the accepted wisdom of many—perhaps all—African peoples. For example, the Bekwel of the Congo have a proverb that says, "Sharing brings a full stomach: selfishness brings hunger."[4]

It is also true that Africans readily share space with others. By this I mean that people spend a great deal of time with others; they are with others almost constantly. They avoid being alone. They prefer to work in groups while farming, or on the job in the city, or in the kitchen—in fact, during virtually all the time not spent sleeping. Even when sleeping Africans typically sleep in rooms with several other people. If an individual has a preference for being alone to a noticeable extent, he or she is considered strange, antisocial, or even to be feared. My wife and I have been in friends' houses, sitting with others when a man or woman would come in to change clothes. The person would strip down to undershorts or panties, and change outer clothes. No one in the room paid any attention. The needs for privacy—that is, the desire to be alone, or to be by oneself, or to maintain a private life, or the need to get away from people—seem to be relatively unknown in Africa.

Westerners who have lived in Africa sometimes ask, "Do Africans have no need for privacy?" I believe they do, but I would argue that their privacy generally takes the form of thought privacy. My experience has been that Africans do not verbally express many things that Westerners express without hesitation. For instance, I have interviewed scores of Africans and asked countless questions. Over and over again, Africans found it difficult to talk about themselves and give their personal biographies in any detail. There were many subjects that they were not used to talking about, at least not with someone outside their inner circle or even their culture. In my research I worked up questionnaires that seemed reasonable to me, but which turned out to include questions people thought were too intrusive, and so the questionnaires were basically unusable.

On one occasion I was in a village employing a local man to help me interview some of the older men. I was after very basic information about the languages people spoke, especially in families where husband and wife were from different ethnic groups. I was interested in learning how their children acquired the several languages spoken in the village. At one point I was interviewing an older man when suddenly a large, burly young man

---

[4]Phillips 1999.

stood directly in front of me, glaring at me. I was very startled. My assistant explained that the older man had not liked answering my questions and had called his burly son to get me to leave. Now of course in these situations there were many elements involved in what took place. But I think it is safe to say that included in these is a general concept that many thoughts and much information is private in Africa, and will be opened up to others only under limited circumstances. This is also doubtlessly true of all peoples, that they have things they do not freely talk about with outsiders. What I am trying to express is that Africans have categories of information and knowledge that are very private. They may be very open and nonpossessive in many ways, but when it comes to what they know, there are many facts that are closely guarded, and will be revealed only in very measured ways.

In some cultures the concept of privacy only refers to social privacy. Privacy is achieved by simply not addressing nearby people and not being addressed by them, for a certain time. Privacy is simply being left alone, even while many others are present. In these situations individuals have social, but not spatial privacy. For Westerners being alone means occupying a certain space all alone, requiring both spatial and social separation from others. The degree of spatial and social privacy needed depends on temperament. Even extroverts have some need for privacy.

In contrast, Westerners share their thoughts and knowledge much more freely than do Africans. The Internet and the countless scientific journals that publish the latest in research findings are archetypal examples, designed in the West and reflecting many Western values. One of these is the belief that society will benefit from a free sharing of information. Extreme examples are seen frequently on television. Some athlete has just won a gold medal, or someone has just had his house blown away by a tornado, and a reporter will stick a microphone in front of him and ask, "How did you feel when you crossed the finish line?" or "What is it like to lose your house in a tornado?" As trivial as these examples are, it seems to me they do reveal an attitude present in the culture that personal thoughts are expected to be shared with others, even with outsiders. All this is not to say that Westerners and their institutions do not hold many facts confidentially, such as trade secrets or patents on discoveries. The restrictions that are allowed on proprietary knowledge for limited time periods are specific exceptions made to reward commercial investments, and do not contradict the general rule that Western society believes it is best served through the dissemination of knowledge.

A case in point is the Chinese building a sports stadium in Dakar a few years ago. It was one of many such projects carried out across Africa as part of China's international aid and public relations efforts. In Senegal, as well as in many other countries, the Chinese brought in scores of Chinese workers, building housing for them near the project. Very few, if any, local workers were hired in spite of the government's efforts to ensure that foreign-funded projects employ a maximum number of nationals. I asked a Senegalese friend what people in Dakar thought was the main reason the Chinese brought in their own people when so many Senegalese were unemployed and available. He said that most people thought it was because the Chinese were using building techniques that they wanted to keep secret, to keep Senegalese and Africans from gaining access to their technology. This reply greatly surprised me at the time. The stadium was a very low-tech affair constructed of reinforced concrete, so could not reasonably be imagined to involve secret construction methods or materials. What people's interpretation did reveal was the assumption from their own culture that knowledge was something one did not freely reveal to outsiders. Many times during our years in Africa I saw this assumption applied to the interpretation of news and actions of Western countries in believing that Africa was left behind because the West did not or would not share its technology.

I have traveled in several African countries where I needed to ask directions of local people. This could be in a city or in a rural area. Very often the person asked is willing to give directions, but wants to enter the vehicle to show the way. This attitude is at first a surprise to the Westerner, as it is something new, and he thinks he will have to return to the starting point to drop off the guide. However, the guide expects to walk back or, sometimes, to take public transportation. Part of this African behavior is based on kindness and hospitality to strangers, but part is based on the belief that the guide possesses knowledge, and knowledge is a salable commodity. Hence, by getting into the vehicle the guide will obligate the driver to pay for the information given and will expect the driver to also pay for the guide's return to the starting point if an expense will be incurred.

Airports are another place where there is a contrast between Africa and the West in sharing knowledge. I have been subjected to flight delays at airports in several countries in Africa. Typically, passengers are not told the cause of the delay, how long it may last, and what services will be provided by the airline during the waiting period. Sometimes this goes on for hours, through mealtimes, and sometimes into the evening or night. Passengers mill around sharing their ignorance of what is going on, rumors abound, frustrations mount. Again, the situations are complex and without one simple explanation, but I believe the cultural trait of not freely sharing knowledge is a significant element in these events.

The role of recipients

13. **The person requesting a thing or money from a friend or relative has a dominant role in determining whether his or her need is greater than**

that of the potential donor, and consequently, of whether or not the potential donor should donate.

Between close kin or between friends, if the owner does not give in to the demand for something, a refusal may well result in an immediate verbal lashing in which the person refused angrily calls the other selfish. Furthermore, one friend may ask for something he or she has no urgent need of as a way of testing the friendship. If the thing requested is refused, the reaction may be open anger and insult to the person refusing the request.

It is virtually the right of a self-defined poorer person to be given what is asked for from a relative or close friend, if what is asked for appears to them to be "donatable." I have heard many Africans complain about this, but all have said they are powerless to stop it, to condemn it openly, or to challenge the system. If they do not yield to people's demands, they will be severely criticized, openly or behind their backs. Yet if they give in too quickly or easily to unreasonable demands, they will be criticized as suckers.

"I need your radio-cassette player." (Observations 13 and 69)

I once had an African friend come to my house and ask if I had any bedsheets or window curtains to spare—even if they were old and torn. His relatives had just visited him and when they left they took all his bedsheets and the curtains at the windows of his rented rooms. I asked him why he had allowed them to take his things. He replied that it was impossible for him to refuse without being practically read out of the family. It was unthinkable to say no. Although such obligatory generosity is required in many African cultures, it is not so in all. Some friends have said such things would not happen in their ethnic groups. When I told this experience to two African friends who both came from the same country, one said that such things happen also in his country. The other said such a thing would never happen there!

I have had a few African acquaintances come to me and simply say, "I need X amount of money." No reason or justification was given. I interpret these requests as being examples of the asker having a right to the giver's resources. These friends assume that because I am a Westerner I always have money on my person. So in their conceptualization of our relationship there is a sense in which my money, or at least some part of it, is or should be their money. My reaction is to reject this claim. My response to one of these requests was, "What do you think I am, your banker?" The reaction was one of real hurt and a look of, "And I thought we were good friends...." In my Western culture only a wife or a husband, or perhaps immediate family members, would expect to have such a claim on the family resources. Certainly no friend, no matter how close, would be so impertinent or presumptuous as to request money without giving a good reason.

The "needy" persons in many African relationships have a dominant say in whether or not the owner of something should give it to them. In some African cultures, even within a family, if someone wants some thing or money that they know the location of, they will just take it, and the owner is virtually powerles to stop such plunder or make an issue of it.

As was explained to me: "In our culture, when the owner of a resource refuses to give it to someone who has judged it to be 'available,' the owner is considered to be ungenerous and not even a friend, or worse. When the request is granted, the receiver sees no need to thank the giver. We do not judge the receiver to be lacking in gratitude; rather, we consider that the owner has only fulfilled his or her obligation." To a Westerner this amounts to socially sanctioned theft.

In contrast to this taking of another's property, it is very common for thieves to be severely beaten. If a person is caught stealing in a market or other public place, or is caught under suspicious circumstances in a house or walled courtyard, he will probably be beaten and otherwise be treated harshly by those at the scene. Evidently, an important difference between a thief and a nonthief is that the first takes things from unknown people and the latter from those of his kin or social circle without asking.

13W. To a Westerner if a person has a virtual right to take someone else's goods, or to unilaterally change the designation of spending of entrusted funds, it amounts to socially sanctioned theft.

Ownership and possession of resources seems to be much more absolute in the West than in Africa. Westerners do not understand nor take kindly to attempts made by solicitors of loans or money, or vendors, to pressure them into giving to them or buying from them and react negatively to such tactics. They categorically reject any claim on their resources by a stranger.

14. A person to whom money or other resource is entrusted has a major say in how that money or resource will be used.

Many thousands of Africans have migrated to Europe and North America. They send large amounts of money to their relatives back in Africa. I know of one African woman living in France who sent back one thousand eight hundred dollars to enable her nephew to join her in France.[5] As the nephew who wanted to migrate to France lived in the interior of the country, she sent the money in care of an uncle who was a government functionary in the capital city. This uncle kept one thousand four hundred dollars for himself and only passed four hundred dollars on to the nephew who should have received the full amount. But even the four hundred dollars was never used by the nephew to buy the intended ticket to France. Only a small amount was used to obtain a passport. The fact that the money was not used according to the wishes of the donor did not seem to bother any of the individuals involved, including the donor.

In another case, money was sent from Europe for a brother who needed an operation. The money disappeared without the operation ever taking place. Also, a Western friend of mine told about the African treasurer of an NGO who let his wife meet a financial need in her family by taking out the equivalent of two thousand dollars from the organization's coffers. To Western friends who know the people involved in these and in countless other cases, yet who are not privy to all the confidential details, it seems like monies mysteriously vanish without a trace.

14W. The designation of how funds or other resources are to be used that is made by the provider must be followed by the recipient or trustee. Only if the provider agrees, and before the resources are used or spent, may the resources be used for another purpose.

In the West the one who provides the assets makes the determination as to how they will be used. A potential provider may choose to discuss with the manager or trustee the ultimate use of the resources, but is not obliged to. It is up to the potential recipient to accept, or not, the terms proposed for use of the resources. If the terms are accepted, the recipient is responsible and honor-bound to follow exactly what was agreed upon. If at any time before the funds are spent, the recipient or fund manager wishes to use them for another purpose, he or she must go back to the provider for prior approval of the changes. If permission is not given, the funds must be used for the originally designated purpose or returned to the provider.

---

[5]Throughout the book, figures are given in U.S. dollars.

Similar principles also hold true for governments and businesses in the West. If a business budgets certain funds for a department, the department manager is obligated to use the funds according to the purposes for which they were budgeted. If he thinks changes should be made, he is obligated to go to his superiors to have the designations changed. If he does not have prior authorization, he cannot on his own authority make changes in the budget. As this study is focused on personal money matters, these comments are just made in passing.

15. People who have many possessions or a "surplus" of money are prejudged to be egoists who are insensible to the needs of others.

In a sense, prosperous Africans must be constantly looking over their shoulders. If they want to remain as esteemed members of society, their use of resources must take into consideration the opinions of potential or hopeful recipients.

The extent to which this operates in many African societies was explained to me in these terms:

> By our reasoning, everyone with many goods certainly has among his relatives those who are poor and needy. Therefore, they think if these wealthy people lived up to their family and social obligations they would not, could not, have amassed so many goods. If in spite of such needs that must exist, they have accumulated so much, it must be because they have chosen to close their eyes to the needs, and their ears to the requests for help, even if the requests were unspoken...
>
> In any case, those who have many goods yet fail to respond positively to the requests of those who want to have such things, are classed as egoists and are usually rejected by the larger society. It is the same for those who fail to attend the various family ceremonies that are important institutions of life. Whoever is conspicuous by their absence from family celebrations risks having very few people present at the ceremonies he or she organizes. This obligation to attend family gatherings of all kinds, beyond the solidarity it symbolizes, is also a gift of self. Everyone who values social cohesion and hospitality will make the sacrifices needed to attend (personal communication, 1996).

Even food kept in a refrigerator can be considered surplus. Some African ethnic groups have a pejorative term for Westerners that means "people who put food in a refrigerator." I have a friend who worked for an NGO that provided him with a house furnished with a refrigerator. Once when I was with him we invited several friends in for a meal and ordered it prepared by a neighbor who had a tiny restaurant. We had a large amount of food left after the meal. I noted it would serve my friend for several meals if he put it in his fridge. He was almost scandalized at my suggestion. He said he would never do such a thing. Rather, he would return the food to the restaurant woman, who would have plenty of hungry people who would eat it. I understood his action to stem from at least two motivations. One, he had a genuine concern for those who might need food. The other, inseparable and probably unconscious, was to live up to his ideal of being a generous person.

According to the Cameroonian Bouba Bernard, the French are quite different from Americans in their use of leftovers. He writes, "in a French home, everything left over goes to the cook, who eats it or takes it home if he wants. In that regard, the Frenchman is like the African in the way he gives."[6]

Budgeting and accounting

16. Precision is to be avoided in accounting as it shows the lack of a generous spirit.

Precision and rigor in keeping accounts show a lack of generosity. It is nontrusting. It is not what a friend does. Moreover, it is foreign, threatening, and indicates a lack of understanding of the needs of ordinary people. People should show confidence in their friends. Consequently, calling them to account is a bad reflection on both them and you. An African friend explained to me that because it is so difficult to replace or repay money that has been borrowed, whether from a friend or from an account under their control, people find it necessary to be very lenient and nonjudgmental with others about matters of accountability.

Another part of the explanation for this avoidance of accountability comes from the fact that in most African cultures it can easily lead to suspicion, mistrust, and confrontation. Such unpleasantness is to be avoided if at all possible. Social harmony is a highly valued goal. Questioning the handling of money and other resources will inevitably lead to tensions and the disruption of surface harmony.

But there is still another, very subtle attitude that seems to be involved. People resent money itself. Somehow it represents something ambiguous, negative, or even evil. I had long suspected that there was widespread ambivalence toward money in Africa, but such a feeling did not make much sense. Africans avidly seek to have money—yet at the same time many seem also to hold it very loosely. Olivia Muchena, Zimbabwean, sometime

---

[6]Bouba 1982:31.

government minister, member of Parliament, writer, and agricultural economist, points to some of the causes of this uncertain attitude toward money:

> Money was forcibly introduced when the colonial powers
> needed workers for their farms and mines. The governments
> introduced poll taxes that could only be paid with money.
> This forced African men to work in the mines or on a white
> man's farm to earn the money needed to pay the tax. The
> result is that money, while essential to life in most parts of
> Africa today, still has an alien and alienating feel to it.[7]

If money at a deep, subconscious level is really considered to be somehow impure or a force that corrupts human values, then its mere use would
verge on immoral behavior. Therefore, giving money undue attention, in
attaining it, hoarding it, spending it, or requiring that its use be carefully
accounted for, would all be negative behavior. This analysis may reflect a
stretch of logic, but the great gulf between Africa and the West as regards
accountability toward money seems to call for an extravagant explanation.

Colonialism left another legacy. During the colonial period African
leaders were not accountable to the people under them, but to their colonial
masters. These in turn were accountable only to their home governments.
The local people were there to be controlled, not informed. Surely this colonial pattern left indelible marks across the continent. Yet the last fifty-some
years of independence have been long enough to develop new attitudes
toward accountability, if this had been desired.

This laissez-faire attitude toward financial accountability, found in so
many African cultures, certainly fosters a great amount of the corruption
that is such a hindrance to development. Huge sums of resources are di-
verted from long-term goals of the country to meet the immediate needs of
those who have access to the funds. The World Bank president emphasizes
the importance of dealing with corruption:

> The very first item on the agenda, the very first issue that
> we address of the things that we think are needed to have
> for an appropriate and equitable development in a state, is
> [attention] to governance and corruption....I don't start with
> finance, I don't start with education—as important as all
> those things are....If you cannot have in a country a sense
> of proper governance within a framework that is unambigu-
> ous in its opposition to corruption...then statements that we
> make will fall to the ground.[8]

---

[7]Muchena 1996:176.
[8]*The Herald*, Feb. 26–28, 1999, Yaoundé, Cameroon.

16W. Precision is essential in accounting; laxity, leniency, permissiveness or flexibility will in the long run be perilous for individuals and for society at large.

For the Westerner the basic reason for insisting on accountability in financial matters is to ensure honesty. Even those without a great concern for honesty believe that accountability is a necessity for practical reasons. In the long run everyone will benefit if dishonest people cannot abuse their access to resources by stealing or misappropriating the funds under their control. Dishonest people are obviously present in all societies, so society needs to protect itself by insisting on strict accountability from all. In this way those who are in direct control of resources avoid being suspected of dishonesty. Only those individuals who are dishonest would oppose the system as they are the only ones who can lose by it.

By requiring careful accounting, (a) everyone's resources are protected from being used or misused by those who have access to them; (b) dishonest people are prevented from misusing resources, or at least may be found out if they do; (c) managers can live in tranquility and freedom from fear of being falsely accused of fraud or corruption; and (d) if someone is accused of dishonest behavior, the strict procedures and records that have been kept will allow dishonest people to be found out, while those that are shown to be honest will be exonerated.

Good accounting procedures for managed resources include not just keeping accurate records, but opening them to the scrutiny of those whose assets are being managed. I have observed African organizations that had accounting procedures in place. The organizations' treasurers were supposed to be keeping adequate records, but at business meetings no members present queried the officers or their reports in any meaningful way. The African members present were evidently loath to ask any questions about the reports or how finances had been handled for fear of offending the officers, or bringing them under suspicion, or showing the slightest lack of confidence in their performance and honesty. To Westerners this only raises suspicions. They think that officers should insist on being given opportunity to account for the resources under their care. Because there is so much dishonesty and corruption in the world, honest people should certainly want to gain people's complete confidence by providing adequate reports and being available to answer any points that are not clear. Skipping lightly over or avoiding these issues creates a reaction opposite to that intended. Secrecy breeds suspicion. If there was nothing to hide, why would people be reticent about explaining how resources were used? To do less is to call into question the organization, its officers' handling of finances, the financial integrity of the organization, and even the seriousness of the members' attitudes toward their own resources.

Even if transparency in accounting matters is not the norm in Africa, it can produce positive results. John Crawford, a researcher in central Africa, reports:

> One young minister in Ghana told me that the giving in his first parish quadrupled when he simply began reporting to the people how much money was given, and how it was spent.

> In many cases, there are no checks and balances on the local church treasurer. Some of them have been known to resent any kind of surveillance of their books (even weekly reports) and feel threatened, or under accusation, if the other church leaders ask for any kind of accounting.[9]

It seems to the outsider that part of the reason Africans are so forgiving of those who misuse the funds in their trust is that they consider themselves to be generous for not making an issue of it. In such a spirit, "generosity" encourages irresponsibility and dishonesty.

"One-pocket" versus "two-pocket" systems. Another reason for the lack of accountability seems to Westerners to be the widespread practice of using the one-pocket system where the two-pocket system is required. The one-pocket system combines both personal and organizational funds in the same pocket, that is, held or mixed together. In the West this could be the case with a small single proprietor business. The owner's funds and his business funds may be kept together. All income goes into one account and the owner takes out monies for personal or business expenses as he wishes. As he is only responsible to himself, he is free to do this. No outside party has a basis for complaint because they have no vested interest in the business.

In the two-pocket system personal funds are taken out of business or organizational funds according to duly authorized procedures for planned expenditures, such as for salaries. Strict records must be kept of all transactions. Personal expenditures may only be made from personal funds. Transfers of funds from the organization's pocket to personal pockets must be duly authorized. The two-pocket system is required whenever outside owners, shareholders, or contributors are involved or have a vested interest in the organization. Much of the misuse of funds in Africa, from the Westerners' point of view, comes from Africans maintaining a one-pocket system when they should have two. When those who have access to funds dip into the one pocket to meet personal needs, it is difficult to tell whether personal or organizational monies are being used. With such a system it is inevitable that at some point some organizational funds will be misused. The Westerner strongly believes that the two-pocket system is the only

---
[9]Crawford 1981:304.

proper way to handle funds at all levels of an organization. In other words, persons who have direct access or control of funds should have no right or ability to use organizational funds for personal ends.

There is irony in observations 16 and 16W. To Africans, Westerners in general are disagreeably independent and deficient in community values. The Western system is understood to be selfish, with each individual out for all he or she can acquire. Africans perceive their system to be community based, with the interests of the individual subordinated to those of the group. Yet to the Westerner the widely practiced African model allows for more self-seeking behavior than their own system. Where money and other resources can be misused for private purposes with impunity, it certainly puts the individual's interests above those of the community. And the high degree of accountability that is required in the West certainly seeks to benefit the community rather than the individual.

The Western viewpoint is summarized by William Barclay:

> ...A man's conduct in money matters is no bad test of the man. If, we might say, a man can be trusted with money, he can be trusted with anything. A man's character, his honesty or his dishonesty, his straightness or his crookedness, can be seen, and nowhere better, in his daily business and financial dealings.[10]

Accounting is not just considered necessary for carrying on ethical business, but also for achieving success in life. Budgeting is considered so important in the U.S. that school children are given courses in "life skills." Some examples of this were reported for the Dallas, Texas, area.[11] In the programs described, children are taught to live within the incomes they receive for class purposes. They plan their budgets, learn to write checks, use credit cards, monitor their expenditures, pay taxes, and plan for health and other emergencies, and to live within their incomes. Parents and pupils greatly appreciate such courses that help prepare children for adult life.

17. Budgeting, in a formal accounting sense, is not an accepted way of handling personal finances.

What is meant here is that people resist making a categorized list of their monthly expenses, comparing it item by item with their normal income, and then adjusting the expenses to match the income. Several people of my experience have complained about being broke and not knowing why, although they certainly realized their income was very limited. They admitted to not being able to adequately manage the finances they did have. Yet when the idea of a personal categorized budget was presented

---

[10]Barclay 1971:161.
[11]Hawkins 1998.

to them rationally, bringing expenditures into line with income, they rejected it out of hand, even though they were offered help in setting one up. To a Westerner it is the logical thing to do. In trying to explain this to myself, it seems to me the basic reason lies in the difference between ideals of individualism and independence that are inculcated in Westerners, and the African ideal of interdependence. Westerners want to make it on their own as much as possible. Africans I have talked to about this are not used to thinking in terms of what they can do by themselves with their own resources. They have always managed all their life, including their finances, in relationships with family and friends. To then suggest that they begin thinking in terms of living independently or autonomously, without receiving from and giving to others, is foreign and worse than unattractive.

This does not mean that Africans exercise no control over their expenditures; it just means that their system is quite different from that usually followed in the West. Probably the most widely used basic budgetary method is to separate financial needs or expenditures into two categories, called in French: the *dépense* and the *ration*. The *dépense*, which translates as 'household expenses', are the daily needs for basic perishable foodstuffs, such as vegetables and fish. Relatively few families have refrigerators, so purchases are made daily at a neighborhood market. The money needed for these groceries is the *dépense*. The husband is responsible for providing the money to the wife who has charge of preparing the meals of the day.

The *ration* relates to nonperishable staple foods that are purchased on a monthly basis. These are bought at the beginning of the month and include rice, cooking oil, salt, sugar, coffee, tea, tomato paste, and tins of milk. The husband is responsible for these purchases, and they typically absorb a major part of his salary. The purchases are made at a neighborhood *boutique*. At the beginning of the month, on payday, money for the monthly *ration* is handed over to the manager of the *boutique*. The amount is entered in a book, and throughout the month family members make purchases which are duly noted in the book. Sometimes the expenditures are made on credit rather than against a sum previously deposited. (I have used terms from Francophone countries in this description, but equivalent terms are used in Anglophone countries.) This system does not preclude the purchase of other items.

The way many Africans spend their money beyond the essentials is frequently a source of tension with Westerner friends. They think too much spending is illogical and uncontrolled, and when they are called on to provide assistance because of what seems to them as a failure to plan ahead, the result is irritation. In the following episode the Westerner's midnight frustrations easily can be imagined.

A Westerner organized a public celebration to announce the opening of a village training center. Food, entertainment, awards, and other festivities were generously provided by the organizer. Even a group of musicians was engaged to come from a city some distance away. The musicians were paid for their services before the end of the festival as the music was to continue into the night. Near midnight the musicians went to the house of the Westerner, woke him up, and demanded money for transport back to their home city. When they were reminded that they had already received payment in full, which included the specific sum they had requested for transportation, they replied, "But we spent all you gave us, and we have to get home so we can go to work tomorrow morning." The Westerner paid them again, largely because it was the quickest way to get back to bed.

18. Africans do not budget for special events; rather, they spend as much money and other resources as they can marshal for each one.

This observation applies to weddings, naming ceremonies, funerals, and other rites of passage.

In their spending for special events, many people borrow from and cajole their relatives, friends, and anyone who can be prevailed upon, the maximum amount of money and other resources. The goal is to have the most sumptuous and impressive event possible. Little thought seems to be given to questions of repayment or how this will impact the future of the individuals and families involved. It is far less important to consider how money, food, animals, and other goods will ever be repaid than to have a celebration that everyone can enjoy at the moment and that the sponsors can be proud of.

A wedding saga. A Westerner was invited to a wedding and traveled with members of the African family of the groom from the capital city to a town far in the interior of the country where the wedding was to take place. The following account of the events related to the wedding may seem exaggerated, but it is reproduced from notes made at the time they took place. Even if it seems a bit extreme to an experienced Western observer, the story is quite typical of the way many family and other events are managed.

The families of both groom and bride are peasant farmers who live in very modest circumstances. The father of the groom probably has an annual income in the order of six hundred dollars, although much of the staple food—corn and millet—is grown by the family and therefore does not require cash to purchase it. An additional source of revenue is money sent home by family members working abroad.

Modu (not his real name), the father of the bride, is the manager of a development project funded by a large international donor agency. His brother is the groom and an uncle of the bride. Modu was financing the wedding with major sums received the previous year from the international agency he worked for. He also received an advance from the agency, gifts from friends and relatives, and monies from relatives working abroad.

The main wedding party traveled from the capital in a vehicle Modu borrowed from a government ministry where the family had connections. They also had government gas coupons from a source unknown to others in the party. The Westerner traveling in the car contributed toward the cost of gas. During the long trip the vehicle had several flat tires. Part of the reason was that daytime temperatures were over 110°F (45°C). The party knew that travel during the hottest hours of the day should have been avoided, but because of delays in getting started, daytime travel was necessary.

Large amounts of money had been spent by the family on the wedding, such as the Muslim ceremony held three months earlier at the mosque, new clothes for all relatives, wedding clothes for bride and groom and immediate family members, long-distance phone calls to solicit more funds, meals and travel expenses for relatives, including many bottled drinks, engagement of professional praise singers and two groups of drummers, rental of a powerful sound system and a professional disk jockey entertainer, rental chairs for all relatives and guests, and rental for a large canvas canopy for sheltering guests against the hot sun.

By the time the wedding party arrived in the town where the wedding was to take place they had no money left. They asked for another advance from the employer to pay for the two wedding cows which were already in the family's possession. The employer refused to provide more money. They kept the cows anyway and ate the beef at the wedding celebration, but later were called before the police by the herdsman, who demanded his money. The family head escaped going to jail by borrowing funds from a friend of the family.

"Pay me for the cows you bought for the wedding!" (Observation 18)

Modu had nothing to give his aged mother upon arriving home, although custom strongly dictated that he bring her a gift. A short time before, the mother had been ill and the family had received money for medicine for her, but the son with whom it had been entrusted kept it for himself.

After the wedding some of the guests did not have enough money left to return to the capital, so Modu was obligated to feed them until they could find the money to make the trip home. In the government vehicle on the return trip, the Africans all claimed to have absolutely no money, so they asked the Westerner to pay all their expenses as they traveled. Some of the stops included repairing and replacing several flat tires. At one point Modu phoned the government minister who had provided the car, and said, "We have no money and no tires." The response was, "Drive slowly on the flat tires."

Before Modu left the capital, where he had one wife and several children, and from the other city where he had another wife with several children, he let friends in both cities know that he had not had money to leave with his families for even their basic food needs and asked them to provide money while he was away.

The story has a postscript: a typical case of "post-celebration blues." For several months after the wedding, the Westerner in the story was incessantly bombarded with appeals for money by Modu and other members of the family. Money to pay for the beeves that were eaten at the wedding but not paid for; money for seed as the planting season was begun and no one in the family had money so they were threatened with starvation later in the year. And money for lots of other things.

How should a Westerner look at this event? To the Westerner, Modu is a derisive figure—someone who aspired to be more than his station in life warranted, who shamelessly used other people's resources in an attempt to build his own prestige, and whose overall behavior was in many ways foolish. It appeared that the wedding was largely a fiasco, financially and management-wise, if not socially.

How would Africans look at Modu and the wedding? One of my African friends became indignant upon reading the Westerner's account. Laying out the facts as they transpired seemed to him to be an unfriendly act. It was an unsympathetic thing to do. He said, "We try to be understanding of people, not critical." He quoted the African proverb, "The gaze of love looks above the faults." Other African friends agreed that events such as those described in the account are common, and lamentable.

The question might be asked why the host was so determined to have an impressive wedding. The answer is tied to the view of identity. To the typical Westerner an individual's level of performance or competence is very important, and if someone fails to perform adequately, or shows signs of incompetence in what he attempts to do, he is severely judged. This probably relates to a person's identity being closely tied to his personal accomplishments, or *achieved identity*. In Africa, identity is much more a question of who you are, and who you are related to, than of what you can do or have done. This is *ascribed identity*, of social circle, family, ethnic group, even race, where solidarity is keenly felt between African peoples. Relationships also are an integral part of self-identity. The African does not have to demonstrate what he is or what he can do to create his personal identity, so personal performance and competence are relatively less important, and failings in these areas are less severely judged. This analysis seems to contradict what is seen in the story. If the host should have been resting on his ascribed identity, why was he so overreaching in his attempt to achieve an impressive wedding for his son? Two possible hints might be: (1) the family was not part of the socially elite of their town; and (2) the more successful members of the family had migrated to cities and abroad and may have absorbed some foreign values related to personal achievement.

The custom described for this wedding—the borrowing, spending far beyond one's means, maneuvering, running out of money, and the post-event scrambling to find resources to cover debts—are the normal, constant, even expected behavior of a significant percentage of the population. For many it seems as though these are necessary means to preserve dignity and honor. This is, to a greater or lesser extent, the standard model followed by people with significant social aspirations. This is the way a great many people see their friends living, and most naturally they follow the same procedures when they carry out their own major family events.

But there are dissenting African voices quietly speaking out for simpler celebrations. I know one African pastor who will not marry young people if they want an ostentatious, costly, debt-producing wedding. He tells the families of the potential brides that his young men offer their love, fidelity and stability in marriage, and hard work, to the bride and family and not unaffordable bridewealth and a costly, fleeting celebration. Families are accepting the pastor's proposals.

Westerners may look critically at these extravagant celebrations, but in many African countries they have been responsible for adding to the extravagances. Even Christian missionaries have been involved. For instance, in one country where the Christian community was very small, the first Christian man and woman to get married were the source of joy and celebration. The missionaries were so pleased at the prospects of the first Christian family being established that they happily put on a Western wedding, with a full-length white gown for the bride, a full "Christian" (in reality, a traditional Western) ceremony, a reception with refreshments, food, and music for all. In sum, it was a very Western and expensive event—one that the couple of very modest means could never have afforded alone, and perhaps could not even have imagined. The Westerners thought it was a beautiful wedding, as did the Africans who attended, but to some observers the joy seemed misplaced. They did not minimize the joy of seeing the couple married, but they regretted many unnecessary and unfortunate precedents that were being established. What would future Christian brides, and perhaps non-Christian ones, desire for themselves? And if the foreigners did not come up with the financing and even the management of the events, would there not be great disappointment, even disillusionment? At the least, expensive, foreign customs were being introduced that would seem to many to lead to a misuse of scarce resources.

Another example of how celebrations are financed relates to another friend who was getting married. He approached me, and other acquaintances who were thought to have resources, telling of his marriage plans. The wedding would cost from eight hundred to one thousand dollars, in the local currency. And would I help? This man had only temporary employment at a salary of one hundred thirty dollars per month; which means he wanted a wedding that would cost the equivalent of more than six months' wages.

To a Westerner such a way of financing a major life event simply does not fit the concept of budgeting. It might better be called "reverse budgeting": working backward from the kind of event one wants to have, and then seeking by all the means at one's disposal to come up with the maximum possible sum of money and other resources. When I explained to another African friend how I had been approached, this friend was irritated at the request. He said he thought it was inappropriate for a man of very modest means to try to have a wedding that a rather wealthy man, or even a government minister, would try to have, and furthermore, it was inappropriate to put it on with other people's money.

A severance payment. Another picture of nonbudgeting is the story of an African, Kamba, who worked on a project for more than ten years and was well paid by local standards. He knew the project was of limited life, and approximately when it would end. Kamba had few marketable skills and lived in a region of his country that was very depressed economically. In the country where this project was being carried on, the law requires that a long-time employee be given a large severance payment, based on the number of years of employment. This is typical procedure in many African countries. In this case, the settlement was equivalent to more than a year's salary. Long before the end of the project, the manager pointed out to Kamba that this would be his chance of a lifetime to buy land, or a house, or a business, so that he and his family would be set for the long-term. The project came to an end. Kamba received his settlement. But within three months he was back at the offices of the terminated project, totally broke, and begging for any possible financial or employment help. The whole sum of the settlement had vaporized with no perceptible long-term benefit to

Kamba or to his family. To a Westerner, he wasted an opportunity of a life-time to establish his economic future.

Certainly not all Africans act only for the short term, as some of these examples would indicate. We know a couple that had an expensive naming ceremony for their first child. The event put them in debt that took a very long time to pay off. When their second child came along they decided to minimize the celebrations and expenses. They deliberately planned to have the baby born in a maternity clinic so there would not be a large gathering of friends at their home. Their major expense was the purchase of a sheep for the wife's parents. For those who came to visit them at the clinic, they served simple pastries that they had brought in their car.

Some African reviewers of the material in this chapter have told me that the extreme examples recounted above are not characteristic of their people. Others, from the same or different countries, said they were very typical and that they could give me examples of even more extravagant celebrations. As was said earlier, people from different countries, or from particular ethnic groups, follow a variety of work ethics and financial practices.

19. Personal spending is quite categorized.

Africans are well aware of how their money needs to be spent, and have mental categories for it such as food, shelter, clothing, and family rites. They expect to cover the essential, predictable categories from their regular income. If extra expenses come up, they will seek funds from someone in their network. So, for instance, it is common for people to ask for help in buying medicines, which are not a predictable category.

A main category is food of course. Salaried people deposit money at their neighborhood boutique, that is, neighborhood grocery store, on pay-day to assure that their basic monthly needs will be met. During the month they buy groceries and other essentials, against the funds they have deposited there. But the catch here is that little money is held back or planned for beyond the current month. Most people feel fortunate if they can just meet essential needs month by month. This is true, yet there is another hidden reality involved. The fact is people typically do have some money set aside for funerals, naming ceremonies, and other special events that are unpredictable yet expected because they are inevitable happenings of life. The monies for these special events are hidden somewhere and are kept secret from family (including a spouse) and friends. A study carried out in 1991 of individual Senegalese not participating in the banking system, found that such personal savings, in cash and valuables, averaged one thousand three hundred dollars (375,000 Francs cfa) in urban areas and eight hundred dollars (237,000 Francs cfa) in rural areas.[12] At this time the average annual income for Senegal was about six hundred dollars per inhabitant.

---

[12]*Sub Hebdo* 1991.

It might be more accurate to rephrase observation 18 in these terms: Africans often do plan their spending, but not at all in the Western sense of making a personal or family budget. They also have a term for those needs that cannot be fitted into their budget for necessities. They are called *dípenses dérobées*, 'concealed expenses', in French; and in Wolof, the dominant language of Senegal, *yidul farata* 'beyond essentials'. The idea is that these are *wants* rather than the *needs* that are essential to survival. Examples are cigarettes, lottery tickets, consultations with diviners and shamans, nice clothing, and kola nuts.

A unique accounting method is used by many cattle-raising peoples across Africa. The cattle owners divide their livestock into categories such as the *cattle of money* and the *cattle of girls*. Complex rules govern how and when cattle of each category can be bought, sold, or butchered, and how cattle of one category can be transformed into that of another. Basically, the cattle of girls refers to cattle used and received in exchanges of bridewealth and cattle of money refers to purchased cows. Many rules govern the use and disposition of livestock in each category, similar to the rules governing designated funds in Western accounting systems.[13]

20. Living beyond one's means and income is accepted as normal, and is almost universally practiced.

Most people are overextended financially. Their monthly expenses exceed their income. This is accepted as normal, even unavoidable. This is true for all levels of society, not just for the unemployed or the poor.

A Westerner friend of mine was frequently being asked by an African friend to loan him money. More than a bit exasperated, the Westerner inquired about the state of his friend's finances, and how much did he owe people, anyway? The man was very open about it and was able to give specifics about the outstanding debts he had that he could remember. The total came to more than a million francs, which was equivalent to about three thousand five hundred dollars. This was in a country where the average annual income was at that time about six hundred dollars.

In Western countries a high percentage of people live beyond their means, but the sense is quite different. In the West living beyond one's means means living on credit, or having expenditures that exceed income. This is possible because banks, credit card companies, and other credit agencies are available to make loans. The borrower must pay off these loans in a systematic way, or be subject to prosecution or loss of his or her assets. Under severe conditions a person may become officially bankrupt, when he gets into a situation where there is no hope of paying off his debts, but this is relatively rare and most Westerners live with large debts that they do pay off, month by month. Some people keep "maxed out," meaning that

---

[13]Hutchinson 1992:294–316.

they keep spending money on new credit as fast as they pay off old credit, so that their monthly payments to credit companies are always at the maximum their income allows. In such situations, if the person loses his or her employment or suffers a major financial reverse, payments on the debts will be difficult or impossible, and there is risk of personal bankruptcy.

In Africa living beyond one's means describes a state in which a person owes friends and relatives more than he can ever expect to repay. Of course if every person was repaid everything that others owed him, he might be able to repay his own debts. But the system is so informal, so pervasive, and without records, that repayment is out of the question. Besides, the system is not designed to be paid off, as credit is in the West.

The pressure for spending and appearing prosperous comes from friends who are of the same social and economic class. Each one has the same needs and the same opportunities, if not the same ability to take advantage of opportunities. This is true in Africa and doubtlessly, around the world. One Senegalese friend explained it this way:

> For certain, the celebration of a millionaire cannot be compared with that of a poor person, but their worries are the same. In either case, an inadequate naming ceremony for a newborn, for example, will be a ball and chain the person will drag around the rest of his or her life. Whenever there is conflict with the social circle, such a person will hear, *Amoo loo wax, ngente wuñla*, 'What you say has no meaning, you weren't even named' (didn't even have a naming ceremony when you were a newborn). Parents will do everything in their power to keep their children from facing such insults.

> On the other hand there is the common expression, *Boroom ngente bu neex ba ngi nii*, 'There goes someone who had a sumptuous naming ceremony'. Such a compliment resonates in the ears like praise, a hymn that reflects on the whole family.

> The foreigner may see in an extravagant naming ceremony little but wasted resources, but behind it there is great concern that those of their social circle think and speak well of them. How else can we explain the behavior of people who don't have the means to make ends meet, yet entertain hundreds of people at a day-long family celebration, when in the following days and weeks they will be drowning in debts? And when we realize that this happens with most events, it is easy to understand how Africans seek advances to their salaries and other means of obtaining resources (personal communication, 1997).

21. When someone goes on an errand to make a purchase for another, if he is given a bill or coin that is greater than the amount of the purchase, the person running the errand will normally keep the change unless asked for it.

For example, your friend is going out and you ask him to get some medicine for you that costs eighteen hundred francs. You don't have the exact amount so you give him a twenty-five hundred franc bill. My experience is that most Africans will keep the change unless asked for it. And if asked, they will seem surprised, as if the change is expected to be theirs without question. Although this observation applies to many cultures, it does not apply to all. One African reviewer told me: "This behavior does not apply to my culture" (personal communication, 1996).

21W. A Westerner expects that if a person makes a purchase for him, any change is considered to belong to the Westerner, and is automatically required to be returned unless he expressly says, "keep the change."

When making a purchase for another person with his funds, if nothing is expressly said, the Westerner considers that keeping the change is dishonest. If the Westerner must ask for the change, he or she is embarrassed and considers it to be a negative reflection on the person involved.

A closely related subject is per diem payments. In the West these are maximum daily allowances that are provided an employee to cover above-normal living expenses while traveling. They are paid to an employee on the basis of documented expenses that must be submitted to the employer. Africans in general expect to keep the full amount of per diem paid to them for their expenses, whether or not they spent the money on expenses. Sometimes Africans even object when the per diem allowance is used to cover expenses.

> Such difficulties stem from how Africans regard per diem. Most see it not as money paid to cover expenses, but rather as payment for their time and attendance, and for them to take home at the end of the workshop.
>
> Per diem is a creation of donor organizations, an incentive to get people to attend workshops they were not truly interested in attending. Today these same donors are trying hard to backpedal on per diem, and some are asking for participant fees. The participants, however, realize that they are on to something good and are reluctant to relent.[14]

For Westerners these small monies are important, for they believe careful accounting is best for society overall. They believe that slippage in small things will lead to carelessness in major matters, so the only safe way to do

[14]Richmond and Gestrin 1998:216.

business is with relative rigor. This is much more important than the minor amounts of money that may be involved. When they record the handling of small sums, it is not a negative reflection on their African friends, but rather their ingrained belief in what is the most helpful way to manage financial matters in the long run. They treat each other in the same fashion.

To an African it seems these small sums are not worthy of attention, or are beneath the dignity of a wealthy Westerner to mention. They think that paying attention to such small things is a sign of their ungenerous spirit.

This seemingly small matter is actually suggestive of some fundamental characteristics of many of the cultures of Africa. On much of the continent, it seems to me, solidarity, generosity, and resistance to every kind of personal confrontation, combined with a sense of being economically disinherited, all work together in financial matters in these ways:

1. Careful accounting is avoided, both for self and for others.

2. Advantage is taken of every financial opportunity—consciously, unconsciously, or habitually.

3. The accepted social norms allow for much slippage in accountability, and not just in financial matters.

4. Unethical people can misuse funds, reasonably assuming that no one will challenge or confront them about it.

5. There seems to be an ever-present yet unspoken pressure on the patron to be generous, with the strong implication that anything less than generosity and the glossing over of details is beneath the patron's dignity.

Other patterns of resource use

22. Many African institutions are well-supported financially.

It is the rule for those who attend naming ceremonies for newborns, wakes, and other ceremonies related to deaths, to contribute to the expenses. The families involved in hosting these events need and expect help, and it is freely, but discreetly offered. Africans do not wait to find out what the financial needs are; they just give, knowing money or food is needed.

Many Muslim institutions are well-supported. Newsweek ran a two-page spread on one of the most wealthy and well-known groups, the Mouride, describing their leaders as very powerful. "Millions of dollars a year—wired through banks and stuffed in suitcases on international flights—flow home" to Senegal, sent by their diaspora that have settled in many countries. "So powerful are the Mourides, who make up a quarter of the country's eight million people, they recently took over the national chamber of commerce."[15] Most of the money flowing into the Mouride coffers are donations made by individual Mouride disciples to their leaders, with the General Khalife being the charismatic epicenter of the brotherhood.

There are literally thousands of independent Christian churches in Africa. Independent means they are organized apart from Western-based organizations, or have severed ties with them. Many, probably most, flourish without financial support from the West. At the same time churches started by Western missions almost universally have difficulties supporting themselves. John Crawford writes:

> While it is hard to generalize here, there seem to be some groups, such as the Kimbanguist Church in Zaire, which have done a good job of supporting themselves. They make no public accounting of gifts or expenses; all is in the hands of their leader. But they have developed and encouraged giving on the part of their members, particularly for building purposes....Congregations are urged to rival one another in giving, and men challenge women in "giving contests." Stewardship and emotion work together with strong results....Most mission-founded churches do not have as good a record. Most are not self-supporting.[16]

David Mann, a researcher in Cameroon, sees the main problem with undersupport of African Christian churches as relating to the impersonal basis in their handling of finances. He writes:

> Any appeal to Christians for an increase in giving must be perceived from beginning to end in reference to a relationship....Also, in this regard, the African church should make certain that there is a public relationship between the supporters and the leaders of the church, i.e., the treasurer(s) and the head pastor....But members will more gladly contribute to the budget of an institution if they have a relationship with a key individual in that institution.[17]

23. Fund raising is frequently done on a neighborhood basis for neighborhood financial needs.

Designated individuals from neighborhood organizations go from house to house soliciting funds. They have notebooks or sheaves of papers with them

---

[15]Mabry and Zarembo 1997:42–43.
[16]Crawford 1981:302–303.
[17]Mann 1990:56.

that donors may examine, and if they make a donation, add their name, date, amount given in cash to the representative, with their signature. Funds are raised in this manner by soccer clubs and other neighborhood youth organizations, for equipment, uniforms, or travel. Funds are also raised for special medical needs or crises. Residents show their solidarity with needs in the neighborhood through their participation.

Foreigners typically wonder whether to give or not when they are approached for a donation. The comments made by one African friend give one experienced point of view:

> These are neighborhood projects and if any fraud develops, there will be a public outcry. Besides this, the neighborhood will only allow young people to solicit funds who are from recognized families. Those who solicit funds for local sports clubs do not do so beyond neighborhood boundaries where they are known.
>
> New arrivals in a neighborhood, Westerner and national citizens alike, will have difficulty distinguishing between beggars, the truly needy, valid representatives of neighborhood undertakings, solicitors for various religious projects, and many others who will ring the doorbell. But when a solicitor carries an official register of donors and the amount of the donations already made, one can ordinarily have confidence that the funds will go to those who are authorized to receive them.

One surprising example of participation in a neighborhood need is one I initiated. Our office was located on a street in Dakar that filled up with sand during heavy rains. We lived some months on the street before we realized there was a paved street under the several inches of sand. Vehicles frequently got stuck and had to be pushed out. One summer a volunteer worker came to help us. He was nineteen years old and was taking a year off from the U.S. Air Force Academy. We had what we thought would prove to be a very unrealistic idea, of getting all the people on our street to contribute to the removal of the sand. The cadet went from house to house explaining the project to each one, showing them the estimate we had gotten from a trucker. He said if everyone in the neighborhood contributed, it would cost each one X amount. To our amazement every one of the residents contributed their share, in cash up front! Our young volunteer hired the truck and several men with shovels. They hauled out thirty-five loads of sand. We reported back to each house, thanking them for their community solidarity.

24. Many products are purchased in very small amounts even though the unit cost is much higher than for purchases in larger quantities.

An African would say:

> If I have extra I am obligated to share. Sure I know that buying a whole sack of charcoal is cheaper than buying it by the little pile. But if I buy it by the little pile and my in-law or neighbor or friend comes asking for some, I can honestly say I don't have any to give to them. I only have enough for this meal for my family. If I have an entire sack, there is no reason not to give them some, and if I don't, hard feelings and jealousy arise.[18]

A friend told me of the good fortune of some young men he knew. They had been able to sell some wood, so they had money in their pockets and were "buying their cigarettes by the gross." When I asked what he meant by a "gross," he said, "You know, a whole package of twenty cigarettes."

"Sell me two cigarettes." (Observation 24)

Some of the most exasperating experiences I have had are those of taxis running out of gasoline in the middle of a ride. Typically in many African countries taximen buy very small quantities of fuel, rather than fill their tanks. For instance, in one city in August 1997 when gasoline was four hundred fifty-five francs per liter, my taximan stopped to purchase six hundred

---

[18]AOC Lecture Notes 1999:3.

francs of fuel, which is only a little more than one-fourth of a U.S. gallon. But at least he did not run out of fuel in midjourney.

People typically buy powdered milk, mustard, cooking oil, tomato paste, dish soap, and many other products in very small amounts—just enough for one meal or one day's needs. They consequently pay much more per unit than they would if they purchased the same products in larger packages. This pattern of behavior is not explained by unit cost. Many people have enough money to purchase larger quantities, though they may not have refrigerators in which to keep perishable items. Even for those who do know how much of common foodstuffs they will use in a week or month and could gradually build up their cash reserves to buy in larger quantities, if they wanted to or were able to, social norms prevent it.

The answer is complex. A few contributing factors doubtlessly are: (1) society in general does not focus on comparative shopping for best value; (2) adults and children are not used to having quantities of food in the house and anything edible or otherwise consumable would quickly disappear; and (3) if relatives and neighbors knew that there were usually supplies of food in a family's larder or household supplies in the closet, it would be irresistible for them to not borrow and irresistible for those with supplies to not lend. Whatever the reasons, the overall effect is significantly to increase the cost of living for most households. And as a Togolese friend told me, "When we buy food in a large quantity, the discipline to manage it is not there. So there is misuse. It finishes before time." (personal communication, 1996).

Summary: Use of resources

To a Westerner the most outstanding characteristic of the African way of handling money and other resources is the way Africans share and support one another. The solidarity between friends and relations is outstanding. Sometimes this sharing is resented or is done under threat of gossip or open criticism, but underneath, Africans believe in their system, even if it is frequently a heavy burden on those who at any given moment are employed or have resources.

Another striking characteristic is the fact that "interest" is an expected part of friendship. Disinterested friendship is in practical terms an oxymoron, even if it is known and practiced in special intimate friendships. In the U.S. there is the well-known proverb, "A friend in need is a friend indeed," so the differences in material involvement with friends in America and in Africa are those of degree, not of principle. And doubtlessly those Americans who live under more precarious economic conditions are more involved with each other than are those who are affluent.

The lack of accountability in financial matters that Westerners see across much of Africa is doubtlessly the characteristic most negatively viewed by them. They think it has much to do with the economic problems on the continent. It is not only on the level of personal friendship that close accounting is not required. The same uncritical attitude is applied to organizations and governments at all levels.

Many times the financing of family ceremonies and celebrations seems unreasonably extravagant and wasteful to Westerners, given the widespread scarcity of resources. Westerners believe more resources should, and could, be applied to long-term projects that would raise everyone's standard of living.

Another difference to note is the mechanisms developed in Africa and the West for living beyond an individual's means. Westerners are no better at living within their means than Africans, but they have very different ways of obtaining credit. In the West credit is obtained impersonally through credit card companies, banks, or other credit agencies, which follow strict accounting procedures. Sooner or later the Westerner must pay off all debts and in the meantime is constantly reminded of them through interest charges. In Africa credit is obtained personally from friends. Eventual, approximate reciprocity is an ideal of the system, but may never be required.

Political structures and personal finances. One of the greatest differences between Western and African societies lies in the very different political systems they are based upon. The Western system has a democratic structure. African societies are, or at least were historically, usually based on consensus. In such societies there is much discussion of issues by the entire group or by the elders. The process can often be slow. Votes are seldom taken. Decisions are made after thorough discussion of all points of view. When the leaders sense that agreement has been reached, the chief or leader announces the decision that the group process has achieved.

The mindset that develops in consensus societies greatly influences social institutions and individual behavior. (The same can be said for democratic societies, of course). For the purposes of this discussion, the effects related to the personal or community use of material resources are of interest. Donald K. Smith, an experienced development specialist in Africa, explains:

> A consensus society tries to keep all people equal and equally involved in the group. This extends to matters outside the normal concern of politics, including wealth or outstanding achievement. It is not considered wise or safe to be too much ahead of others in the group...
>
> It is well to remember that this is the ideal held in a consensus society—that all share equally, and that no one advances too far ahead of others. But the ideal is not always

kept. The real practice may be only a little different from the ideal, or very different...

The ideal of unity in all things also hinders a few from becoming wealthy while most remain poor. Being the richest man does not necessarily give status. Status is gained by willingness to share the riches with other people. Consequently, it is not possible to accumulate wealth and still be an accepted part of society. Accumulation of wealth without sharing is considered anti-social, a threat to the community and a cause of disunity. Such a person will often be ignored by the community or forced to leave.[19]

Personal savings in Africa. The discussion presented in this chapter may lead readers to think that Africans have no way to put away savings, that all income is immediately spent or loaned out. This is not the case. Many Africans do save, although the average annual income for sub-Saharan Africa is one thousand thirty-six dollars.[20] An African consultant at the Ministry of Commerce in Senegal, El Hadj Diop, describes a picture of savings in Senegal that differs from the one regularly presented by the media. This economist has given special attention to those Senegalese who are outside the formal banking system.

> Although the national average income is about two hundred thousand francs per year, many people have earnings far above the average. Many of the occupations that seem humble and escape the attention of economists are, in fact, well paid. Examples are street barbers who with a chair, table, and small mirror, operate in the shade of a tree. One study showed that on average they have thirty clients per day at five hundred francs per haircut. This gives them an annual gross income of over four million francs with very low overhead expenses. Similarly, "shade tree" mechanics, cabinet makers, fabricators, and welders of window grills and other construction materials made of steel earn enough to generate considerable personal savings. Even car washers, vehicle guards, and shoeshine boys, who live communally in order to economize, are able to save and send money back to their village families. Also the profit margins of shops located around city markets, are considerable (personal communication, 1997).

---

[19]Smith 1984:113-115.

[20]Central Intelligence Agency 1999. Calculated by the author for the thirty-eight countries of sub-Saharan Africa, less South Africa. This figure contrasts with thirty-one thousand five hundred dollars for the United States.

These statistics relate to cash savings, which do not provide a complete picture. The economic anthropologist Parker Shipton, who has carried out extensive research in Africa, writes, "The first and most basic point about saving in The Gambia is that most of it does not take the form of money. The most important material forms of saving include animals, stored crops, jewelry, tools, and household goods."[21] Doubtlessly, Shipton's findings can be applied to much of Africa.

These facts seem to contradict the economics of spending and borrowing that Westerners living in Africa observe on a daily basis. I think both pictures are true: most people live precariously in economic terms, but others are able to get ahead. The ones who are quietly getting ahead are far less noticeable than the others. The people who get ahead become the patrons while those who fall behind become the clients.

---

[21]Shipton 1995:249.

4

Friendship

Interpersonal relations between Africans and Westerners in Africa may be friendly and even cordial, and typically are, but developing significant friendships on a personal level requires considerable effort. For many Africans it is difficult to forget history, the relationships of power that the white man represented and still represents, the economic disparities, the color of skin, and perhaps above all the great cultural differences. Of these the most significant one is the important place that material resources are given in African friendships.

In terms of the observations presented here, African cultures practice friendship in ways that are quite different from those of the West. Anthropologist Robert LeVine describes the differences:

> There is [a] dimension of [interpersonal behavior] that Africans emphasize when describing relationships of equality or inequality, namely, obligations to give material goods— food, gifts, financial help, property, and babies. Relationships are frequently characterized by Africans primarily in terms of the type of material transaction involved: who gives what to whom and under what conditions...
>
> In contrast with the Western attitude (genuine or hypocritical) that the emotional component in interpersonal relations is more important than any transfer of material goods involved (the latter being thought of as something incidental), Africans are frankly and directly concerned with the material transfer itself as indicative of the quality of the relationship...
>
> In considering the part...material goods play in African social life, several points should be emphasized. (1) A certain amount of material giving is obligatory in a

relationship, particularly in a kin relationship, and is not dependent on how the individual feels about, or even how well he knows, the other person. (2) Persons are evaluated partly in terms of how much and how freely they give to others; those who give more than the obligatory minimum may be better liked as generous persons or may become special friends or leaders of others. (3) Failure to meet the material obligations of role relationships cannot be compensated by a friendly attitude or emotional warmth and support; since the relationships are conceptualized in terms of material transactions, attitudes and feelings are concomitants but not substitutes. (4) Relationships that have goals of obtaining valued resources generate competition, particularly when the resources are limited, the scope of obligations wide, and the rules for allocating resources somewhat ambiguous. Potential recipients or heirs are naturally competitive with one another, and Africans grow up in an interpersonal climate in which such competition is ubiquitous, although held in check by a variety of social controls.[1]

The key to appropriate gift giving is to understand how it works in any particular society where the person resides. Find out the local rules involved. Gift receiving is also important and the rules for it must also be learned locally, as the following account illustrates:

Our neighbors kindly brought us lunch every day—millet mush with sauce made from ground tree leaves. They did for us what all Fulani would want done for them when they visit another village.

There was too much millet in the bowl for us to finish. We wanted to be polite, so we did for them what we would have wanted done for us—in North America, if you give a neighbor a casserole or pie, they should thank you and later return the clean dish. So we transferred the leftover millet into a container, which we snuck to [our friends'] hut at nighttime to feed to the chickens.

But in Fulani culture, what you are supposed to do is eat your fill of the gift food and promptly return the leftovers to show that you got enough. Eating all the food in the bowl is impolite—hinting that the portion was skimpy. We watched with dismay as each day more and larger bowls of millet were brought to our hut. The neighbors were following the

---

[1]LeVine 1970:288–289.

Golden Rule, but it made us stressed instead of happy, as we feared what would happen to our Christian witness if they found out we gave their food to chickens. Finally we learned enough language and culture to know to send back the leftovers.[2]

In the West the emotional component of friendship is emphasized. Even kinship relations are defined largely in terms of their emotional content or value. In these relationships the exchange of money or possessions is mistrusted and avoided except in unforeseen or special circumstances. Gifts are exchanged at birthdays and Christmas, but these are more symbolic than a significant sharing of resources. Disinterested friendship is the ideal.

Friendship in Africa is much more than friendly relationships between two or more people. It involves concepts of solidarity, hospitality, sharing of resources, obligatory frequent interaction, and living as community, that is, practically as a large family. A normal circle of friends includes many people. In the West friendship can probably be defined as normally being restricted to a relatively few people. Perhaps Westerners can best understand friendship in Africa as combining into one category what in the West would be separate categories of friends and business associates.

Following are eleven observations about the role of friendship in African culture. They are numbered 25-35.

Networks

25. A network of friends is a network of resources.

Friendship and mutual aid go together. A Kenyan told me, "More friends means more security." A friendship devoid of financial or other material considerations is a friendship devoid of a fundamental ingredient: mutual dependence. A disinterested friendship is something without sense. It is only natural to expect material benefit from friendships.

To a Westerner this comes close to buying friendship, or of seeking and having friends for what one can get out of them. I have talked to African friends about this, and they emphatically do not accept any suggestion that their practice of friendship involves "buying friends." How then do we explain it?

The concept of close friendship found in some African ethnic groups makes clear that it would be a caricaturization to consider such relationships as involving buying friendship. Take for instance the Wolof of Senegal who have two words for 'friend': *xarit* and *wóllëre*. *Xarit* is the general word for any kind of 'friend'. A *xarit* is a minimally known person with whom one

---
[2]Crickmore 2011.

has less than a close relationship. A much stronger and closer relationship is expressed by *wóllëre*, who is

> a friend with whom one is tied by a long and profound relationship of mutual assistance. Two persons are *wóllëre* to each other if they have a long history of friendship, mutual help, exchanges of hospitality, and of solidarity tested through difficult situations. It is a tie stronger than simple friendship *(xarit)*, a tie that requires that each party be always ready to come to the defense of the other, even at the price of painful sacrifice. It is founded on reciprocal esteem. Whoever commits a fault that gravely dishonors such a friendship, risks being subjected to social isolation. The Wolof is willing to sacrifice anything, except his dignity. He never shows solidarity with someone who is dishonorable. He carefully watches out for his respectability and his appearance of being honorable.[3]

So the problem is not that Africans do not have the concept of real, disinterested friendship, but that Westerners who live in Africa find it difficult to make such friendships. There are many reasons, which include barriers of language, customs and values, temporariness of residence, economic disparities, and many other factors. In whatever combination these are present in any two-way relationship, they make the formation of true, meaningful, and satisfying friendships difficult to achieve between Westerner and African. This is not to say it is impossible, but that it requires effort and commitment on both sides to bring it about.

As for the type of friendship called *xarit* above, too often the Westerner sees it as an attempt to buy his or her friendship. Although the Westerner wants to have African friends, when a request for money comes too early and before a bond of respect and trust is established, he sees such requests as manipulation. He considers that the supposed friendship is being used to get something out of him. He thinks the African believes he has his pockets full of money, more than he needs, and therefore should be willing to share it with even a newfound "friend" who has great material needs. Even though Westerners in general have access to money, it is usually budgeted and committed: for end-of-the month bills, car payments, income taxes, the family vacation next summer. One reason Westerners are so uncomfortable with requests for immediate financial help is that they like to plan ahead with their charitable giving as well as with other areas of their lives. Of course Westerners have considerable money available for discretionary spending, but they do not walk around ready to hand out cash to relative strangers.

---

[3]Sylla 1978:89.

In Africa the use of money is much more immediate. In general, people are thinking of the current month. And if they have the rule, "first need has first priority," and their friends are included in this rule, then a disinterested friendship can be seen to be abnormal.

25W. Disinterested friendship is the ideal in the West. Any friendship that includes material considerations is suspect.

Western friendships are built on, or valued for, mutual interests, easy social interaction, loyalty, emotional support in times of crisis—but not normally on finances. Westerners are very careful in choosing close friends. The differences are:

1. Westerners seek a relatively few deep, emotionally and psychologically satisfying, real friendships. Having a lot in common has a great deal to do with friendship. Loss of a friend is relatively traumatic, probably in part because the psychological, time, and emotional investments have been very great. Quality of close friendship is seen to be incompatible with quantity, that is, a person is thought not to be able to maintain many close friends.

2. Africans seek to have a multitude of relatively casual or superficial friendships. (No negative judgment is intended in using these terms.) Quantity is not seen as incompatible with quality of friendship. There is a great quest for increasing one's network of friends. There is need to be greeted and to greet many people, thereby demonstrating affirmation and respect. Africans probably spend much more time with a larger circle of friends than do typical Westerners.

I have had many Westerners ask me, "How can Africans get satisfaction from friendships when they know that money is a major component in them?" and "How do people get satisfaction from having/visiting friends when they know that money is involved?" Westerners consider these kinds of relationships not as friendships but as self-seeking manipulation. Real friendship must have a balance between self and other, whereas in Africa, they believe, the emphasis is on what the self can get from the other.

Westerners believe that true friendship is friendship for its own sake. If money enters into their friendships they believe it is impossible to determine if the other person likes them for who they are, or only for the material good they may obtain. If the friendship is at all based on money, then it is a business relationship, and the purpose falls in a different category from personal friendship. For the Westerner a main goal of personal friendship is the assured support it provides, that a friend is a friend because he enjoys the other person's company for what he is as a person.

It is helpful to consider several factors that lead to the doubt about relationships. First, when these questions arise, it is good to remember that the Westerner and the African live on very different socioeconomic levels, with the African considering the Westerner to be rich and himself to be poor, with much cultural behavior flowing from these differences. Second, many Africans are ready to use casual meetings or acquaintanceships as a means to gain personal profit. The Westerner can summarily reject such personal encounters and the people who make them, or expressed more constructively, can candidly accept them as facts of life in Africa. The latter course of action allows the Westerner to move forward to work out the negative and sometimes positive possibilities that derive from relationships with particular individuals. Third, Westerners often fail to distinguish between Africans who come from higher socioeconomic levels, who are not importunate and annoying as are the many opportunists who try to gain the Westerner's attention. Very different relationships can be built with them as socioeconomic equals. In these relationships it is often the Africans who represent higher economic and social classes than do the Westerners.

In the West many people have business friendships where personal and financial interests merge, but they recognize that such friendships are based on business interests first and personal factors second. So if two business associates enjoy playing golf together and have other interests in common that they talk about, they establish a friendship. But underneath they realize that if they change their business or employment or move away, or if the mutual profitability ceases to exist, their friendship will end. It is business that brings them together, and each expects to gain some kind of economic advantage from the association. They recognize the primacy of their business connection and that the friendship came about because they happened to meet in the business world, and that its persistence depends upon their continued business interests and connections. Westerners should recognize that many friendships in the West are far from disinterested. So in the Westerners' world, personal and emotional needs are met with friends of personal choice, financial needs are covered with business associates, and a multitude of services are easily available in the society on an impersonal basis.

Africans build friendships in somewhat different ways. Many Westerners have the impression that because African friendship normally includes material considerations, it must follow that such friendships are devoid of significant emotional satisfactions. I do not think this is true. I cannot presume to speak for Africans in this matter, but it is obvious that they get a great deal of satisfaction from friendships. However, their friendships are largely between socioeconomic equals, while the problem of "interest" in friendships as typically encountered by Westerners, arises from their associations with Africans who are on a very different socioeconomic level. This skews their understanding of relationships in Africa.

Certainly Africans have close friends. To doubt this would be absurd. African women gain great emotional satisfaction from one another. Dorothy Hammond and Alta Jablow studied women in thirty ethnic groups from across Africa and write, "it is abundantly clear that women form highly significant relationships with one another based on common interests and affection."[4] Women also receive great satisfaction from their children, and African men are typically very close to their mothers. A classic description of a child's highly affectionate relationship with his mother is described by Camara Laye.[5]

African men get much satisfaction from greeting friends (by name), being members of the village or neighborhood assembly of men, where they have place, voice, respect, acceptance, honor, and where they may become elders. They get pleasure also from spending time with friends in small talk, discussing serious subjects, keeping up with the local news, gossip, and being in the know. They also like to demonstrate solidarity with friends and neighbors at family and village rites—deaths, weddings, naming ceremonies, religious holidays, and countless other events.

Africans receive great satisfaction from having many friends with whom they can share the everyday experiences of life, and who will be there to meet primary needs, or who may have connections, high or low. Connections are essential so that there is someone to turn to in case of need in any of a multitude of problems that are bound to come up, and for which people are the only way that solutions can be found. When public institutions and services are weak, ineffectual, corrupt, or nonexistent, and therefore impersonal means of meeting basic needs and services are unavailable, friends are the resources needed for achieving a decent life. It is entirely understandable and logical then that friendships take on very different meanings in the West and in Africa. Satisfaction in friendships comes from the way that friends can meet basic needs in each case.

Perhaps we can say that in the West where economic needs basically are met outside of and independent of personal friendships, Westerners can live so autonomously that they are free to cultivate friends solely for emotional ends. They separate emotional needs from economic needs as the two are met in such different ways. In the old pioneer days in the U.S., neighbors were friends, providing each other both emotional and practical support. I, for one, lament the "progress" in interpersonal relationships that has so much isolated Westerners from the needs and lives of neighbors.

Edward Stewart makes some helpful comments about friendship in America:

---

[4]Hammond and Jablow 1976:111.
[5]Laye 1954.

> The generalized 'friend' of Americans, standing for anyone
> from a passing acquaintance to a life-time intimate, is
> maintained according to activities. The company of a
> friend centers around activity, a thing, an event or a shared
> history....The various compartments of friendship are kept
> separate, so that a friendship that is centered around the
> office does not intrude into the relations with friends who
> participate in recreational activities....These patterns of
> friendships...signify more often the American reluctance
> to becoming deeply involved with other persons. In
> circumstances where a foreigner might turn to a friend for
> help, support or solace, the American will tend to search for
> the professional, preferring not to inconvenience his friends.[6]

Another way of describing the differences between Africa and the West
is in terms of the economic principles under which societies are organized.
Anthropologist Paul Bohanan and historian Philip Curtin describe these
principles and their outworking in society in this way:

> They are the market principle, the principle of reciprocity,
> and the principle of redistribution. Taking the American
> economy as a model, we can think quite correctly that we
> live in a market economy. Most of the transactions that take
> place are transactions according to market principles of
> price determined by supply and demand, with more or less
> government "interference." However, we pay taxes, which
> is a form of redistribution: wealth moves toward a political
> center and is redistributed from it...
>
> In Africa...there will be a different sort of emphasis
> among the three principles. In the subsistence economies of
> western Africa, the principle of reciprocity or of redistribu-
> tion is to this day likely to be dominant and the principle of
> market peripheral: the market exists and products go into it,
> but it is like gift-giving in the West: it could disappear with-
> out chaotic results.[7]

In the West people expect that personal financial transactions will be almost exclusively carried on through the market economy. Redistribution is
handled impersonally by governments at multiple levels, and by charitable
organizations. When Westerners arrive in Africa and find that redistribution
is largely handled on a personal level, and that reciprocity involves much
more than giving gifts at Christmas and on birthdays, they undergo culture

---

[6]Stewart 1972:54.
[7]Bohanan and Curtin 1971:169-171.

shock. They do not understand the system and consequently are unsure how they should even attempt to cope with the unfamiliar realities.

Besides the confusion created when foreigners are implicated in a reciprocal system when they are ignorant of the unwritten rules, there is an inherent mismatch.

1. Relationships are supposed to be mutually dependent, but if the Westerner is always the giver, a basic requirement of the system cannot be met. There really will never be reciprocity. The Westerner will never be in a position to be on the receiving end, as his or her material needs will never be greater than those of the borrower.

2. Part of the dynamics of the system is that the donor receives prestige and "big man" status, but for Westerners this can never be the case. They do not feel an enhancement of their prestige through this type of giving. The intangible rewards associated with giving by elite members of society will have little or no meaning to them. Besides, they could not fill the role of an African big man even if they wanted to.

I have discussed point 25 and 25W at length because it is a major problem to Westerners living and working in Africa. The discussion has only touched on the way Africans combine material interest with friendship. They actually go much further with this than is indicated in the discussion above. They have developed a unique way for people of material means to relate in personal, satisfying ways with members of society who basically are without means. It is expressed by what is called the patron-client relationship (see discussion of clientelism in chapter 2). In the West I believe we have never achieved this.

26. People constantly work at maintaining and enlarging their network of friends.

Africans not only have many friends, they actively and continuously cultivate new friendships whenever there is the least opportunity. They never seem to tire of meeting new and more people, with no limit. It goes beyond simple gregariousness and extraversion, although it is my observation that Africans are generally gregarious and extroverted. Africans were active developers of social networks well before it became a subject of study in the West.

The desire to increase friendships can be seen in several ways. Driving in rural areas of many countries of Africa, we see men and children frequently waving at the people in the passing vehicle. And if those in the vehicle have a question, or a problem, the people are immediately present and ready to help and to make friends with the strangers. One time we went to visit a waterfall. We had not seen anyone for some time in this remote area, and decided it was a good opportunity to take a family picture. We lined up to the side of the falls when, to our amazement we had several children at our side, wanting to be part of our family picture.

Another indication of the wish to network are the frequent requests Westerners receive for their address. I have been asked for mine many times in many places, mainly by young men. And I have sometimes obliged. Almost invariably after doing so, I will receive a letter or card in the mail, with the person wanting to initiate correspondence. Sometimes an African will specifically ask for the address of someone in "America," as they would like to have an international pen pal.

One consequence of Africans' focus on making new friends is that they generally remember people's names much better than do Westerners. By this ability many African opportunists take advantage of Westerners who live in Africa. I have been approached countless times, in several countries, by someone who greets me with wide-eyed surprise, holding out his hand, and saying something like, "Hello, friend, how are you? It's been a long time since I saw you." When the man sees a puzzled expression on my face, he will say reproachfully, "You don't remember me, do you?" All the time, he is trying to get me to say my name or give any other piece of personal information. If I do give my name, frequently including it without thinking, the opportunist will seize upon it, to begin to address me with it, as if he knew it all along. Or the opportunist will attempt to solicit the name of a city or place where we have supposedly met. If I say, "Did you work at the American Club?" he is ready to use this as a piece of information he can build on. Invariably, he will attempt to use our supposed past connection to wheedle something out of me. But sometimes the African really did meet me years ago, and really does remember my name, when I have totally forgotten him. It is these occasional encounters with the prodigious memories for face and name that intimidate Westerners and provide the opportunists an opening.

27. Friendships and other relationships are built and maintained with gifts.

Gift exchange is a major factor in building relationships and friendships. Across the continent this is a basic characteristic of African societies.

The Wolof of Senegal provide an example that is quite typical. Their extensive specialized vocabulary clearly demonstrates the importance they place on gifts.[8]

añu njëkë	Sum of money given by a woman to her sisters-in-law at the time of a naming ceremony or marriage

---

[8]Sylla 1978:86

jaxal	Contribution given to a friend or relative who is in mourning
ndawtal	Contribution given to a friend or relative who is having a major family celebration
ndéwénël	Gifts given to children at annual feast days or holidays
ndokeel	Gift or expression of sentiment addressed to someone that has just gone through a major difficulty
reeru goro	Sumptuous meal given by a woman periodically to her in-laws
sangu	Clothing or sum of money given to cousins at the time of a family funeral
sëricë	Gift given upon returning from a trip, given to those who come to greet the traveler
wàllu bàjjan	Share reserved for the paternal aunt
yeelu maam	Special share given to grandparents at times of family festivities

They even have a specialized vocabulary just for gifts related to marriage.

can	Bridewealth, the totality of the gifts and material goods that the groom gives in exchange for the bride
dekoore	Gifts given during the *jébol*
feccoo	Giving of gifts to the bride on the sixth day after the wedding
jébol	Rich banquet given in honor of the relatives of the bride
ndarufar	Monthly gifts given to the participants during the time of the engagement
ndobin	The part of the bride-price received by the father of the bride
nibol	Ceremony held two to three months after the wedding night, when gifts are given to the bride's female companions

warugar   The part of the bride-price reserved for the *bàjjan* 'mothers' (that is, the aunts and female friends of the mother), the *ndey-njàkke* 'sponsors' (that is, the sisters of the father), and the *njëàkke* (sisters and female cousins)

Gift giving is frequently institutionalized in Africa. The Lebu fishermen of the western coast share the dangers and risks of ocean fishing through an elaborate system of gift exchange. In very simplified form, the main gift categories are[9]:

dëwyeew   Fish given to the survivors of men lost at sea or victims of other disasters

mboole   Fish given to retired or old fishermen

neeral   Gift of fish given to members of a family who have lost their male source of support. Eligible people are given a certain part of the catch if they meet a particular boat at the time it returns from fishing at sea. The fish is sold at the market and the profits sustain the family

njaaylu   Collective work (fishing) days, with the proceeds going to finance large projects, such as replacement of lost boats or nets

In Muslim cultures it is the custom to give selected friends a choice piece of meat from the animal sacrificed at the annual feast *id al-Adha*. In Senegal many Christians have felt that they needed a way to respond to the Muslim gift giving. One ethnic group, the Sereer, have transformed a local delicacy into a traditional gift. *Ngallax* is a thick drink made from pounded millet, peanuts, and sugar. At Easter time it is now the custom for Protestants and Roman Catholics to prepare an especially delicious ngallax, made with millet, peanuts, and sugar, with the addition of dates, raisins, and other special ingredients. They make large quantities and give portions to Muslims and other friends. Muslims often express much appreciation for this Christian gesture of friendship, and the fact that it is done by the Christians to commemorate the resurrection of Jesus, just as they share from their celebration of Abraham's sacrifice of a ram.

   In some communities gifts are expected to be given by people traveling, when leaving on or returning from a trip. It is not obligatory to give gifts, but when the traveler does so, especially to close friends, it is greatly appreciated. Commonly, when a person returns from a trip, people will ask, "What have you brought for me?" This is a form of welcome as much as an

---

[9]Sud Quotidien 1997.

expression of hope. When my wife and I lived in a village we often returned from an absence with a sack of fruit which we would pass out to the children that came to greet us. Fruit for them was scarce and expensive, so this not only helped us to make friends but to augment their deficient diets as well.

Certainly gifts must play an important role in the lives of all peoples. The unwritten rules followed in each culture are complex, far beyond the scope of this chapter to examine. But there is a common American expression used in relation to gift giving that contrasts with African custom. Under certain circumstances Americans say, "It's the thought that counts." If an American is late in giving a gift, making a phone call, sending a greeting card, or gives a gift that is smaller than would be expected, the polite recipient will use this expression, meaning that having been remembered, whether early or late, or with something large or small, is more important than the value of the gift. Even token gifts provide evidence that the recipients have been in the thoughts of the givers, that their welfare is of concern, and that they are important to them. I venture to say that Africans would not have come up with this expression. In Africa, you do not forget or neglect your friends. If you forget them or are too busy to take time for them, words cannot make up for your having put them, in effect, into a category of secondary concern.

28. Visiting is concentrated on friends and acquaintances who are actively part of a person's economic network.

This observation is difficult to demonstrate as valid without systematically studying visiting patterns of Africans, which I have not done. However, it is logically reasonable. Most people are (a) overextended financially, (b) dependent upon friends to bail them out of frequent financial difficulties, and (c) great developers of social and economic networks. These facts would indicate that people have good reason to keep their circle of friends and acquaintances in constant repair.

My own experience confirms this. Several times I have had African friends who visited me frequently, but whose visits stopped when I was no longer their employer, or disburser of organizational funds, or I had declined to give a person something asked for. I do not believe the visits stopped because they repudiated me or my friendship, but that in their need to secure resources they found it necessary to concentrate on members of their networks who were more potentially forthcoming. The realities and necessities of life required them to concentrate on productive relationships.

29. Most networking is done horizontally or "up" and seldom "down" socially or economically.

When we first arrived in Africa and needed to drop off or pick up friends at the international airport, often in the wee hours of the night, I was amazed to see many pedestrians along the streets. When I queried an African, he told me people were out visiting friends, which is a major activity. That is, they were visiting their networks of friends, and he said people always go to visit those who are higher than they are socially or economically. He lived in a modest part of the city, and he said none of his more affluent friends had ever visited him there; rather, he always had to be the one to pay the visit. This is consistent with the etiquette of the greetings system: "Ideally, one greets 'up': it should be the lower-ranking party who greets the higher. Acceptance or refusal of the role of initiator is of major importance in how one handles the greeting situation."[10]

Etiquette

30. Africans are more hospitable than charitable.

Hospitality, as meant here, is personal and spontaneous. Africans are extraordinarily hospitable. In my experience, and in that of countless other Westerners, there is nothing more classically African than being invited—with insistence—to eat a meal, when happening to drop in on people at mealtime.

"Come eat food!"
(Observation 30)

---

[10]Irvine 1989:169.

30W. Westerners are more charitable than hospitable.

Charity is defined here as giving that is impersonal and planned. Europeans and Americans collectively give billions to charitable organizations, but individually may not want to offer a meal to someone not invited or planned for. In contrast, Africans will offer a meal to all who drop in, but give little to charities. As a general rule we can say that Africans are generous in a hospitable sense but are not charitable, whereas Westerners are charitable, but not hospitable to everyone who comes to his/her home. What does this mean? Let us start with an example from a personal experience.

Our acquaintance Abdou told us that he can go to stay with any of his extended family, or even with friends' families, and they will offer him his meals as long as he is there. It is a "law" to be generous in this way. And this applies even more so in his father's households (his father having more than one wife). But food and lodging are all he will get. Even if the clothes are falling off his back, he will not be offered more. Abdou went on to explain that Westerners are different. If you go to their house, they may well not invite you to eat with them, even at mealtime. They are not generous in this way. But they may help you in other ways. If you need clothing, if you need help with your school fees, if you need seeds for planting, they may help you. And, he said, Senegalese will rarely help you in these ways.

Westerner taking a charitable contribution to the Red Cross.
(Observation 30W)

Hence I am saying that there is a difference between hospitality and charity. The Western way is to be hospitable only within a small circle, but to be open to being charitable to any need in the world. Africans are open to being generous/hospitable within certain limited domains, but are not very open to helping with major needs that are outside a limited circle, or outside of what could be called their zone of personal interest.

An African friend explained how important hospitality is and to what extent it is practiced:

> The Wolof word *teraanga* is a core concept that includes elements of hospitality, civility, honor, consideration, and always living in a manner that brings praise from others. In relation to foreigners it could be called a form of "temporary solidarity," which leads to treating foreigners visiting or living in the country in such a way that they will not return home with bad memories. In relation to Senegalese who are less fortunate economically, *teraanga* is "permanent solidarity." In principle, it would even be an affront to put on a big party at one's house, knowing that at the next door neighbor's the wife has not even "boiled the cooking pot" that day. Such solidarity leads Senegalese society in general to ill judge those who amass wealth (personal communication, 1998).

> There are also the cases of visitors who arrive at any time of day or night. When I still lived at home we sometimes gave up our food to visitors who arrived without notice, telling them we had already eaten or that we weren't hungry. We were sometimes also forced to sleep in the hall, even on the floor, in order that the visitors could sleep in our beds. Sometimes the visitors stayed for long periods, during which time we always had to be the last to lie down and the first to get up so that they would not see how we were living. If they saw how we were living they might cut short their visit and that would have shamed us. This is just one personal example of how all Senegalese, from all ethnic groups, live out the concept of *teraanga* (personal communication, 1997).

Very often there are tensions between Africans and Westerners because of the Westerners' lack of hospitality in inviting people to eat with them. Westerners need to be sensitive to this, and adjust, and frequently prepare extra food if they think an African friend or even just an acquaintance may drop in at mealtime, which some frequently do (and sometimes even purposefully).

At the same time Westerners can understand themselves better if they realize that their culture teaches them more about being charitable than about being hospitable in the ways that Africans are. The Western way is more a planned, budgeted, giving-for-long-term good, whereas the African way is to be more generous spontaneously, not thinking of the long-term.

Some great differences between African and Western cultures in the area of hospitality have been shown in many receptions and similar gatherings I have attended. The African concept of hospitality includes the idea that invitees should be served until they are satisfied. A good host will do this, even if it means financial ruin. So when the food is served in a self-service style, the first Africans to arrive at the table will take all they want to eat and drink. If the host or hostess or organizer has not expected so many guests, or people eat more than has been expected, or there have been budgetary constraints on the amount that could be afforded, both food and drink can easily run out long before all the invitees are served. I have seen events where the last half of the invitees found only scraps of food left for them.

In such a situation it is a negative reflection on the host. It is the host's responsibility to have more than enough so that everyone will be completely satisfied. It is not the responsibility of the invitees to ration themselves to ensure that there will be enough to go around, or to take only a small portion until all have been served. This is especially true when the host has the means to make ample provision for food and drink, which they would certainly consider to be true for wealthy Africans and all Westerners.

The Westerners are, however, probably more attuned to evaluating the situation and acting accordingly. Upon approaching the food table, they would mentally estimate the amount available, and have a good idea of the host's expectations and financial means. And they would limit themselves if they thought the food would run out before everyone was served. Or they would look at, say the platters of sandwiches, and say to themselves, "It looks like the hostess planned for everyone to have two," and then take only two. The African will rather think in terms of his or her hunger, and take as many as desired.

There are perfectly satisfactory ways the Westerner can use to avoid running out of food, to limit the amount each invitee receives. However, the hostess needs to know how to do it when planning the event. Instead of having people serve themselves, they can be served predetermined amounts. This could for example be done by using servers in a cafeteria line, or serving plates of food and drinks after people are seated. In these situations the Westerner hostess needs to know the local customs and what is acceptable. These observations do not reflect negatively on Africans, but are merely expressions of different cultures each of which has positive qualities and results. The African system is more spontaneous, the Western one more planned.

A classic example of the differences between the two cultures was shown to me in a church service I attended. I happened to sit behind the pianist, who was a Western missionary. The choir was made up of Africans, who sang hymns in several African languages. The pianist had before him a large sheaf of music which I was close enough to see was very complex, requiring a high degree of expertise to play. The choir sang from memory, using a drum and several simple percussion instruments to set the rhythm of the music. The piano represented a complex, planned, rehearsed, highly developed musical tradition. The choir represented a very different, spontaneous, emotive, participatory tradition, which also comprised great rhythmic and other complexities and was very enjoyable. Both traditions have made profound contributions to world music, yet in very different ways.

On a very practical level of hospitality and entertaining guests, Westerners frequently are out of sync with African cultures by offering choices to their guests.

> Offering choices is foreign. When you have visitors in your home country and you offer them something to drink, you might say, "Would you like coffee or tea?" When you say this to African guests, two things happen. First, they might assume you don't really want to offer anything. Otherwise you would have brought it out, and used a command form (of the language), "Drink!" or "Eat!" Secondly, they will probably answer "Yes" to this either/or question. It would be more appropriate to bring out what you have to offer, and let them indicate what they want.[11]

31. Compliments are frequently given indirectly in the form of requests for gifts or loans and are often formulated as questions.

Examples are: "Why don't you give me your blouse?" Or "Give me your trousers." These mean that the blouse and trousers are really nice.

Typical compliments and acceptable responses are like these: "I like your shirt." Response: "I will give it to you when I take it off," or better yet, "When it has a little brother I will give it to you," meaning, "When I have another I'll give it to you."

---

[11]Hill 1996:11

"When will you give me your blouse?" (Observation 31)

For the average Westerner some of the answers that are frequently given seem to be a bit dishonest, or at least deceptive. A case would be saying that the shirt will be given when taken off, yet having no intention of doing so. Africans understand such responses as replies that mean No but that are more considerate of feelings than would be a blunt "No, I won't give it to you." It may seem strange that these compliments are given as requests, and the responses are given as though they were real requests. The Westerner may think that if these are compliments, why not just answer with some form of, "Thank you for the compliment, I'm glad you like my blouse." But this is not how the game is played. The rules of the game dictate that the response to the compliment be given on two or three levels. The first level is to appear to take the request seriously as a request. The second is to fend off the request with a polite and phony excuse as to why it will not be granted. And the third, if the one receiving the compliment is capable of responding on this level, what most delights Africans is to have a joke made out of it in a clever way. And better still is to be humorous or clever and in addition mildly embarrass the other person. In countless ethnic groups, playing word games of this kind is one of the joys of conversation.

One time when I was with a group of men, one of them asked me, "When are you going to give me your pickup truck?" He, of course, had not the slightest thought that I would ever do so. I answered, "I'd be happy to give you my truck, but I know you can't drive and would just run it into the ditch." All the men around gave a big guffaw. I had not just answered, but with a bit of humor, and had turned the tables on the one who gave the compliment. This kind of one-upmanship is a much appreciated part of the game. Had he thought that I was competent in the language, the man might have come back with a response that put me on the verbal defensive, which would then have given me opportunity to get back at him. But this is beyond the scope of this chapter to explore.

Here are some sample responses that can be given to compliments:

"Not today."
"You're kidding" (suitable for children only).
"You have more than I" (said with a smile).
"If I give it to you, what will I have left?"
"What will you give me?"[12]

One of the most imaginative responses I have heard of was given by an anthropologist friend. When she was once hiking in northern Cameroon she came upon a cattle herder watching over his animals. He admired the watch she was wearing and asked her to give it to him. She said, "Gladly, and I'll take one of your cows in exchange." The man was incredulous, "One of my cows?" She responded, "Yes, but since the watch doesn't keep good time, you can give me a cow that limps." At that point they both began to laugh, and each went on their way content with having had a pleasant verbal exchange.[13]

There is a reasonable explanation for compliments not being made directly except between friends of mutual confidence that applies to many African cultures. Traditionally there was much fear of evil tongue, evil eye, or evil touch. So, for example, it was taboo to tell parents that their child was pretty, or even to ask how many children a woman had. Even today if you compliment a relatively unknown person directly, the response in the local language may be something like, "Do not eat me." This is a magical formula believed to have the power to counteract any evil intent or effect that might be contained in a compliment. In these belief systems, saying something complimentary can be a disguise for wishing evil on the person.

Direct compliments are greatly appreciated, but basically they are only given to close friends. There needs to be a high degree of confidence and social relationship between people before they will openly comment on positive things about each other. But where confidence exists, in many African cultures compliments are freely and frequently given and appreciated. Special social gatherings are even organized with friends which include designated times of openly complimenting one another, to give mutual support and express appreciation for each individual.

---

[12]Thanks to Marilyn Escher for these examples.
[13]Thanks to Marian Hungerford.

31W. Westerners are not accustomed to compliments being formulated as requests, and easily misinterpret them and take offense.

Some of the reasons that Westerners misunderstand compliments being given as requests are the following:

1. In their own cultures compliments are virtually never given as requests. The closest equivalent situation I can imagine would be a wife expressing to her husband profuse admiration for a gift a friend of hers received, hoping to alert her husband to something she herself would like him to give her.

2. In many African cultures or countries, Westerners are constantly approached by people requesting money, aid, or loans, that are real requests. They feel bombarded by these requests, which are unpleasant for them. So after a time in the culture area they become conditioned to quickly react negatively to all requests, not understanding the subtle differences between importunity and compliment.

3. Even when they learn that some requests are actually meant to be compliments, they do not know how to distinguish compliments from real requests, and under the circumstances find it difficult to appreciate the intended compliment.

The foreigner in Africa frequently is asked for favors from strangers or near strangers that seem to be a mix of request, an indirectly expressed compliment, and a deep desire that the asker does not expect will be granted. Examples are, "Can you take me to your country?" Or, if the stranger is known or seen to be an American, "Can you help me get to America?" Or, "Will you teach me English?" Certainly the asker would like to have these requests filled, but when the foreigner being addressed is almost a total stranger, he knows it is very unlikely. I understand these requests to be conversational openers, attempts to establish a friendly relationship, expressions of admiration for the thing requested, and verbalization of the recognition that the person being addressed has access to resources, position, and power.

32. If a Westerner has a misunderstanding about finances with an African friend, it is virtually impossible to straighten it out directly with the offended individual.

When the Westerner tries to explain the matter from his viewpoint he will not be believed, basically because in face-to-face discourse, it is the African rule that people should say polite, nonoffensive things. Difficult issues are not handled through direct confrontation. Therefore, to resolve misunderstandings it is necessary to go to a mutual friend and explain the matter, asking him or her to convey the explanation to the offended party. In this manner your explanation will be given credence and will be accepted. The reason your explanation is believable is that, instead of attempting to justify yourself and criticize the offended party behind his back, which is the expected behavior, you are demonstrating that you really did not mean to offend and that you really do want to be on good terms with him.

When Africans have misunderstandings with Westerners, many will assume the worst. (And many will not do so.) The "worst" means they will be quick to interpret the misunderstood behavior as being motivated by racism. I know the leaders of an NGO working in an African country. They followed a strategy of establishing social centers where they taught sewing and other practical skills to women, maintained sports facilities for young men, and such. Their centers employed quite a few Africans. After several years of effort, they saw that the centers were not accomplishing their stated goals and decided to adopt a completely different strategy. They dismissed and settled with all their employees. I also knew some of the employees and heard their explanation of the dismissals. They said the NGO was racist and let everyone go because the Westerners did not want Africans to get ahead financially. Doubtlessly the NGO did not adequately communicate the reasons for their change in programs, but in any case the former employees were ready to blame racism.

In contrast, at the depths of the apartheid era in South Africa, I had African friends tell me that they recognized that racism was not the basic problem in that country; rather, it was the self-interest of whites in protecting their dominant economic position.

33. Africans prefer to apologize symbolically, rather than verbally, when they have made a mistake or feel personal shame.

A typical experience of symbolic apology is recounted by Delbert Chinchen.

> Liberians and Malawians prefer to symbolize, rather than verbalize, important messages, especially those that reveal personal weakness or indicate vulnerability....When constructing [our training college], the Liberian head carpenter made a major mistake in the pitch of the roof he was building, requiring that wasted time, energy and money be spent to correct the error. The researcher, then construction supervisor, let the carpenter know of his displeasure with the situation. The next morning, the carpenter brought several pineapples to the researcher's door. Nothing was said but the implicit message was: "Let this gift put our relationship back on course." (1994:35) [14]

Westerners may not even recognize such a symbolic gesture as an apology. Or if they do realize that they are somehow related to the person's

---

[14]Chinchen 1994:35.

regret over an unspecified previous failing, they may not think them adequate to the offense, or that the person lacks courage and directness to bring up the matter in a more acceptable, explicit way. The Westerner should, however, understand that these are fully acceptable and adequate means of making amends for past faux pas in Africa.

In many African cultures the maintenance of dignity, honor and similar personal qualities, and the avoidance of shame and humiliation are extremely important. So direct apologies, which might be construed as admissions of weakness, insufficiency, or ineptitude are avoided, yet are obliquely admitted through symbolic apologies. Assane Sylla well describes this behavior:

> For the Wolof man, his dignity is without price. In order to safeguard his honor, without which life is not worth living, he is always ready to do battle. Whoever suffers a humiliation or an affront, and retreats without reacting, will be condemned and reprimanded most severely...
>
> [The Wolof are] preoccupied with problems of proper behavior, proper living with others, with meriting respect, and with shouldering their own dignity. All of these concerns impact even the simplest acts of daily life. The multitude of shades of meaning they encompass are reflected in fine points of their language and rules of behavior. Verbs like to work, to look, to walk, to speak, etc., all have several alternatives that express elegance, tactlessness, liveliness, hostility, etc.[15]

A number of times when an African associate or employee has made a rather major mistake, I have looked for an apology or some kind of acknowledgement of fault or regret—usually in vain. For example, I was researching the possibilities of using seeds from the moringa tree as a source of edible oil. I sent my assistant out to collect a quantity of seeds, telling him to not pay more than half the agreed-upon amount to a collector for a set quantity of pods, from which we would remove the seeds. On one occasion he came back, having contracted for a certain quantity, but informed me he had paid the man the complete sum before he had collected one pod. In response to my obvious unhappiness, he assured me that the collector was a person of confidence and I would have all the pods agreed upon. Weeks and months went by, with my bringing up the subject and sending him out to see what was happening, but I never received a pod. And I never detected the slightest apologetic attitude in my assistant. Probably, I was too obtuse to detect a symbolic action, but I did not.

---

[15]Sylla 1978:91.

I mention this because similar experiences are a common cause of friction between Westerners and Africans. It seems that the Westerner is much more ready to admit fault, apologize, and even make amends, than is the average African. So even as it is considered a weakness to admit fault, it is a very delicate matter to have weaknesses pointed out. If a Westerner wants to succeed in calling someone to task, the utmost tact and understanding of how the culture operates in this area of interpersonal relations is needed. And probably it will have to be done by an African, not by a Westerner.

In one African country where I worked, our organization was involved in giving technical advice to an African association. The association called a public meeting to discuss some of the members' questions. The matter was potentially delicate politically, so we as a foreign organization did not participate in the planning, but agreed to be present to provide some technical information. The ministry in charge of national security heard of the meeting and ordered it canceled. I was called in, without a stated reason, to the office of a subminister. We chatted for some time about our organization, and other innocuous subjects. Finally at the end of a reasonable time, the official stood up, indicating the end of the audience. He escorted me to the door of his office, and as I was walking out, casually told me that we should never be involved in the kind of meeting that the association had wanted to hold. The major point he wanted to make with me in calling me in as the representative of a foreign organization, and concerning a subject that got the attention of very high levels of his government, was handled very casually, low key, and seemingly, almost as an afterthought. The experience actually frightened me, as I realized how easy it was for me as a Westerner to not hear communications that African officials or friends might be sending.

34. Many Africans in need are very discreet about asking for assistance, only hinting at their needs.

Because Westerners are so bombarded by people seeking money or other kinds of financial or material assistance, they begin to believe that all needy Africans are out and about aggressively asking for help. This is far from being true. In many African cultures, the most needy people are the most hesitant to ask for help. In contrast, more aggressive, blatant requests are typically indications that the petitioner is manipulative, professional, or at least more practiced. Whether needy people are restrained or bold about asking for help seems to depend a great deal on the person's culture, religion, individual scruples and values, and, of course, on his self-definition of "needy."

In contrast to discreet petitioners are Muslims. Western friends of mine who have traveled in most countries of Africa note that where Muslims predominate, begging is very common. This probably comes from the fact that giving alms is one of the five pillars, or essential practices, of Islam.

Therefore, beggars enable Muslim believers to fulfill their religious obligations, and begging becomes almost a recognized profession.

In many African cultures it is shameful to be in need, let alone to beg. In these cultures Africans are very sensitive to the needs of others, and those who have more resources seek to share with those they know are needy. People who are in need in such cultures have indirect ways of communicating those needs to their friends and kin. If people are attuned to the way needs are made known in these cultures, they understand the hidden or double meanings contained in everyday exchanges such as:

> "How are the children? How is life with your people?" Within the conversation, there may be hints at the need for assistance: "We are hoping to build a hut..." or "We are hoping to make a farm..." or "We are hoping to repair the roof..." These are indirect signals of request for assistance.[16]

When in such a culture a person has made his or her needs known, it is up to the hearer to decide whether to act on the knowledge or not. For the Westerner who is used to bold requests for help, such low key appeals may go entirely unnoticed. Also, in such cultures, if the hearer understands the message and wants to provide help, the response needs to be just as discreet as the request. If being in need can cause shame, so being given to in an open, insensitive way can cause at least as much shame.

Almost opposite to this is a concept present in many African cultures that "It doesn't hurt to ask (for money, to borrow something, for a gift, etc.)." Many people from these cultures seem to have no hesitation in asking for anything that they would like to have, even if they have no expectation of the thing being given to them. It is almost a game, or perhaps, a belief that even if the request is not granted, they have done a positive thing in paying a compliment to the owner of the desired object.

35. Africans find security in ambiguous arrangements, plans, and speech.

Part of the social code is the use of ambiguity and the indirect approach, for it provides allowances for the uncertainties of life. It allows for "bargaining for reality," or expressed more precisely for sub-Saharan Africa, "flexibility for changing realities" or "keeping the options open."[17] It also gives ample allowance for saving face, that is, for avoiding embarrassment for oneself or others.

The following are areas where ambiguity is often seen.

> 1. Borrowing money or other resources or goods, which leaves open when, how, or if return or repayment will be made.

---

[16]Chinchen 1994:150.
[17]Rosen 1984.

2. Not having fixed prices. This maximizes the possibility of making greater profits; keeps the potential customers in the dark, with the seller maintaining the advantage of knowing his or her bottom "last price" below which he will not sell; and the potential buyer having the option of negotiating a better last price. It also allows for the inclusion of personal relationships and other subjective factors in pricing decisions.

3. Allowing for the renegotiation of agreements in the light of changed facts, or a hoped-for basis for claiming a better agreement.

4. Not keeping accurate or precise financial records.

5. "No" being an unacceptable response in many situations where it expresses a finality that is considered to be negative and even hostile, easily leading to a rupture in relationship.

6. The arriving or starting times for meetings or gatherings being indefinitely later than the announced times.

7. Reticence to register for seminars or courses before the closing dates, which involves a commitment to attend.

A basic desire for ambiguity can even be seen in African use of time. In the words of a Ghanaian who spent some time as a student in the U.S.:

> When a group of (my) people meet for a social development project, discussion is not always with an agenda but is open-ended. This could bring long discussion, deviation from the main topic with everyone expected to make a contribution, no matter if the contribution is relevant or not. Decision by such a group is normally by consensus.
>
> In contrast to this, I discovered that in America, when people meet together for class, church, or a party, everything is programmed and each activity has to be done in a certain order and finished by a certain time. For example, at school when it is close to the time the students expect the lecture to end, all begin looking at the wall clock or turn to look at their wristwatch. When the time is right on the dot, they close books ready to leave. The lecturer has to stop, whether finished or not. My observation is that paying close attention to time gives Americans a sense of security, whereas it causes a lot of anxiety to me as a foreigner.[18]

Reference was made in chapter 1 to the prevalence of micromanagement in Africa. It seems clear that the area of ambiguity relates at least in

[18]Mogre 1982.

part to micromanagement. The definiteness that Westerners consider essential to the expeditious handling of personal or commercial business seems to be absent in many of the actions of Africans. For them the importance of interpersonal relationships, avoiding the possibility of offending others' sensitivities and leaving plans open so as to allow for last-minute developments are of greater importance than expeditiously handling business.

Many of the observations in this book involve ambiguity as a cultural preference. For example, consider the cases referred to under observation 17 in chapter 3. These Africans rejected the Western way of attempting to match monthly expenditures to income by paring expenditures to bring personal budgets into balance. They much preferred to keep finances fluid. They always managed to get through a month the way they had been doing it and liked to continue that way rather than live in the grip of a rigid budget.

In one African country I was responsible for planning construction for a training center. I needed to be able to study the local building code so that we could plan such things as the best type of construction to use, the layout of buildings, and how many floors we could have. I spent several days trying to track down the building code. Finally, I ended up in the office of a high government official who told me there was no book. He said, "I am the book in this country." In other words, for the whole country what was allowed to be constructed was based on subjective criteria, not upon carefully worked-out standards that would be known and followed by everyone.

We lived a couple of years in a middle-class neighborhood in an African city. The neighbors on one side frequently pestered us to give them things, from money, to food, to ice water. This went on for many months when, to our surprise, they sent over a quantity of fresh fish fillets. No message was sent with the child that made the delivery, no explanation was given. Was this simply an expression of neighborly generosity? A way of expressing thanks? A symbolic apology for their importunate demands? Were they reciprocating for the help we had given? There was never a verbal explanation of any kind, but we interpreted it as partly involving amends for their frequent demands.

An experience that at first seemed ambiguous as described by Carole Unseth leaves no doubt about the meaning of a nonverbalized action:

> We had been living in a Majang village in southwest Ethiopia....In spite of my...training, however, some things really irritated me, especially that nobody seemed to ever say "thank you" for anything. In fact, they'd come to the door without any greeting and just demand, *"Deyaa maaw!"* (Give me water!). I'd give them some out of our precious supply carried from the river. They'd drink it, and then leave without a word.

This went on for some time, and since I noticed that they did it to each other as well, it didn't bother me quite as much.

Then one day, a special friend, Maryam, had a daughter who was behaving strangely, and the family wanted (my husband) to take her into the nearby town to the clinic...

A few days later...our friend Maryam arrived at the door of our little round house with a bundle of sticks tied together to make a broom. Without a word she walked in and proceeded to sweep out the many clods of dirt that had come into the house on visitors' feet. She finished the job and again, without a word, but with a little smile, she left.

I've often thought since then that Maryam's thank you, though not verbal, was much more eloquent than what we often lightly say to each other when a favor is done. I think she really meant it.[19]

The comments by Yale Richmond and Phyllis Gestrin speak to the point:

Ambiguity is an art in Africa, and imprecision is its first cousin. Africans speak naturally, with eloquence, and without hesitation or stumbling over words, but their language is often imprecise and their numbers inexact. Every personal interaction becomes a discussion which establishes a basis for the relationship between the two parties. Westerners should probe gently for specificity and details until they are reasonably satisfied that they understand what is meant even if not stated.[20]

Richmond and Gestrin also offer this advice:

Westerners should be watchful for...roundabout approaches by Africans they meet or work with. An expatriate, for example, was once puzzled when an African with whom he was working complained to him at length about the behavior of someone from outside the office. The expat could not understand why his African counterpart should complain so much about an outsider's behavior. The African, however, was trying to explain indirectly what the expat himself should not be doing.[21]

---

[19]Unseth 1995:3-4.
[20]Richmond and Gestrin 1998:85.
[21]Ibid., 129.

An indirect approach is also needed between employers and employees. As Harriet Hill tells us:

> The confrontive, direct approach that many of us have been trained in is inappropriate here. First of all, you won't pick up what people are trying to tell you. Secondly, people will find you offensive.
>
> If your employee is trying to tell you something, he will go about it in a roundabout way. This will take more time, and it might take a while before you catch on to the point he is trying to make. It is your role to discover the issue and verbalize a solution. Africans love symbolism, proverbs and double meanings, not straight-forward speech.
>
> Likewise, if you need to communicate something to an employee, you need to beat around the bush. To confront him or her directly would be inappropriate. Among the Adioukrou (of Ivory Coast), when a person gives an outlandish opinion or idea on an issue, you respond first by congratulating him and praising his oration. This is very flowery. At the end, you add "but it's also true that..." and say what you really want to say. A flat 'no' in response to a request should also be avoided. For example, if someone is trying to sell you meat at your door, compliment the meat, their kindness, etc., and then say that you regret that today you don't need any.[22]

35W. Westerners find security in clearly defined relationships, arrangements, plans, and speech.

This observation is especially true of Americans and Northern Europeans, and less true of Southern Europeans. American idioms express many characteristic attitudes toward clarity of communication and directness of action. They like to "lay their cards on the table," "face the facts," "get on with the business at hand," get their information "directly from the horse's mouth," "call a spade a spade." People are told to "fish or cut bait," and "stand up and be counted." They don't like those who "beat around the bush," or "pass the buck."

Edward Hall, who has spent a lifetime studying and helping people in international business relate more effectively to each other, observes: "Many foreigners comment on the American low-context legalistic approach

---

[22]Hill 1996:8–9.

to things; everything is spelled out and put on paper.[23] Two-thirds of all the lawyers in the world are practicing in the United States."[24]

American business has "three key characteristics: (1) clear lines of authority, (2) detailed instructions for subordinates, and (3) constant feedback on individual performance."[25] These all imply ideals of clear, open communication, not only "down" from those in power and authority, but also "up" from those in subordinate positions.

Present and Future Orientation. The different experiences of Africans and Westerners have obviously molded their attitudes toward ambiguity. Africans' experiences have taught them that much of life is uncertain, including the future; therefore, caution is needed. Much that goes on in the halls of power at all levels is ambiguous, shrouded in secrecy. Government is all-powerful, and the goals and policies of those in power are largely unknown. Transparency is much talked about but little practiced. The rule of law takes a back seat to the rule of power. Available resources are very limited and there is much hidden competition and conflict over their control. This state of affairs is both the consequence and the cause of the situation. The highest levels of society operate this way because the lowest levels, and those in between, also do. Consequently, to commit oneself to a future action or to the use of personal resources is very hazardous or even reckless—who can tell what will happen after a decision is made that will affect one's resources, the rules, and even the playing field? So the successful strategy is to delay final outcomes as much as possible. Ambiguity gives security, because flexibility is built in, contingencies are allowed for. People have learned from experience to be present-oriented, preferring to focus on the present and deal with the uncertain future as it comes along.

In fundamental contrast to the African experience, Westerners' experiences, and their education, have taught them that those who plan ahead get ahead, in this way achieving more of what they want from life. The conditions of their lives, their governments, and institutions have been stable and predictable; they assume they will continue that way. They have found that it pays to carefully budget their resources, time, and activities. Ambiguity causes worry because future plans need to be settled now. If something is determined to be advantageous now, take advantage of it. Conditions or opportunities may not be quite as advantageous in the future. Besides, when

---

[23]Low-context situations exist when background information relating to an event or a matter needs to be made explicit to the participants. In high-context culture, normal transactions in daily life do not require that detailed background information be given—the participants are already informed about the people involved so little information needs to be made explicit.

[24]Hall 1990:149.

[25]Stewart 1972:159.

one matter is settled and therefore concomitant obligations are known, plans for other matters can be negotiated and resources be committed to them. Ambiguity causes worry because of a need to know what future actions and commitments will be. Ambiguity prevents Westerners from planning for the future. Being future-oriented, they need to make detailed plans for the future. When they cannot do so, they are frustrated.

Summary: friendship

Hospitality is a very important part of friendship in Africa. Westerners are frequently amazed at the lengths that Africans will go to be hospitable. This is clearly shown in an experience some Western volunteers had soon after their arrival in Cameroon:

> Last Sunday we attended a house church. It meets in a tiny, shabby building, adjacent to a hairdresser's; plaster peeling, walls unpainted, ceiling decrepit. We were given pride of place on chairs at the front. Everyone was crammed into two small rooms. After the meeting, we went outside to chat with people, and when we came back in, there were about 12 large metal platters with rice, manioc, huge fish, fried plantains, etc.!
>
> We sat to eat, everyone else sitting around the walls of the room in silence until we'd had plenty. What a banquet! The food was superb. Then pineapple juice and fruit salad. We were treated as kings. There was really nothing that they could have done for us that would have been too much—the pastor's wife kept on piling our plates up again and again, and was obviously delighting in the role of hostess. It was not until we had almost finished eating that the others began to eat. What a lot we have to learn from our African friends about hospitality (personal communication, 1999).

5

The Role of Solidarity

Solidarity means interdependence rather than independence. It also means living in community rather than living in social or spacial isolation. Though he was speaking about Poland, the eloquent words of Krzyszt of Kieslowski, the well-known Polish film director, provide a keen insight into some fundamental differences between Africa and the West:

> Question: "Is man more isolated in affluent Western countries than he was in Poland and the other Eastern-bloc countries under the Soviet empire?"
>
> Kieslowski: "Without a doubt. Because suffering unites people, while affluence and riches divide people. In our time success is very fashionable. Strength is fashionable. And in order to be strong and successful you have to throw away all of your scruples. And when you do this, you become alone, because you lose all your friends. Weakness is not fashionable. Compassion is not fashionable. Yet these are the qualities that bring people together." [1]

Sharing resources

36. **Showing solidarity with friends at such times as funerals, naming ceremonies, feast days, and weddings is extremely important. This is primarily done by attendance at these events and by contributing financially.**

It is a great honor to have many people come to a man's or woman's death observances. Typically across Africa the evening radio news includes death notices from around the country. One of the first and most important

[1]*Newsweek* 1995:56.

things for a family to do at a member's death is to telephone or otherwise immediately notify the national radio administration of the person's death, giving the name, village or town, and dates of observances. These death notices are probably the most closely listened to of any programming in each country. When people hear of the death of someone they know, they immediately notify others who knew the person to make sure they are aware of the fact. And if they are related by kinship or friendship, they immediately make plans to visit the bereaved family, whether located near or far. Even if they are not close kin, they will take the time and bear the expense of personally presenting their condolences. It is a great shame on the dead person and his or her whole family if few come to pay their condolences.

It is difficult for most Westerners to understand the degree of importance that Africans place on attending funerals and other family ceremonies. I have found that even my research into these matters in my quest to better understand African customs and attitudes, and my surprise at learning of their importance to African thinking, are taken as evidence of Western indifference to the pain, sorrow, and loss of others. How else would I even think to ask about things that are basic expressions of living in human community?

Sharing grief at the time of a death. (Observation 36)

Africans easily interpret the behavior of Westerners as evidence of being such victims of individualism that they do not care to show solidarity with others. For instance, it is considered insensitive that a Western associate would not take a day off to attend the funeral of a friend, or that a Western employer would not allow an employee to take one to three days off with full pay to go to his native village to pay his respects at the time of an honored villager's death.

> The financial implications are only one aspect of social-cultural life that require a certain amount of diplomacy. If in a neighborhood a family has recently suffered a death, if they do not feel the solidarity of their neighbors and friends, this emptiness and lack of support will cause them much more suffering than the loss of their loved one. They may think that perhaps the deceased did some evil thing in life that they were not aware of, or perhaps the whole family is ill thought of in the neighborhood. As a bad reputation could have many causes (sorcery, witchcraft, loose morals, thievery, etc.), it is easy to understand the bitterness a family could experience. If such a thing happened, the family would do all within their power to move away within a few months. These cultural traits are very much alive and anchored in people's collective thoughts.

> It is important to realize, in this context, that the financial implications related to a death are of secondary importance.

> The speech itself of men and women at these occasions reflects their state of mind. Even though the expenses will be very heavy, no one in the family would ever ask the question, "What is the total of the expenses we have already incurred?" Rather they will use euphemisms, such as, "How are we coming out?"

> The visits of condolences begin the day of the death. Those paying their respects will leave amounts of money, small or large, as a sign of their solidarity. But it is not obligatory to leave money. The physical presence of friends and relatives in such a circumstance is most important in demonstrating their ties to the family (personal communication, 1996).

Giving fish to widow of a fisherman lost at sea. (Observation 36)

37. A great many economic needs in Africa are met or alleviated through the solidarity and generosity of relatives and friends.

The importance of solidarity and generosity to Senegalese society was expressed by Assy Dieng Ba, a prominent Senegalese theatrical producer, in the course of an interview:

> The conduct and morals in our society get worse and worse. Youths are abandoned to fend for themselves. Women are losing their values. The spirit of helping others is under severe attack. The European way of life, 'everyone for himself and God for us all,' is more and more followed. Our parents and old people are neglected rather than assisted, protected and venerated, as was the case in the past.[2]

Although an outside observer would clearly see the undeniable positive personal and societal values that are demonstrated through social solidarity, such an observer would at the same time probably conclude that some of the consequences are less than positive. Some of the side effects are described in some detail by Régine Nguyen Van Chi-Bonnardel, giving a historical perspective to the discussion. She provides background to the development of customs relating to the imperative need to share

---

[2]*Sud Week-end* [Dakar] December 14, 1996.

resources. Such sharing is essential to showing solidarity and being generous, but it also has some negative effects:

> During the whole colonial period the peasantry of the peanut basin lived by means of advances extended by the merchant-buyers and collected from the peasants at harvest time. The peasants became so dependent on these advances that they became indispensable to simple subsistence.
>
> Such a long-established habit of living by credit could not, for sure, be uprooted by the suppression of private merchants from the peanut business. No serious effort was made by Senegalese society after 1960 to transform the credit mentality. In any case it would have been hard, given the realities of increasing difficulties: low income and buying power deteriorating from year to year. The farmers continued, therefore, to borrow, but under conditions that were less favorable than ever, as peanuts lost their long-established value.
>
> Indebtedness is a gangrene, not only in the rural areas, but also in urban areas where multiform credit is essential to urban commerce. One can assert, simplifying matters only a bit, that buying on credit now constitutes, throughout Senegal, the principal stimulant to the economy.
>
> As the value of goods in circulation is much larger than the cash available in the economy, and as such an extremely weak economy in no way justifies people—urban or rural—living above their means, the whole country is in the grip of an economic crisis. The constant increases in prices, the low monetary revenue, the steady decrease in buying power, the chronic indebtness, all these obviously make it impossible to put any savings aside, whether in the country or in the city, and at any economic level...
>
> Naming ceremonies, weddings, circumcisions, funerals, religious and community feasts, all continue to be the source of ruinous expenditures that ordinary income cannot cover....Besides these celebrations, simple social relations and the requirements of hospitality demand that expenditures be made to maintain prestige. There is no question of avoiding them except at the cost of losing honor. Such expenditures are considered "exceptional," but in fact they are very common and they are a major source of family expenditures,

even if their unpredictability requires people to call on resources they do not have, and consequently, must borrow.[3]

Thus, we see that the habit of living by credit extended by merchants
has been transformed into living by credit extended by family and friends.
It is carried out under the pressures and name of solidarity.

**37W. Westerners greatly admire the high degree of solidarity and
generosity they see between African friends and relatives, but they
find it difficult to become full economic participants in the society.**

There are many factors that limit Westerners' involvement in society. They
feel....

They feel they are continuously bombarded with requests for financial help, which they are culturally and psychologically unprepared for and
do not know how to deal with. Even where there is not a question about
whether or not they are financially capable of meeting a need, they question
whether or not their assistance would be a long-term help to the person and
even to society as a whole, and what their giving priorities should be.

Even if they are disposed to give away everything they have and that
their friends back home have—and this is certainly not the case—they
strongly believe it would only make matters worse in the long run. Until
economic structural changes are made, they remain skeptical about giveaways. They have seen many governmental and private charitable programs
in their own countries that have had a largely negative impact on the recipients themselves and on society as a whole. And aid programs, including
giveaways with crosscultural boundaries are even more difficult to admin-
ister than those within a given country.

Although Westerners highly value generosity and loyalty to friends and
kin, they believe that generosity with others' resources is not really generosity, but an abuse of friendship or kinship. A person who shares his or her
own resources with others is admired. But if a person has to borrow in order
to be generous, with little likelihood of making repayment, the Westerner
sees this at best as unethical, and at worst as immoral. Westerners cannot understand how generosity with something borrowed can be a good
thing—that it could be something that a person needs to do in order to
be considered a good person in any society. They cannot understand how
this could possibly be considered showing solidarity with the receiver, and
that not doing it could be considered to show a lack of solidarity with that
person. They also fail to understand how a host can feel personally honored by providing for his guests when he knows that his hosting is done
with someone else's resources. In fact, the Westerner would believe there
would be more shame in putting on a false front of prosperity done with the

---

[3]Van Chi-Bonnardel 1978:443.

resourses of someone else, than just admitting one's financial limitations. To the Westerner it is not a dishonor or a disgrace to be in economic hardship.

Most Westerners come from societies and families where budgetary discipline and control are idealized and practiced. A recent study in the United States showed that an overwhelming percentage of American millionaires live very normal and relatively frugal lives. The comparatively few flamboyant millionaires—especially the stars of Hollywood and the entertainment and sports figures who are constantly in the world's media—represent only a small fraction of wealthy Americans.[4] Bill Gates, the richest American, and known the world over, is an example of the flamboyant type. But the second-richest man, Warren Buffett, is more typical. He and his wife still live in the unassuming house in the modest part of the city that they have been in since before they became very rich. So if even rich Westerners are relatively frugal, it at least suggests that prosperity in the West is largely based on budgetary restraint, and that Westerners understand restraint as a principle that if followed will result in at least a degree of prosperity for any practitioner. And that the lack of such restraint will ultimately bring economic hardship or even ruin.

Westerners are basically very sympathetic to the economic needs in Africa, but believe the system of living in debt, that Westerners are asked to participate in, only encourages further economic woes. Westerners are sympathetic to the needs of current consumption, but not to the needs of social consumption. (Current consumption refers to basic needs for food, shelter, clothing, and health; social consumption refers to expenditures for feast days, celebrations, maintaining one's place in society, from the French *besoins de la consommation courante* and *besoins sociaux*, respectively.) Outsiders are mostly unwilling to participate to any great extent in expenses that will be used mainly to avoid dishonor or shame or loss of face.

Westerners are very willing to contribute to, or seek contributions from their home countries for, endeavors that they have confidence in and where they believe their assistance will provide long-term help. They believe that they are accountable for seeing that any help they are involved with does not go to unworthy causes and that they will share part of the blame if their help is used unwisely. They believe it is their responsibility as potential donors or intermediaries to evaluate the worthiness of the cause needing or requesting assistance.

Westerners believe there is a general lack of financial accountability in African society. This negatively impacts their incentive to help or to seek help. They believe that the requirement of detailed and rigorous accounting is not a negative reflection on a person or organization, but is a safeguard for donors and recipients alike. It is practically an impossibility for Westerners to understand that Africans might lose face if required to provide careful

---

[4]Stanley and Danko 1998.

accounting. Westerners also find it contrary to their values to be indulgent in matters of accountability.

As an example of expecting accountability, consider what happened in the United States during the presidency of Bill Clinton. For many months the president and his wife were under investigation. Many of their fundraising and personal financial activities were examined, and several of their close personal, business, and political associates were found guilty of misusing funds and in other ways of breaking the law. Several were sent to prison. Others have been publicly criticized for unethical, if not illegal, activities. Whatever degree of political motives lay behind these proceedings, Americans strongly believe that their president and leaders are accountable to the American people and should be subject to the laws just as other citizens are.

To Westerner there is a downside to the admirable African qualities of solidarity and generosity. They consider that there is such a high degree of unquestioning solidarity in society that it has a tendency to breed parasitism and irresponsibility in some individuals. And it seems to many Westerners that part of their frustrations and culture shock comes from their being the attention of a disproportionate share of such opportunistic and irresponsible people.

Most Westerners probably believe they and their friends have been deceived by some Africans. (They certainly realize they have been deceived by many of their own countrymen. However, such deception may not worry them because they have grown up learning how fraudulent behavior works in their own countries. But a major part of their problem in Africa comes when deception is carried out in other languages and cultures they have not mastered, and by very different rules. In these contexts in which they are foreigners, the problems seem more worrisome and are more thought about than would be similar problems at home.) Deceptions include misrepresentation of financial needs, failure to keep promises such as a promise to repay a loan on the prearranged date, asking for assistance for what seems to them an unnecessary expense, failure to seize available opportunities for employment, requests for help in dire situations that were later found out to have been fictitious, and encounters with charlatans whose main source of income derives from a systematic finding out Westerners' names, where they live, and then finding ingenious ways to fleece them of their resources.

Although Westerners realize their bad experiences have been with only a small segment of society, these experiences make them wary of providing more help, as they see themselves being incapable of separating valid needs from questionable needs.

Westerners see that it is unjust that they have so many material goods while many of their friends and fellow workers do not. Yet they do not know what the solution is to this problem. Of course Africans struggle with inequity, too. But that many Westerners struggle with it may be largely unknown and come as a surprise to many Africans. The first edition of this book and of these financial observations attracted attention across Africa, precisely because Westerners living in Africa wrestle so much with these issues, practically every day. The discrepancies in living standards create huge problems, but what should be done? Westerners have not found many workable solutions.

Westerners have seen and heard about many people and projects that were hurt by receiving funds where there was inadequate planning, training, management, and accountability. They believe the funds were largely wasted, at least as far as long-term benefits to local people were concerned. They do not want to further contribute to waste and failure. Some examples follow.

This handling of funds is a very delicate matter, and sometimes African and Westerner perceptions and conclusions regarding many of these things are very different, even diametrically opposed.

An African who worked in the office of an NGO was paid according to the government-established scale for his education, responsibilities, and experience. The man frequently told Westerner workers in the NGO what a hard time he was having financially. They felt sorry for him that his wages were not higher, and several of them regularly gave him money, to the extent that he was able to rent a better house than his employment and station in life would normally justify. He was also able to put several children in private schools that he would not normally be able to afford. And in other ways he was able to improve his life style. There came a time when his Westerner friends became unhappy with some of his behavior and stopped giving him extra money. But he had become accustomed to the gifts, even depending on the supplementary income. At some point he began to embezzle in major ways from the NGO, and was finally dismissed, making an appeal to the labor court which found in the NGO's favor, but still sour relationships and feelings were left all around.

Some NGOs have carried on literacy work using volunteer teachers. They have followed the method pioneered by Frank Laubach, of "each one teach one," or other strategies based at least in part on volunteer teaching. Probably millions of people around the world have become literate through these efforts. More recently as governmental aid programs, the World Bank, UNICEF, and other major donors have championed and begun to fund large-scale literacy programs, the results have been mixed. In some areas, where volunteer teacher programs had been in place, teachers have at the least complained, believing they should now be paid after some organizations began to pay attendees. Some nonliterate people even refused to attend literacy classes without payment. The claim has been made that in some of these cases in order to quickly obtain impressive statistical results attendees were paid, whatever the long-term benefits of this practice would be.

This desire to be paid is very understandable from the local point of view. People desperately need employment. But some of the long-term consequences may be unfortunate. It is doubtful that there will ever be enough foreign money and programs to pay everyone to become literate. So if people do not learn to help themselves with things they can do themselves, their development will be limited in the long-term.

Finally, I want to comment on the concept widely held in Africa that was expressed by Assy Dieng Ba, above, that European culture can rightly be characterized as "everyone for himself and God for us all." There is a sense in which most Westerners would agree with this sentiment, as we do see that there is a general decrease in neighborliness, and in personal care for parents and friends. But what are the facts?

The studied opinion of at least one experienced researcher portrays a very different view of American concern for others than that painted by Assy Dieng Ba. Edward Hall writes:

> Americans can be extraordinarily generous to others. They contribute billions of dollars to charity each year (nearly $90 billion in recent years) and are easily moved to respond to the misfortunes of others, both at home and abroad. This generosity is matched by no other country we know. Business leaders are among the many Americans who spend a great deal of time and money on charitable and civic activities. As one American banker said, "The sense of altruism and its concomitant commitment of time runs through all levels of U.S. industry."[5]

Why, then, is the African perception of the West so different from what is arguably the American reality? Although there is massive help provided for the less fortunate or poorer people in Europe and America, the help is largely given impersonally. Perhaps this is a major source of the misunderstanding. Help is not so much people to people, immediate and visible, as in Africa. This may be the greatest reason that so many Africans consider that there is no concern and help at all, that in Europe and America each individual is left to fend for himself or herself, without help from any quarter. This understanding is far different from objective reality. The differences between micro-and macro-solutions are also involved. In Africa help to less fortunate people is largely given on a micro, that is, on an individual or

---

[5]Hall 1990:153. Total private philanthropy in the United States in 1994 was $129.9 billion. This included $105.1 from individuals, $9.9 from foundations, $6.1 from corporations, and $8.8 from charitable bequests. These are conservative statistics as they were derived from income tax returns and much charitable giving is not reported for tax purposes. Source: The American Almanac 1996–1997.

family level. In the West the approach is much more macro, that is, society is organized to give people the opportunity to have a good education, to earn a good living through free enterprise which encourages the formation of employment, striving to give equality of opportunity to all. In this context people are expected to work hard and to be relatively self-sufficient. But when misfortune strikes, or when certain individuals are unable to prosper in the system, there are private and governmental agencies that are prepared to step in and help. This help, in the United States alone, was about one hundred thirty billion dollars just from the private sector in 1994, as was cited above. Besides this, government at federal, state, and local levels provided many additional billions of dollars.

But even if one concedes that Westerners are generous, in their own way of being so, there is one area of giving that is largely outside their scope of concern, sympathy, or generosity. For them, if the African call for solidarity and generosity means helping people who are, for example, organizing a wedding or funeral, or putting on a newborn's naming ceremony they believe is extravagant and beyond the family's own resources and what by an objective standard they can afford, then they will probably fail to measure up. In this case, the cultural divide between Africa and the West would be fairly unbridgeable.

38. When people ask for help, they will usually be content with being given a part (sometimes even a small part) of what they are asking for.

Frequently, even typically, when a person has a need for a sum of money that exceeds his or her resources, the person will make the rounds of kin and friends, asking for assistance. The normal pattern is for each person solicited to give a part of the sum needed. No one individual is expected to supply the whole amount. Consequently, the solicitor will be content to receive even a small fraction of what is needed, say, for a medicine, a trip, or a funeral.

Part of the system is to have a network of friends who are available to contribute at least something when there are special or unforeseen needs. Friendships or family relationships do not require that any one person in the network has to provide the entire help that any one particular need necessitates.

Westerners new to Africa usually do not understand this system. So when they are approached by someone they have met, or perhaps by a total stranger, asking for a fairly large sum and describing the origin of the need, they feel that an unreasonable demand is being made of them. Sometimes the solicitor will say, "Anything you can give to help will be appreciated," but more often will not make that explicit (these being high-context societies). The Africans believe most people can afford to help someone a little bit. Probably the need is real, as real needs are very common (as is seeking help). Even if the need is fraudulent, the donor has not lost a lot, and a small donation is not worth spending time and research to determine the veracity of the need. Once they know the system, Westerners are often willing to help even total strangers, even if they have no way of knowing if the need is true as presented. For one thing, making a small donation is the easiest and quickest way to get the solicitor to move on.

39. Offers or exchanges of gifts, food, or hospitality may involve unspoken obligations; likewise, failing to accept gifts, food, or hospitality may have negative implications.

The observation states that offers may involve obligations. They do not always do so, especially when invitations to eating are involved. As Sue Smeltzer writes from Mali, "If people are eating, whether a main meal or just a handful of fried plantain, they will invite you to eat or to take some. This includes people that one has never met in one's life and will probably never see again. You cannot not invite someone to share food. It would be just too shameful."[6]

It is generally, if not universally, considered impolite across Africa to refuse a gift, or offer of food, or hospitality. An example of Westerners being overwhelmed by African generosity is given at the end of chapter 5, under the summary of friendship. The rule is always to accept gifts. It may be polite in Western cultures to protest, "You're too kind—you shouldn't have done it," but it is not polite to do this in an African setting. There are always means of returning kindnesses at a later date. Still, Westerners need to be informed about the implications of gift giving where they are living. They may involve an obligation to establish a relationship with the giver. Gifts may be given now so that when the donors come in the future to ask for something, the recipient will be obliged to give it to them.[7]

The following example is written by a Kenyan working among the Boni, an ethnic group not his own. It may be extreme in describing a people that share to a greater extent than the average. But it graphically illustrates the importance of exchange in African societies, even if usually practiced on a smaller scale.

> Even though I am Kikuyu, I was brought up in a neighbourhood of mixed ethnicity in western Kenya. In my childhood, the neighbourhood lived in communal ways, borrowing basic items from each other such as salt, sugar, milk, and paraffin. For example, my mother would put a cooking pot on the fire and then when she had started to mix the flour into the boiling water, she would realise that there was not enough flour to make *ugali*.[8] She would then send me flying to the

---

[6]Schmeltzer 1997:10.
[7]Hungerford n.d.:7.
[8]*Ugali* is a popular food in Kenya made from maize flour.

neighbourhood to borrow some flour to finish the recipe. This is the kind of background in which I was brought up...

At first I was amazed by how much the Boni share things. I first noticed this from one of our team members. I gave him a shirt and after some time, I saw his cousin wearing it. Another time, I met his father wearing it. Soon I discovered that most of the men in their household had worn the shirt. When I asked him why he was giving his shirt to everybody, he told me that whoever woke up earliest could choose to wear any of the clothers in the house. Since the shirt was good, it was naturally the choice of most of the men.

Then I discovered that the Boni share more than just household items; they share anything that can be asked for, whether tangible things or services. Another thing that struck me was the quantity of asking; it was much more than I was used to! Also the Boni aren't ashamed of who they ask things from; they literally ask for anything from anybody they relate to. One would expect that they would be shy when asking for things, but that's not the case; to them, asking is quite natural. They would ask me for money, shoes, clothes, pens, a ride on the motorbike (most often, for the sake of it), soap, planting seeds, maize flour, and so on. On a single visit to a Boni village, I would be asked for at least ten items. Once a man even asked me why I did not ask for things from them. I was beginning to grow weary of being accosted with requests, but then I realized that they asked even more from each other than they did from me!...

Sometimes...(the) pattern of asking for things brings about tensions that have the potential of stirring up strife in households, villages, or between villages. This occurs mainly from a lack of reciprocity in the sharing of goods. Two small and very different factions within Boni society create these tensions. The first are those who ask for things and often receive, yet they themselves do not give when they are asked. These people make enemies easily and are not cooperative. The second group are those who do not ask for things. Interesingly, they cause as much strife in the community as the stingy ones. The community perceives that this second group does not ask for things because they do not want to give. Without a doubt, I belong to this second group.

I have realised that to relate to the Boni in a way that doesn't cause strife and confusion, I am under obligation to ask them for things. I ask for things that are easily available, such as walking sticks, baskets, mats, cassava, maize, honey, etc. After all, asking is not only a way of life to the Boni; lately, it has become my way of life, too![9]

40. When you give to beggars, they are doing you a favor by allowing you to gain credit with Allah.

This observation applies principally to countries or regions where people from Muslim cultures are present.

Do not be surprised if beggars do not show appreciation; it is not required, although many do express it. Many are also very aggressive about asking, insisting—virtually demanding—that a person give to them. It is my opinion that part of this aggressiveness comes from the fact that society allows a self-defined needy person to have some sort of valid claim on the resources of those in society with means (cf. observation 13 in chapter 3).

The point of view of this subject by one African is illuminating:

On this point it would be incorrect to say that beggars are not grateful. One should remember that Africans are very conscious of their religious beliefs and that they believe in a Supreme Being who will recompense those who do good and chastise those who do evil. Hence, to thank someone verbally would mean to "rob" them of part of the heavenly recompense such an act would bring them. It is not rare to hear a donor repeat, while making a donation, "Don't thank me." The donor is thinking that a future divine recompense is better than a verbal thank you.

The person who does not verbally thank a donor may well formulate an interior prayer that when that person experiences a need it will be granted, and without being subtracted from that person's heavenly reward. Part of this behavior stems from a belief in "evil tongue," the idea that an evil effect may be generated by eulogizing someone. Although this and similar beliefs in many African ethnic groups are part of African traditional religion, they have carried over widely into Islam and Christianity.

In the West the one who has the resources makes all the decisions related to a donation, and it falls to the solicitor to accept the terms, or not. Once the donation is made, the

---

[9]Mungai 1997:3–4.

recipient is obligated to thank his benefactor, as society dictates that this is the correct behavior. In at least some African cultures it would even be considered humiliating to require a verbal expression of thanks. In facing such a requirement, the one requesting help might well say or think, "He showed me his muscles," and would withdraw the request.

Which is right, the Western or the African way? I am not saying that Africans are more "spiritual" than Westerners, but one thing is certain: the Divine occupies a greater place in their lives than in the lives of Westerners. Thus, if in the West the donor-beneficiary relationship is bipolar, in Africa it is tripolar, donor-beneficiary-Divinity. As the donor is receiving much more materially from the Divine in this life than can reasonably be expected by the solicitor, he accedes to the latter's demands. By so doing he only increases his future reward.

In some cultures, especially those with major Muslim populations, the occupation of beggar is a profession on a parallel with journalism and real estate management, for example. These professional beggars are for the most part lepers, blind, cripples, albinos, and the mentally ill, but they also include some in good physical and mental health (personal communication, 1996).

A custom exists in some regions of giving regularly to specific, professional beggars of the kind just described. In this way needs are met and personal relationships are developed in a kind of symbiosis. The donor provides regular support that the beggar is lacking, and the beggar provides a known, rightful outlet for the donor to discharge a religious duty. Thus it becomes charity with a human touch.

Effects of solidarity

41. In many rural communities, and less so in urban neighborhoods, people are afraid to accumulate more goods or property than their neighbors and kin, for fear of creating jealousy which may lead to reprisals being carried out against them on an occult level.

It is common for certain people to use occult means, through the mediation of shamans, *marabouts, mallams* (Muslim ritual practitioners), or other workers of magic, to cause the failure of competitors, to achieve their own success, or as a leader to ensure that people will agree with him or her. There is general fear of such reprisals, and a significant amount of economic development is held back because of it. Much of the migration of youths from village to urban areas is attributable to fears of being subject to such attacks. As occult rites are carried out in secret, people never know who may be taking action against them, even from within their own family.

I knew a village woman who was hired as a household maid by a Western family in a certain city. The woman's friends in the village were so jealous of her having regular employment, and of her now "getting rich," as they expressed it, that they went to shamans to have curses put on the employed woman and the whole Westerner family.

42. Money "corrupted" is not expected to be paid back; accountability is not enforced; restitution is not practiced.

Personal accountability is discussed under other observations, such as observation 16 in chapter 3. Restitution is practically an unknown concept, in government, among friends, in Islam, even in many Christian churches.

A church was in need of benches. A Westerner made a donation, but was told sometime later that the money had disappeared, the church treasury having been cleaned out by the church treasurer. Church elders also informed the donor that the treasurer had just bought a new radio-cassette player. The donor suggested they sell the radio-cassette player and put the proceeds back in the church treasury. The elders exclaimed, "You wouldn't take a radio-cassette player away from a poor man, would you?"

A reliable source told me that the director of a private school made off with most of the sizeable balance in the school's bank account. The account had required two signatures on every check, but the money was gone. The man was dismissed by the school board, but no attempt was made to investigate how the check was cashed fraudulently, to bring the man to justice, or to recover the large amount of money involved. The school remained in serious financial straits, but the ex-director continued to live with impunity in the same city.

The newspapers in one city reported, at least three times over a period of several years, on the construction of a very large mosque, and the raising of funds for it. The first time the money disappeared the faithful were urged to again bring in their contributions. They did so. The same thing happened twice more. No explanations were asked for or given, as far as I could find out.

A friend of mine asked an African friend of his how families handled situations in which one of their members, perhaps a son or a husband, was known to be receiving money corruptly. He was told that in some families there would be quarrels for a week or so, but "*never* would anyone in the family let the name of the household be discredited by revealing such facts outside the house" (personal communication, 1998).

The Wolof of Senegal have a special word *sutura*, which ordinarily means 'discretion', but has a deeper level of meaning which refers to hiding personal secrets or weaknesses. It is described by Assane Sylla as that which hides from the view of the public the weaknesses and faults of someone, so that what is visible is only that which renders the person respectable. It is an appearance of purity, honesty, competence, etc., behind which are hidden all faults and weaknesses. An absolute precept of the Wolof requires that one respects the *sutura* of others, that is, that one does not divulge whatever one knows of the failures of others, without very compelling motive. A proverb says it well, *ku xaste yaa ñaaw*, 'whoever denigrates another debases himself'.[10]

43. A major function of government is to provide money and other resources to those members of society who are in power or have a close relationship to those who are in power.

This unofficial role of government is widely observed in Africa. Many of the conflicts, the wars, and leaders' clinging to power are a direct result of the practice.

The words of the Prime Minister of the Central Africa Republic are very revealing. His explanation of the background of the army mutinies in his country was quoted in a Dakar newspaper:

"In Africa, it is misery above all that rips our countries apart. In our country, as in Liberia or in Rwanda, when the cake becomes too small, those dancing around it bring out their knives. The cake is the State, the only feeding trough our poor countries have," declared Jean-Paul Ngoupande.[1112]

A report from Somalia had this to say: "Bureaucrats, civil servants, and those well connected to the government were positioned to channel the significant resources of the state into their own pockets."

The media in Cameroon echoed the same theme in an account written by B-P Talla:

The State lacks credibility and fails to establish its moral authority. Every citizen looks at the public treasury as a "cake" of which he tries to get the biggest piece, to the detriment of the others....If there is one priority arena where Cameroon should double its vigilance in order to become believable, it is that of the present impunity enjoyed by those

---

[10]Sylla 1978:89.
[11]*Sud Quotidien* [Dakar] 1996, Decembre 6.
[12]Besteman 1996:585.

who are guilty of corruption and the fraudulent diversion of government funds to private use.[13]

Dancing around the "cake." (Observation 43)

The pressure is immense, from above and from below, on individuals in government and business to use their positions for the direct benefit of themselves and family members. An example of this was described in the Dakar newspaper *Le Temoin* (January 21, 1997) where the dismissal from office of a high government official was described as having been motivated by his refusal to allow his staff to profit personally from their positions—to feed directly on the cake—in spite of the exemplary direction and management he had provided his department. His dismissal was obviously mandated by even higher levels of government.

This desire for direct financial support rather than for assistance in developing their own resources and institutions is characteristic of many Africans. They look not only to governments, people of power, and more wealthy Africans, but also to nongovernmental organizations (NGOs), and Muslim and Christian organizations.

Such desire of people in government to profit from their positions is, of course, a universal problem, but in Africa there may be a more generally expected and accepted role for government in this respect. This contrasts with the high purpose and philosophy of government as expressed by President Abraham Lincoln in the phrase contained in his Gettysburg

---

[13]Talla 1997:68–73.

address, of "government of the people, by the people, and for the people." That is, that the purpose of government should be to provide laws and infrastructure that give opportunity to *all* the people of the country in a fair and equitable way, rather than primarily to serve a privileged few.

44. Giving preference to the employment of kin over nonkin is a normal expression of family responsibility and solidarity.

Nepotism is the practice of showing favoritism to relatives, especially in hiring individuals or appointing them to desirable positions. In the West giving such preference to relatives is considered to be a misuse of authority and position. Such misuse is considered to fall in the category of corruption. In many African countries, perhaps in most, nepotism is also officially considered to be an evil, and detrimental to the proper functioning of government and commerce, but in practice it has been difficult to eradicate.

Nepotism is not the only way that position and authority can be misused. Closely related to it are: communalism, where tribe, clan, or community are the bases of giving preference; favoritism, where people are given positions on the basis of friendships or other personal relationships; and sectarianism, where people of the same religion are favored.

Some of the main reasons for condemning such practices are:

1. Personal, family, or other private interests are placed before the larger organizational or public interests.

2. People who are underqualified tend to be employed for particular positions, as private interests are placed above qualifications and competence for accomplishing the purposes for which the positions were supposedly created.

3. Accountability is lessened, as loyalty to private interests is placed before the accomplishment of official tasks.

4. Motivation to work conscientiously is lessened, as people are hired because of who they are, not primarily what they are capable of doing.

5. Standards of honesty, service, and morality are subverted to private interests.

6. Power, wealth, and influence become concentrated in the powerful few, rather than being distributed justly.

7. Smaller entities are put at a disadvantage in the competition with larger ones because they have fewer human or monetary resources.

8. Planning is not carried to implementation, and priorities are not followed, as the rational use of resources is subverted to private interests.

9. Hypocrisy, cynicism, and duplicity are generated in society as people see that those who operate at levels of influence follow double standards: one for appearances and another in fact.

It is clearly more difficult to avoid the pitfalls of nepotism, and related forms of partiality, in underdeveloped countries than in those that are developed. Where, for instance, a manager has relatives in great material need and employment opportunities are extremely limited, it is very difficult for him or her to choose to employ individuals who are unknown, in the name of the national good. This is especially true where relatives in high places are expected to provide for their own, and where not doing so is seen as a betrayal of the highly placed person's group, however it is constituted. In these situations the people involved see nepotism as being more ethical than failing to provide for the family.[14] Yet even if it is understandable, widely practiced partiality has serious negative effects on economic development and on society in general.

> Developing countries literally cannot afford corruption.... For corruption saps development and makes nonsense of planning. This is especially true of those plans which are intended for the benefit of the weak and underprivileged. Corruption weights the already over-weighted scale in favor of the rich and the privileged....It vitiates policy, weakens administration and undermines public confidence. Implementation is the essence of economic planning, and corruption has an almost fatal effect on the efficiency of execution.[15]

Blaine Harden describes nepotism and other forms of reverse discrimination in even stronger terms:

> Not only does family loyalty gum up African governments, it can hobble the careers and limit the achievements of individual Africans. Jealous relatives often harm each other. Gossip, curses, land disputes, homicide, and witchcraft are aimed at successful relatives whose remittances to the family fail to meet expectations. Aggrieved kin demand not only a share but also influence in spending a relative's income. A continent-wide survey of family studies has found that kinship "squabbles thwart the individual's initiative and creativity and interfere with his efficiency."[16]

---

[14]Chinchen 1994:97.
[15]Venkatappiah 1968:274–275.
[16]Harden 1990:69.

45. An unjust settlement of a dispute is better than an offended complainant.

Observation 45 and 45W are discussed together.

45W. For the Westerner settlements need to be based on a fair interpretation of the terms of the relevant law or contract. Personal feelings or other subjective considerations should be subordinated to objective facts.

The following story illustrates what Westerners would consider an unfair practice.

An employee in a Central African country claimed to be owed sixty thousand francs because of an error made in a settlement. The history of the claim was as follows: The employee was let go because his job category was being phased out. Various documents were prepared by the employer relating to the case. A settlement of seventeen thousand francs was agreed upon between the employee and the employer, and this amount was typed on several documents. Some weeks passed before the payment was made because a new personnel officer was being put in place by the employer. At this point the employee claimed to be owed sixty thousand francs. Trying to settle the case, the new personnel officer examined the documents. He noted that the amount of sixty thousand francs was entered on only one document, while the amount was seventeen thousand francs on the others. Being concerned about this inconsistency he went to a labor inspector to show him all the documents. The inspector agreed that it was a simple typing mistake and that the correct amount was seventeen thousand francs. But this was a different inspector than the first one who had originally approved the seventeen-thousand-franc settlement.

When the first inspector learned that the personnel officer had gone to another inspector with the problem, he became angry. He issued a summons to the personnel officer to appear at the labor department. A meeting was called, with the two inspectors, the personnel officer, and a union official to be present. The first inspector did not question the fact of the typing mistake, but said that the personnel officer would have to pay the employee thirty thousand francs. (In the inspector's opinion thirty thousand francs was an equitable compromise, with the employee receiving only half of what he wanted and the employer being required to pay only half of what the employee wanted.) The personnel officer objected, saying the settlement had been agreed at seventeen thousand francs, and therefore that was all the employer should have to pay. The people present said, "All right, then how much will you pay?" (In other words, they wanted to renegotiate the settlement.) The personnel officer said he was not willing to discuss a change in the settlement; all he was prepared to pay was seventeen thousand francs, as had been agreed upon. All the Africans present exploded in anger, asking incredulously, "How can you refuse to negotiate?"

The inspector then told the employment officer that (1) it is not good to have the complainant unhappy and holding ill feelings toward the employer; (2) the employer has lots of money and can well afford to pay the amount; (3) the employee is a poor man and will be without employment, so he should not be refused a bit of help; and (4) if the employer takes it to court, he may not win his case and in any event lawyer and court costs will be greater than thirty thousand francs. The employment officer agreed to pay the required thirty thousand francs.[17]

To many Westerners it seems unjust to be required to pay when their position is clear and in the right and an employee is in the wrong. If the employee is in the wrong, or if an agreement has already been made, the employer should not be obligated to pay anything more. Yet in the U.S. and in other countries many disputes are settled out of court in a similar way. Without admitting to any wrong-doing the second party will agree to a settlement with the first party; first, because it will cost less than taking it to court, and second, because of the good will that will be established or maintained between the parties.

Other types of unjust settlements are certainly known in the U.S. Juries award punitive damages that would be considered unjust by a majority of Americans. A notorious case was that of a woman being awarded two point three million dollars for a cup of hot coffee that she spilled on herself through her own carelessness. In such cases the settlement is not made to keep a complainant from being offended, but because a trial lawyer is able to convince a jury that the defendant, usually a large corporation, was negligent.

I am personally not convinced of the rightness of many such settlements in the U.S., or wherever they are made, when considering their long-term effects. In the short run they may constitute speedy, practical, and cost-effective solutions to conflicts. But in the long run they do not contribute to building a just society. People are taught that they can use the system for personal gain, irrespective of the merits of their complaints. If an ethical attorney is involved in such settlements, he will consider the precedent being set which will likely make similar cases more costly in the future.

Another example of interpretation of a contract even more difficult for a Westerner to accept is when an African employee or friend uses the Westerner's money to keep another African from being upset, unhappy, or in disagreement. This sort of experience has happened to me many times in the course of working in Africa. Here are examples of this.

---

[17]Two actual cases of employee-employer conflicts were combined in the account described here. Thanks to D.T. for providing details and to attorney B.V. for legal input.

I send Ndembe out to undertake some anthropological research. We draw up an itemized budget with designated amounts for travel, food, lodging, a per diem for extraordinary expenses, such as honorariums for village elders who will provide the information being sought, and other expenses. On one such occasion a man who was assisting my researcher Ndembe claimed he should immediately receive an extra allowance "because the trip involved risk." The man had previously made a trip to the same area and had not raised the issue before starting the trip; it had not been part of the employment agreement, and there was nothing in the budget for such an item. Ndembe realized it was an unwarranted demand, but to avoid conflict with the man he took money from the transportation budget, giving him all he asked for. Ndembe had, without question, considered it better to misuse (in the opinion of the Westerner) the funds in his care than to create hard feelings with someone. His attitude upon returning from the trip was that he had done only what was necessary. He seemed to have had no concept of having misused someone else's money. Solidarity prevailed over accountability.

Another illustration of settlement on a nonobjective basis is the following experience. One time we were traveling by train and upon arriving at the station we were beset with baggage handlers. We had already made arrangements with one handler to carry for us; if he needed help it was up to him to get it. We tried to stop the group (minimob) of handlers, but they opened the trunk of the taxi against our attempts to keep them away. Each piece of baggage was grabbed by a different handler, with us trying to stop them so as to entrust the bags to our designated man. Once in the train station we finally got the mob stopped, as they could not go through the gate until we produced our tickets. We had quite a row, trying to put the bags under the control of our man. All of the handlers finally agreed except for one who was especially obnoxious. He insisted loudly and physically that he was going to carry one bag. When we finally got to our compartment, he demanded more than the official rate per bag, the rate printed in large letters on all the handlers' official shirts. We insisted we would only give the official rate. He made a scene, demanding more money. We refused to give it to him and finally he left.

Westerners watching their baggage being carried to the railroad station.
(Observation 45W)

An African on the train who had observed the scene, said to us, "You are very hard. Why didn't you give him what he was asking for, as you obviously can afford it?" We overheard another African mutter sarcastically, and not so quietly, "Such *poor* Americans!"

On another occasion we were taking a taxi from the train station. We engaged a baggage handler while we were still on the train. We told him we would pay only the official rate, three hundred francs. He agreed to carry one bag to our taxi for this amount. Once at the taxi he demanded one thousand francs. We refused to increase the amount we would pay, and another minor row broke out. Our taxi driver gave the handler sixty francs, a very small amount, but the man took it and left. I asked the man why he did that. He said he wanted to calm the man's spirit. Richmond and Gestrin recount one experience that clearly shows how a simple problem can be viewed surprisingly differently by Westerners and Africans:

> An expatriate relates how he once hired an artist to prepare a poster, having reached an agreement with him beforehand on job specifications. When the completed poster turned out to be different from what they had agreed on, the expat said that he would not pay, to which the artist retorted, "Since we reached consensus on what the job specs would be, we must also have consensus on whether or not you pay me!"[18]

---

[18]Richmond and Gestrin 1998:82.

Richmond and Gestrin give advice to Westerners as to what they should do in similar situations:

> This need for consensus calls for prudence on the part of foreigners. Confrontation should be avoided, since it inhibits the achievement of consensus. If differences are openly aired, Africans may believe that you are trying to pick a fight with them....Never say "That's not true." Rather, propose an alternative while recognizing the sincerity of your interlocutor's concerns and needs. "The best remedy for a dispute," a Chuana proverb says, "is to discuss it."[19]

These experiences are recounted because I think there is a deep-level clash of cultures here, perhaps one of the most difficult and irreconcilable areas of cross-cultural relationships that Westerners encounter in Africa. The amounts of money involved may be small, even insignificant. In many instances we can afford to pay them. We could give beggars along the street greater sums. The problems are, to Americans at least, the several principles that are involved.

(1) If there is an officially established rate for performing a service, and it is even printed in large letters so everyone will know what the government believes is a valid amount to pay, then we should be able to pay this amount without causing an unfortunate and uncomfortable argument. The governments of Africa, at least, know that squabbles with foreigners in this way are bad for the image of Africa and discourage tourism.

(2) If someone makes an agreement he should keep it, and we do not want to contribute to the formation of a society that puts so little value on keeping one's word. The principle is the same whether the amount involved is large or small.

(3) Generosity is a very high value in Africa, and should be a high value with Americans. But Americans see generosity to people who in their opinion are making unjust claims or whose behavior should be sanctioned as misplaced generosity. Generosity should be shown to people who deserve it. Africans believe generosity should be shown to everyone, good and bad alike. Many Africans would have little more than contempt for Americans who in their eyes act very ungenerously, as in the experiences described here.

(4) Rewarding a rogue by buying him off will not be good in the long run. More rogues will be created, seeing that it pays to break one's word or to create a scene. The more that people reward rogues, the more roguish behavior will spread through the society.

(5) If people in a society generally buy peace at the cost of justice, the whole society will suffer, and this is part of what we think is going on in

---

[19]Ibid.

many situations in Africa. One little incident would do little damage, but when multiplied from baggage handlers to many other classes of workers and officials in society, the effects are very negative.

(6) Buying a quick peace through unjust means, even if only small injustices are involved, is not good for society.

(7) Certainly any half-thoughtful American would recognize that baggage handlers are poor men who are struggling to make ends meet and they would like to see them improve their economic well being. But the American almost instinctively believes that the way to help baggage handlers, and society in general, is not to reward unjust behavior, but to find other ways to achieve just economic development. To appeal to an American that he should pay off a petty vagabond because he can afford it, immediately and viscerally strikes him as a very bad way to operate an economy. It strikes him as something that is bad for the whole system, and he feels he has almost a civic duty to not contribute to it. For one thing, where do such payoffs stop? If the easy way out is the correct thing to do with a small sum, how about larger sums with people with greater authority or clout who could cause more than a minor row? Where and when would it stop?

It seems to me there is here a clash of cultures on yet another level. The American believes he is acting on principle. The African likewise believes he is following principle. The American also believes that principles should come first, and these are the principles of justice, right conduct, and acting in the overall interests of society. If such principles are consistently followed, even if individuals are not satisfied at some points, overall all individuals and society in general will benefit in the long-term. Africans believe they are following an overriding principle, that of putting the welfare of the individual ahead of other considerations. They believe that if all individuals are treated with consideration and respect, then society will in the long run be a peaceful one where people live together in mutual dependence and solidarity. That there are rogues, everyone is aware, but even they should be shown consideration and respect, and their unreasonable demands should be catered to, as one would treat a child. This they believe is the only way society can achieve harmony for all. To refuse to help a rogue, right or wrong, is unacceptable behavior.

Summary: the role of solidarity

A Senegalese proverb, with very similar ones found in cultures across Africa, states, "The remedy for man is man" (*nit-nit ay garabam*). At the other end of the continent the Tswana of South Africa and Botswana say almost the same thing, "A person is a person through people" (*motho ke motho ka batho*).[20] These mean that whatever the nature of anyone's problem,

---

[20]Morgan 2000:44.

the main support and curative benefits will come from people; or stated conversely, that without people to support an individual, he or she will be unwell. Africans do not want to be independent or autonomous. They want to live in interdependent community. They want to share material goods—both receiving and giving—with those near them. People are generous with others, materially sharing with them and in making allowances for their faults and weaknesses. They expect from others of their group the same indulgence. Mostly people do reciprocate, but they do not give to all failures. Some failures lead to sanctions. A short list of serious lapses would include:

> Failure to show respect to someone as a human being, and especially to someone of advanced age;
> Becoming publicly angry;
> Having an open confrontation with someone; and
> Causing someone to lose face in front of his or her peers.[21]

Showing respect, even to rogues, is perhaps quintessential Africanness. This may well relate to what countless Africans believe and deeply feel about past centuries of being a people oppressed, denigrated, and given no respect in the world. So for them there is nothing worse than being treated or treating someone disrespectfully. To treat even a rogue disrespectfully is to put oneself on a level below that of the rogue.

I am not an economist, but hazard the following observations. The economic problems in Africa are not primarily due to a lack of natural and human resources. Africa has huge resources, but they are underexploited. Part of the current economic problems stems from the legacy of colonialism, and part is due to the present inequalities of world trade. But beyond these historical and structural problems, much could be done to ameliorate economic conditions with the resources that Africans have at their disposal.

Although economic hardship is endemic, there are many signs that financial means do exist. In Dakar, for instance, the greatest construction boom in Senegal's history has been underway for several years. The streets are almost clogged with Mercedes-Benz and BMW automobiles owned by Africans, but there is very little African money going into enterprises that create the crucially needed long-term jobs. Too many of the available resources, it seems clear, go for expenditures that build prestige rather than into investments that increase employment and economic growth.

Individual Westerners and Africans alike are small actors, and each one can do little to effect change in the national or continental situation. Nevertheless, the cumulative effect of individual decisions, to consume, save, or invest, has overwhelming influence on the development of national economies. Governments and societies provide the overarching economic

---

[21]Haibucher 1999b.

environments, but individuals make the choices which together add up to national outcomes.[22]

It is interesting that the help given in Africa and the help given in Europe-America are both taken advantage of by certain individuals who become parasites on the system. Such people rather prefer being provided for by others to having to work for themselves. Such parasitism is in no way restricted to race or continent.

Another quotation from Van Chi-Bonnardel's classic study of personal economics in Senegal clearly expresses the issues:

> The requirements of hospitality effectively create a situation that leads to family parasitism. A man that receives and treats his guests well creates a flattering reputation. People say that he has *téguine* if he is courteous and jovial with guests. He has *bakhe* if he is generous and indulgent. And he has *yévène* if he is totally generous.
>
> (In some regions of Senegal, if) a guest enters a house, he should be offered, besides a chair and a glass of water, two red cola nuts and two white cola nuts, then a meal of which the wife incites the guest to eat as much as possible. The guest is lodged and fed for as long as he wants, provided he does not establish a permanent residence there. When it comes time to leave, the whole household comes to say goodbye to the guest. They give him provisions for his travels, fruit, *mburaké* (a Senegalese kind of granola), and cola nuts. He is accompanied to the minibus station or to the main road. With only a few changes in details, all the peoples of Senegal, in all regions, practice this kind of hospitality, which, in poor families, is done only by means of great hardship.
>
> In the city the requirements of hospitality create the fact that, during the long dry season, the urbanite has permanent guests with him whom he must house, feed and otherwise provide for. These are relatives or friends from the country who pass the slack time of the agricultural cycle traveling from one city to another, from one relative to another, without having to pay or provide for a thing.[23]

These guests even receive money for bus fare to their next destination, as it is in each host's economic interest to pass them along to the next quarry. This exodus from rural areas to the cities and travel from one city to

---

[22]See, for example, Britan and Denich 1976.
[23]Van Chi-Bonnardel 1978:475–476.

another are major strategies that rural people use to conserve their meager resources of food and other scarce goods. Whether or not this is defined as parasitism, it is a very heavy burden on most city dwellers.

6

Society and People of Means

Most of the discussion of personal finances in this study centers on the nonwealthy members of African society. The more wealthy or better-positioned Africans are represented in a large literature. They are often referred to as "elite Africans." The impression may be given that all Africans are ready to part with their resources, and that there is no end to their generosity. This is of course not the case. David Jacobson studied the elites of Uganda some years ago. His findings have remarkable similarities to many economic practices in Senegal, on the other side of the continent. But his observations clearly show there are limits to African generosity. One of his experiences is typical of general attitudes of many elite members of society:

> Elite Africans do see their non-elite kinsmen in town, but not frequently and usually not if they can avoid them. Kinship obligations connect kinsmen in the two classes, but upper-class Africans do not always acknowledge or meet these duties. They assist their poorer relatives, but with reluctance. For example, I was with an upper-class informant when he was confronted by a kinsman. It was late afternoon and we were riding in his car on one of the town's main avenues, when a shabbily dressed man rushed into the street and wildly flagged us down. At first I thought there had been an accident and that someone was in desperate need of help. My informant did not respond with any urgency, but rather slowed the car to a halt, muttering to himself. Just as the man reached the car, my informant turned to me and asked,
>
> "Does this ever happen in your country?" The pedestrian was a distant relative (a clan brother) who had come into town for the day and who was now on his way home, some

forty miles from Mbale. He had seen the car, waved it to stop, and wanted to be driven home. My informant refused, argued, and then agreed only to drop him off at the bus depot, from where he was to get home on his own. After we let him off, my informant complained that his kinsmen were always demanding too much, that he was going to cut himself off from them and that the next time he would not even stop.[1]

"Hey, cousin, give me a lift home!" (Observation 46)

Although the observations enunciated in this section focus on African attitudes toward individuals with means, similar attitudes exist toward institutions and governments "with means." Zimbabwean Olivia Muchena expresses it well:

> Where once the community felt responsibility to care for the needs of people in the community, now they look to relief and development organizations to care for those needs. Where once communities sought to improve their lot through their own work and resources, now they think that the only way to develop is to get money from someone else. Why do the work yourself when there are development

---

[1] Jacobson 1973:57.

agencies with more money than you will ever see in a lifetime looking for places to give it away?...

African individuals, communities, and countries become dependent on donations.[2]

People of means

46. The place in society assigned to people who are perceived to have ample financial resources is that of givers and/or loaners, and not of receivers.

In Africa those with greater means are supposed to pay more than poor persons, and otherwise to be generous with their relative wealth. If a well-dressed person bargains too hard for a lower price, he or she may be reproached with, "You wouldn't want to pay a poor person's price, would you?" Equal prices for all is not an African concept.

According to Western thinking everyone should be treated the same. Justice should be blind, with everyone the same before the law. This means prices for goods and services are public information and applied to everyone. Of course there are exceptions. Large retail chains are given lower prices than small retailers, but in such cases the difference is claimed to be based on the lower costs of selling in large volume.

A singular approach to social organization is found in many African societies. In these, people are classified as either givers or receivers. Actually, most people are both givers and receivers. They are givers to those with fewer resources and receivers from those with more. Judith Irvine describes the very interesting giver-receiver relationships she witnessed in a Wolof village of Senegal.

> The Wolof greeting clearly divides into two dissimilar roles: the Initiator-Questioner and the Respondent. The more active speech role (Initiator-Questioner) coincides with the greater physical activity (person who enters or approaches). These roles correspond to low and high rank respectively, because both physical activity and speech activity are duties which low-status persons perform for persons of higher status. Accordingly, informants state that "A noble does not go to greet a *ñeeño* (person of low caste)—it is the *ñeeño* who must come to greet him." The same could be said of older and younger brothers, of men and women, and so on. To visit someone's compound, or to enter his room, is to show him great respect; and it is the person who enters, or who moves

---

[2]Muchena 1996:177.

toward the other, who must speak first. It is, moreover, out of respect for another that one asks questions about his welfare. A set of associations emerges concerning the two parties to a greeting, associations which recall cultural stereotypes of noble and *griot* (or noble and low-caste) behavior....The Wolof notion that the low-ranking person travels about more and talks more than the high-status person is here replicated in the status-differentiated roles of the greeting.

As a result of the status associations of the greeting, any two persons who engage in an encounter *must* place themselves in an unequal ranking: they must come to some tacit agreement about which party is to take the higher-ranking role and which the lower. This ranking is inherent in any greeting no matter how abbreviated, because the mere fact of initiating a greeting is itself a statement of relative status.

A Wolof proverb summarizes the principle of social inequality and the element of competition inherent in the greeting: "When two persons greet each other, one has shame, the other has glory."[3]

The point of including this long quotation is to show that in many, perhaps most, African societies people do not assume that all people are to be treated as equals. To the contrary, they assume that there are inequalities of social rank, and in any relationship it is necessary to determine relative rank in order to build a proper relationship. In some societies, such as the Wolof, as has been seen, social hierarchy or inequality is so pervasive in the culture that it is even reflected in the greeting system. Westerners need to be alert to the forms of inequality present in any particular culture, as there are wide varieties in Africa of concepts and practices related to inequality.

However, one attitude always true is that Westerners fall into the giver's category. Foreigners who are employers have heavier financial burdens than most national employers. See observation 50 below.

This sense of the giver/receiver dichotomy in all African relationships allows for a mutual **exchange**; relationships are never one-sided. The receiver gains the help needed, or even the means to live. The giver receives prestige, honor, and deference for services rendered to the receiver. The problem for Westerners is that they feel irritated rather than honored when they are continually asked to perform in their assigned role of giver. And in other ways their relationships are indeed one-sided because they are outside of much that is going on in society.

One aspect of the giver/receiver mentality is that when people are social and economic equals or nearly so, the giver and receiver categories are

---

[3]Irvine 1989:169.

subject to negotiation, depending upon personal need, estimated current means of each person, and the negotiating strategies and opportunities that are available.

There is something of the giver/receiver mentality in the U.S., where juries award huge damages to accident victims, especially when the defendant is a large business corporation as General Motors, State Farm Insurance, or such a giant. The concept is that these major companies have deep pockets, that is, lots of money, and therefore the little guy, who has had a problem that can be construed to be tied to a perceived negligence or fault on the part of one of these big guys, should be very handsomely rewarded. And of course there is the English legend of Robin Hood, the hero who robbed the rich to give to the poor.

47. People typically receive satisfaction from being asked for financial help, whether or not they are disposed to provide it.

A friend explained to me that in general, Africans are flattered when they are asked to provide help. This gives them a sense of being useful, of thinking people have need of them. They are honored. He said such requests make one feel as though "people are looking at me, and that gives me pleasure" (personal communication, 1995).

Some Africans consider that the Westerners think that way, too. In northern Cameroon some Western volunteers found that people were asking for medicines they really did not want, because they wanted to honor the foreigners as richer, stronger people. They threw the medicines they had begged for into the bush a short distance from the Westerners' gate.[4]

47W. Westerners are largely annoyed by requests for help, and find it hard even to imagine receiving enjoyment from being solicited, or from taking the role of a patron.

Most Westerners are *not* flattered by being asked for help, although I have run into a few who did enjoy, or at least received satisfaction from, being involved with people and their problems.

48. The reputation of people of means is enhanced through the frequent visits of their clients.

Whether the visits are simple social calls or requests for assistance, the fact of many people coming to the person of reputation and means is proof that the person is important. I have been to the homes of "big men" where many people were in the house and in the yard, calling on him, waiting, hoping that they would be able to have an audience with the important person. The way such people were received, or not received, indicated in turn their relative importance to the big man.

Delbert Chinchen writes for Liberia and Malawi:

---

[4]Hungerford 1998:6.

Visits are attempts to thicken the relationship and to reciprocate for knowledge received. Visits are considered symbolic, intangible gifts. The client is thinking, "My presence in your home, as a visitor, elevates your status as a patron. I am here to let you and everyone else know that my loyalty is with you." Wealth is in people. The more people the patron has surrounding him/her, the more visits the patron receives from his/her clients, the more affluent and reputable that patron is perceived to be.[5]

Out visiting friends and patrons at night. (Observations 48 and 48W)

Frequent visiting is essential to maintaining friendships. African friends see each other at least once a week. Friendship equates with frequent visiting. City streets teeming with pedestrians at night are a testimony to this. Visits are not just made to those of exceptional wealth or influence. Visiting is the principal social and economic activity of most people. The large numbers of people out walking, driving, or taking taxis to all hours of the night testify to this. Although some younger people would be involved with entertainment such as dance clubs, the vast majority of people are just out visiting friends, kin, and patrons.

---

[5]Chinchen 1994:149.

48W. Foreigners are typically frustrated and inconvenienced by frequent, uninvited visits of African friends and acquaintances.

This observation is very similar to 47W. The difference between them is that here the focus is on *visits* that Africans make, whether to their friends' homes, offices, or other place of employment. But in 47W the focus is on *being asked* for material help, whether in the form of money, or in some other way. Perhaps these observations can be summarized by stating that the Westerner wants to set his own agenda of activities, including choosing the people he or she sees or will take time with. Unsolicited visits are mostly unwelcome.

This is very different from typical African attitudes, as described by Chinchen:

> Just as one receives a monthly statement from one's bank to assure the customer of the security of his money and to keep the customer informed of deposits and withdrawals, so visiting gives assurance to the client that all is well with the relationship with his/her patron. Clients do not need a reason to visit you, the patron. Visits are intended to simply maintain or improve the relationship. Foreigners, unfamiliar with visiting etiquette in Liberia and Malawi, often become frustrated by the frequent visits and requests of clients. Foreigners do not realize that a visit from a client, as observed by other Liberians and Malawians, is an enhancement of their patron reputation, not an inconvenience.[6]

49. Leaders in society (religious, political, and business) are expected to be people (mainly men) who have a retinue of followers, who distribute resources and in other ways provide for their followers when they have needs. They also ideally have commanding personalities.

Followers provide prestige, loyalty, services, political support including votes, and other intangible benefits to leaders.

---

[6]Ibid., 148.

The Big Man addresses his followers. (Observation 49)

When a young African becomes the employee, assistant, supervisee, political or religious supporter, or even student (in higher education) of someone in a relatively high position, he often does so with hopes and expectations that are of great personal significance to him. First, he tends to exaggerate the power, wealth, and skill of his leader....Second, he tends to have conscious fantasies that this great leader will use his power to raise his devoted follower from obscurity and make him into a great man too. He may actually propose this to the leader, while asking for help to support his self-improvement efforts in education or business. Third, and more realistically, he expects the leader to be generous with food and drink when his followers spontaneously visit, and to give them financial aid to meet urgent family obligations and pay debts. Every African of relatively great wealth is besieged by potential devoted followers seeking financial assistance and hospitality; a man with political aspirations must satisfy as many as he possibly can, straining his resources to the utmost.[7]

Attempts are frequently made to draw Westerners into this system of clientelism, whether or not they think of themselves as leaders or as people

---

[7]LeVine 1970:291–292.

who have or want followers. I have had African acquaintances broadly hint at offering to be my clients—telling me they appreciated my wisdom, my age, and would like to visit me often for the advice I could give. Unstated but understood is that I would reciprocate by providing financial resources when the need arose. That these were implicit offers to be my clients was confirmed when, after declining to give them money or a requested good, they never again sought me out for my good advice!

A very common experience for a Westerner is to be approached by African friends or even complete strangers, and be asked to help in obtaining employment, or in getting to the United States, or for other favors. Sometimes an American who has no particular link to the U.S. government is asked to intervene at the local embassy, assuming that all Americans have influence there. Often those related to a nongovernmental organization or a mission will expect, even insist, that the NGO provide training so that the African will be prepared for his future when the relationship with the NGO ceases.

50. A person or organization with financial means is basically expected to pay a higher price or make a larger contribution to individuals or society than is a poor person or organization.

For many things there is a poor man's price and a rich man's price, a poor man's law enforcement and a rich man's law enforcement. Many times a Westerner will interpret this class discrimination as antiwhite behavior. In many but probably not all African countries, I believe this is not the case. The basis for such treatment is the person's ability to pay, not race. If whites are subjected to such treatment out of proportion to their numbers, it is because they are assumed to be people of financial means.

This seems to be the usual case, but there are many exceptions. Some Africans appear to resent white people deeply, for whatever reasons they may have. Some of the experiences I have had with this are:

1. Being charged more for public transportation than the posted price which was supposed to apply equally to all passengers.

2. Two Western friends and I arrived late at night at a bus stop. Some taximen tried to take gross advantage of us. They argued vehemently with some African fellow passengers who at an instant literally protected us and accompanied us to our lodging to make sure we were safe. The taximen had argued, "Here we have an opportunity with these people, and you, our brothers, are keeping us from it."

3. I was robbed of my wallet on a bus full of people. Several people told me they saw it happen, but no one called out "Thief!" or

otherwise exposed the pickpocket, as would be normal in such situations in Africa.

Examples of areas of economic life that often follow two standards are: minimum wages that an employer is obligated to pay, hours of work per week or month an employer can require without being required to pay overtime wages, social security and other taxes for employees, vacation time given to workers, the mechanical condition required of a vehicle to pass inspections, and at times even police fines.

In Dakar in 1997 the government-owned water company officially charged three point four times more per cubic meter for water used by a large household (in a villa) than for water used by a small household. In both cases the water was measured by a meter. Where people do not have running water in their houses but fetch it from communal taps, there is no charge at all for the water.

A Kenyan friend gave me his opinion about what people should pay, relative to their means on a scale of 1 to 10. It can be charted as follows (personal communication, 1998):

Class of persons	Relative price they should pay
Tourists	10
Senior government functionaries and rich people	8
Middle class or average people	5
Poor people	2–3

Practicing the system

51. Success in life is attained through personal relationships, through connections with people in positions of power and authority, and through spiritual means.

Where the structures, institutions, and traditions of a country are designed more to meet the needs of the elites than those of the average citizen, then having connections with those elites is the sine qua non of success.

Getting ahead through one's own efforts, by planning for the future, and by saving and investing one's money are not seen as the keys to success. Rather than be produced from one's own hard work, success is believed to have its origins in spiritual, esoteric (that is, occult) power. Assane Sylla sums up the concept:

> Of two adversaries that are in competition (politics, sports, gaining influence, etc.) or two enemies that fight, the one that concentrates on himself the greatest mystical force will

of necessity gain the victory. He is described as *mop ëp bopp* 'he has more of a head than the other'...

Success in life is considered to be a supernatural gift, realized on the basis of the charismatic potential of a person rather than on his or her personal qualities. Success is the result of the direct intervention of the transcendent in the affairs of an individual. It is analogous to magnetic waves and magnets. A successful person is one who has the qualities of a "magnet." Therefore, the transcendent power of "magnetic waves" that generate success will naturally cause the charismatic alignment necessary for the achievement of success.[8]

Traditional Africans who hold to these beliefs are arguably right. With very limited economic opportunity and upward mobility, without equal protection under law, with national instabilities, and countless other economic and even social problems, it is indeed unlikely that mere hard work will ensure success. As for crediting esoteric means with being able to provide what hard work is unlikely to do, the answer is beyond the scope of this book to try to provide.

Not only are personal relationships essential to success, if they are neglected or thought to be less important than conscientious work, such neglect will normally lead to failure. W. Penn Handwerker, who has extensively studied development in Liberia and elsewhere in Africa, writes:

Managers whose primary concern is the production of quality work tend to be isolated and unorganized. If they do not accede to the demands of people placed higher or people with higher-level patrons, they bring trouble on themselves in the course of doing what they see as a good job, for they find themselves compelled to raise objections to projects proposed by incompetent or self-serving superiors. Even if subordinates do not have higher-level connections than their supervisors, they can—and occasionally do—falsely claim inappropriate behavior on the part of supervisors they do not like. Thus, **more often than not, merit is not merely ignored, it is penalized.** People who seek the public welfare rather than the welfare of patrons and clients (both kin and friends) create enemies and stay impoverished, even when occupying very high government positions, because they eliminate the possiblility of significantly augmenting their low official salary. [emphasis added][9]

---

[8]Maranz 1993:58.
[9]Handwerker 1987:332.

51W. Success in life is attained through ability, hard work, education, and delayed gratification, established within the framework of a just society.

Westerners, Americans at least, strongly believe that hard work, perseverance, good judgment, and personal capability will lead to success in life, barring some unpredictable disaster. While this may well be true in America, it is not necessarily true in Africa and in many other parts of the world.

Americans often fail to recognize how much their realization of personal success is dependent upon elements outside themselves: educational and employment opportunities, a dynamic and entrepreneurial economy, stability of government, the rule of law, and countless other factors.

A very important concept is delayed gratification, or future preference, as it is termed technically. This is a concept very important to President Bill Clinton, according to his biographer.

> As much as Clinton and his classmates enjoyed the Plato lecture (famous at Yale University), it was (Professor) Quigley's lecture on future preference that stuck with them. "The thing that got you into this classroom today is belief in the future, belief that the future can be better than the present and that people will and should sacrifice in the present to get to that better future," Quigley would say. "That belief has taken man out of the chaos and deprivation that most human beings toiled in for most of history to the point we are at today. One thing will kill our civilization and way of life—when people no longer have the will to undergo the pain required to prefer the future to the present. That's what got your parents to pay this expensive tuition. That's what got us through two wars and the Depression. Future preference. Don't ever forget that."[10]

Future preference is a valid economic ideal—where economic, social, and political stabilities justify it. It is doubtlessly less valid where the past was unstable and unpredictable, and the future appears to rational people to offer more of the same. In such an economic context, something like present preference may be entirely justified.

52. People who are without ample financial resources typically seek to have a long-term client relationship with as many people, patrons, as possible from among those with resources.

The only way to get ahead in many African societies is to attach oneself to someone as high as possible in society. This is in many instances the only way up economically and socially. With educational, employment, and all

---

[10]Maraniss 1995:59–60.

other avenues to upward mobility closed to a majority of the population, the only way open is to attach oneself to someone in a position of influence, trusting he will reward loyalty, service, and labor with long-term benefits.

Even many employed Africans will seek out Westerners, hoping to find a reliable source of extra income that can be called upon in case of special need. And as special needs are always arising, for medicines, for travel back to the home village, for deaths, for religious ceremonies, and countless other things, the quest for patrons is constant and intense. Westerners working in Africa, who are frequently asked for financial and other kinds of help, often become weary with such continual solicitation.

Many times gifts are presented Westerners, such as a carving, a goat, a sheepskin, even a beautiful black colobus monkey hide, as was once my experience. Sometimes the gifts are token, but they may also be substantial. These serve to establish or solidify a relationship that is hoped will be long-term.

53. Financial matters involve a great amount of strategizing and gamesmanship.

One strategy, or consideration, is to size up people's wealth and their degree of displaying it. If they are ostentatious, they will be asked a lot. If they give appearances of economic modesty, they will be asked little. If they are known to be unemployed, they will not be asked.

One often-used strategy is to ask for financial or other help when adequate means to cover the expense are actually in hand. This is not to say that the people who do this are exactly dishonest, but that their level of anxiety or insecurity is so high that they will seize upon an opportunity to ask for money to fill a prescription for medicine, when actually they have at that moment adequate funds to fill it. By seeking money for a prescription they know they are more likely to arouse sympathy and receive a positive response than if they were to ask for money to cover the rent. And if they receive money to cover the prescription, it frees up money for other uses. African people are very familiar with these strategies, and they expect to have detailed knowledge of the person before they request aid and therefore before any substantial aid is given, or at least is given willingly.

54. When a person has a financial need, the most appropriate and likely candidate is mentally selected and then approached for help.

The process of selecting whom to approach involves a mental review of one's personal economic and social networks, the weighing of the recent and past history of the relationships: when help was last given to or received from each one, what one's projected future needs will be and who might meet them, the current financial means, personality, and temperament of possible benefactors, and past obligations that have never been repaid, and such considerations.

We can say that choosing a candidate is something like choosing which credit card to use; hence, the process is not totally different from the Western system.

55. People with moderate to extensive means can be divided into the *hiders* and the *revealers*.

If you are a person with means, you need to choose between being a hider or a revealer. Which you choose depends upon what you want from the system, or what image you want to project.

Getting the Mercedes out of sight in the garage of the modest house.
(Observation 55)

Many people with some means make a serious effort to keep their assets secret from neighbors, relatives, and sometimes even from spouses (especially in polygamous households), as well as from the government.

> One can no longer count the Africans who have bank accounts but who tell no one, not even their wives. The idea is the less people know, the less they will ask for financial help. The common opinion is that money that is sleeping in a bank is not being actively used and so is "available." They don't understand the concept of investments. Consequently if people with bank accounts cross paths with someone they know while waiting in line at a bank, they will say, "You didn't see me here!" (personal communication, 1996).

On the other hand, there are the revealers, those who flount their wealth with big cars, luxurious houses, expensive clothes and jewelry, a big ram at *id al-Adha*, and in other forms of ostentatious living. Some languages have a special word to describe someone whose behavior is ostentatious and proud, and who flaunts his or her possessions. Typically, the emphasis, or implicit criticism, is on the attitude and not on the possessions per se. For example, the Mossi of Burkina Faso describe an ostentatious person as *wiligi menga soba* 'the owner of show-off-ness'.

Parking the Mercedes in front of the beautiful house. (Observation 55)

56. The only means of accumulating savings that is available to many employees are cash advances from their employers against future work.

The worker "deposits" his future work with the employer and withdraws funds when needed (provided that the request for an advance is honored by the employer). For the employee, his "deposit insurance" is the reliability of the employer. The employer assumes the risk of the employee falling sick or dying, or not continuing to work satisfactorily.

This system works very well for the employee. No relative or friend can borrow, steal, or lose his future earnings. Countless Africans live with the constant threat of serious loss from illness, drought, chronic unemployment, and various kinds of disasters. Family and friends make claims on available resources that cannot be refused. Saving money from current earnings is impossible. So, in effect, savings are pushed into the future by borrowing today from tomorrow's earnings.[11]

In a way this is similar to credit cards or other credit arrangements in the West (or in Africa, for that matter). Although credit is obtained in both systems, there are fundamental differences. In Africa these include: personal, long-term relationships that allow for the vicissitudes of life, the credit-giver assuming most of the risk, the expression of trust in the employee that is implicit in the advances, the flexibility of making repayment, and the absence of a profit motive for the creditor.

Summary: society and people of means

People of means are especially important to the functioning of countless African societies. They are found at different levels, from those at the top of the social and economic hierarchy, to others under them who control fewer resources, and so on down the economic ladder. Thus, a client at one level will be a patron to others of lesser means.

Where economic and governmental institutions are weak and the rule of law is often flawed, the most reliable way to gain access to major resources is through personalized means. Individual skills and abilities count for less than connections. The people of means are the gatekeepers of the resources that everyone in society wants and needs. Economists use a number of terms to break down the complex economic and social activities found in these societies into more understandable parts.

1. *Gatekeepers* are individuals or organizations that control access to desired resources. They may be "big men" who have access to major resources, or simply employment managers who have the authority to accept or refuse an individual seeking employment.

2. *Channels* are the routes or means that are available to people through which they can acquire desired or strategic resources. Thus a person of means or a business firm that offers employment opportunities is a channel. In many African countries the employment channels are very limited in number so the national treasury becomes a much-used channel, as was seen in observation 43.

3. *Hierarchy* of social relationships refers to the various levels of position and authority that exist along the channels or routes between people with needs and the resources they desire.

4. *Resource control* is the power exercised at various levels of a hierarchy to deny or grant people access to goods or services

---

[11]Hill and Hill 1990:57–59.

that they desire. An example is a patron who exercises control over the number and qualities of the clients he takes on.

5. *Resource seekers* are those at any level of society who are involved in obtaining resources they do not have but want.

6. *Access costs* are those expenses in goods or services that are incurred by those who establish and maintain relationships with those higher in the hierarchy. A low access cost would be incurred by a client who had simply to pay visits to his patron in order to be granted access to particular goods. An example of high access cost would be a demand by a government minister for an exhorbitant bribe when awarding a government contract.

7. *Competitive channels* are the different ways available to people for obtaining resources. These typically include government, business, and foreign aid, either of which provide functionaries or employees access to salaries and other material benefits.

8. *Single-channel* resource structures refer to an absolute control over resources. Similarly, multi-channel structures refer to economic environments where there are many paths or channels available to people for obtaining resources.[12]

The terms seem reasonably self-explanatory, providing a sense of the system and how individuals operate within it. They point to the complexities, pervasiveness, and importance of people of means to the functioning of African society. Thus, the observations in this chapter relate to major components of African management of personal money matters and other resources.

Not all Africans are involved in this hierarchy of patrons and clients, but it is probably safe to say it is the dominant economic system in sub-Saharan Africa. Many local variations exist, but general principles apply across the continent. Pastoralists, the few hunter-gatherers that are left, some subsistence farmers, and various egalitarian societies would be outside the system.

---

[12]Handwerker 1987.

7

Loans and Debts

Loans and debts in Africa represent not just economic activity, but integral elements of social interaction. They constitute some of the strong social ties that bind people together. They form a part of everyday life that Westerners would not imagine. The Westerner has clearly defined categories and meanings connected with loaning, borrowing, and asking. In Africa the terms are used loosely, with great overlapping of definitions. Part of this African ambiguity stems, it seems, from an element of shame in admitting to a need. So it is partly disguised in asking for a loan rather than a gift. In the West loans and debts are mostly business matters, carried on with banks and other lending institutions. These transactions are not managed on a personal level. Lenders are obligated, officially at least, to treat all potential borrowers equally. The conditions set for one person are supposed to be the conditions set for all adult members of society. Once loans are made, there is strict collection of debts, with little tolerance of delinquency. In Africa most loans and debts are handled on an individual basis and are inseparable from personal relationships and social life. To be sure, banks exist, but most of their customers are medium to large-scale businesses, governments, and international agencies.

The reader will note in the observations in this section that there is an implicit, pervasive, and consistent bias in the design of some of the rules on the level of personal finances. They favor the less fortunate and less wealthy members of society. At least this is how it seems to a Westerner. For example, creditors have to seek out their debtors. At other levels of African society, those with means and those with political or religious position are definitely advantaged, but such matters are outside the consideration of the personal financial matters which are in focus in this study. In the capitalist West the general, built-in bias favors those with means; the poor are usually disadvantaged economically and legally. Progressive, liberal, and socialistic governments seek to change this imbalance by instituting various mechanisms for income redistribution or at least a rearrangement of economic opportunities.

Following are fourteen observations (numbered 57–70) about loans and debts in African culture.

Debt and funding strategies

57. When an African has a need for money or some good, the normal and acceptable way to get it is to ask for it from a relative, friend, or acquaintance who has it.

Africans want and expect to depend upon others and they want others to depend upon them. Interdependence is a high value. They fear social isolation, and the only way to avoid it is by being involved with others, and social involvement includes money and goods.

African history probably has played a major role in the development of this culture trait. When people are living on the margins of existence and even survival is at stake, it is understandable that the social rules would allow people to be able to ask for what they lack in the way of essentials, and that pressure be brought to bear on those who have an excess to share them. Whatever history we can imagine for this feature of countless African societies, the present reality is that many people see nothing wrong with asking, and others feel a great obligation to share. An expatriate friend of mine living in East Africa went to the market with an African friend who bought a goose. On the way home the friend asked the expat to carry the goose; otherwise, if someone came along and asked for it, he would be obligated to give it to him.

Another friend was telling some Sudanese men that Westerners do not usually ask for things. The Sudanese had worked for expat NGOs for years but had never understood this. He went on to explain that Westerners believe people should work for what they get, that asking is considered to be a sign of weakness and of personal insufficiency. He explained that when Westerners do ask, it is only of those they are close to, who know them well and understand their need, because it is considered humiliating to be unable to meet one's own personal needs. The Sudanese men were astonished to learn this about Westerners. They felt comfortable asking whenever there was opportunity and where there was even a chance of receiving. They were also not offended when they were turned down.[1]

---

[1]Some of the examples used in this book have been collected and used at the Africa Orientation Course of SIL International, held for many years in Cameroon. They come from the experiences of many anthropologists and NGO staff. I thank especially Marian Hungerford, Jon Arensen, Dick Bergman, and others who have provided examples from across Africa.

57W. Asking someone for money or some material object is considered impolite or an imposition. People are expected to take care of their own personal needs.

Middle and upper class Westerners do not look to relatives or friends to meet material needs. It may be different for those who are less affluent. Westerners highly value independence. To directly ask someone for something would be considered to be demeaning. Doing so would normally indicate personal failure.

Westerners are basically unused to being asked for things, and when direct requests are made of them, they react negatively. They are embarrassed for themselves and for the asker. It is not so much that they are ungenerous or unwilling to give to someone in need, but they do not know how to evaluate a direct request, to know if the need is legitimate. The situation is still more difficult for them if the person is a stranger. But even with people they casually know, they feel unable to evaluate the need adequately. In their home countries they expect that governmental services or charitable organizations will handle such things and that the average citizen does his or her duty by giving to charities that are expected to determine needs objectively. They think that if they give to someone who is on drugs or is an alcoholic, their contribution might actually add to the problem rather than alleviate it.

In the West it is acceptable to ask for minor, nonmaterial help from a friend, a neighbor, or even from a stranger. Examples would be assistance in starting an automobile with a jump start when a driver finds the car battery is dead, helping a handicapped person cross a street, or assisting a neighbor who is unloading a heavy crate.

58. Old debts are forgotten and are not expected to be repaid, neither by the debtor nor by the lender.

These are some of the factors that go into debt forgetfulness: (1) Loans long forgotten serve to strengthen bonds of friendship. Such loans can be of money, goods, service rendered, and other tangibles and intangibles. (2) Outstanding debts obligate the receiver to reciprocate on at least an equal scale. (3) Receiving a loan puts the recipient into a position of obligation. An example would be a worker who parks his moped in a yard while at work, paying a small amount monthly. The owner or person responsible for the yard borrows money from the moped owner. This allows the moped owner to go many months without paying the monthly fee. No detailed accounts are kept, but the moped owner's nonpayment of parking fees will exceed the amount of the loan.

59. There is a strong sense in which people want to be owed money by their friends.

Being owed money indicates that a person is accepted as part of the community and that he or she is a contributing member of society. Not being owed money indicates that an individual is socially isolated, a condition that is greatly feared. It is also rejected on philosophical grounds, that is, people believe that social integration is an essential ingredient for living a happy, constructive life. So people want, in one sense, to be owed money because they need to be part of a system that really requires it. At the same time, many of them resent the need to live this way. One African expressed his fervent desire to win big in the lottery for which he frequently bought tickets. He said that if he won he would be a free man for the first time in his life. Then in the next breath he admitted that even if he won, he would not be able to escape the system.

I have on a few occasions offered to help African friends open a savings or bank account when they have complained about the claims made by others on their finances. In all cases my offers have been rejected. One friend stated that he would prefer to invest in his future by helping others, which was more sure than savings institutions, and which would also indicate he was a better human being.

There is also a strong sense of Africans wanting to owe money for reasons other than financial. What is meant is that borrowing and owing money helps develop long-term, interdependent relationships. And such relationships are very highly valued. In some ways they are at the heart of being African.

Observation 59 contrasts with observation 3 in chapter 3, "Money is to be spent before friends or relatives ask to borrow it." In both, the focus is on the interpersonal use of money. Number 59 points to the advantage of having people in your debt—it is good insurance for hard times. With number 3, people are thinking of the advantage of spending money on themselves versus having the money go for "insurance."

60. There is some sense in which people want to be without money so that they can more easily refuse a request for a loan.

Of course people do not really prefer to be without money, but I believe there is a pervasive feeling that when a person has money there is little choice but either to spend it or to lend it. Just having it in one's pocket or purse is hardly an option. Yet money lent is not completely gone—money so used is in some sense "deposited" in a "savings account."

Parker Shipton describes this contradictory attitude:

> Cash in The Gambia is an odd commodity surrounded by
> ambivalent attitudes (Shipton 1989). As in some other parts
> of Africa south of the Sahara, nothing is more sought after

than money, but nothing is more quickly disposed of than money. Indeed, money is even seen as something to get rid of, something to convert into longer-lasting forms. Several features besides those already noted make money into an unstable form of wealth in The Gambia: its nearly universal fungibility, divisibility, and portability. These features make money contestable. Everyone needs it for something, particularly in the lean season from June to August; and one with money will usually have an almost infinite number of relatives or neighbors with pressing needs. Though few farmers have the means to measure inflation, nearly all are aware of the process. Rural Gambian saving strategies are mainly concerned, then, with *removing wealth from the form of readily accessible cash, without appearing antisocial.* In communities in which one has many relatives, as is usual, this is a delicate balancing act, and besides any ethical issues involved, the "squawk factor," the potential for complaints and accusations, must enter every individual savings decision. [emphasis in the original][2]

Observations 59—that people want to be owed money—and observation 60—that people want to be without money—may seem to say practically the same thing. Although they are closely related, the first speaks to insurance for future needs. It is like money in the bank. Being owed money is an asset that can be called upon when there is a pressing need. If a person does not have outstanding credits, it indicates he is friendless and without recourse in the day of trouble, which is sure to come sooner or later. As for the second, it refers to the heavy burden of social interaction. People want to borrow and loan in order to be functioning, contributing, and respected members of society. That is their overriding concern, but it does not mean that in the immediate moment they enjoy seeing their resources disappear. Consequently, being without money obviates the need to make decisions, to feel the conflict of wanting to be generous and yet wanting to use one's money for personal or family needs.

Even Africans do not always feel "it is more blessed to give than to receive." The process of loaning money can be painful, but being without money may provide the only way possible in good conscience to refuse to make a loan. So in a sense, life is more comfortable when there is no money in pocket.

61. The unwritten rules governing the loaning and sharing of money and goods, and the extreme social pressure on individuals to conform to

---

[2]Shipton 1995:257.

**these rules or face sanctions, serve as leveling mechanisms to keep
people from getting ahead of others.**

The underlying basic principles regarding the sharing of money and other
resources are quite similar across Africa, but the practices and ethics differ
in detail from one ethnic group to another. The persistence, pressure, or
aggressiveness normal to individuals of one group seeking the resources of
other individuals may clash with the practices of another. I know a family
from one ethnic group that lived in a neighborhood dominated by another
group. The latter group was much more aggressive in making demands
than were my friends from the first group. After several years of suffering
importunateness, they sold their house and moved to a section of the same
city where people of their own ethnic group were in the majority. The
family head composed these lines (translated from his own language) that
clearly reveal his irritation:

> Give me a gift!
> Make me a loan!
> Or if you won't
> Leave me alone! (personal communication, 1987).

Besides unambiguous requests for things, there are many ways that
various groups use in seeking material benefits from others or that they use
to keep others from getting ahead economically. I will call these *leveling
mechanisms*: ways that are used in societies to keep people from getting
ahead financially or of achieving something that most people would desire.
Some are individual ways while others are characteristics seemingly built
into the culture.

Fatalism is a common leveling mechanism. On one occasion a mission
hospital ship was in a particular port, and offered free reconstructive sur-
gery to anyone in the area who had a cleft palate. A pastor friend of mine
knew a family that included a young boy who suffered from such a condition. The pastor spent many evenings with the family, trying to convince
them to send their boy for treatment. They were very opposed because, they
said, "It was the will of God and the spirits for him to be born this way and
we dare not interfere with God's will."

Reciprocal obligations are a brake to keeping people on the same economic level. On the one hand, if one person has more goods or wealth, he
will be expected to contribute more. On the other hand, if others cannot
reciprocate on equal or similar terms, hard feelings or jealousy will result.
George Foster describes the way this may operate in a group:

> Reciprocal obligations are most effective in maintaining a
> society when partners have essentially the same access to
> resources, when their economic well-being is at the same
> level. Only under these conditions can equality be maintained

in the long run. However, reciprocal patterns tend to be incompatible with the trend toward individualization that characterizes urbanization, migration, and industrial or plantation or mine work, for not all villagers make progress at the same rate of speed. Those few who begin to make economic progress find that their relationships are no longer in balance: More is expected of them than they will receive from their partners. Progressive individuals are thus faced with a cruel dilemma: If they are to enjoy the fruits of their greater initiative and efforts, they must be prepared to disregard many of the obligations that their societies expect of them or they must expect to support an ever-increasing number of idle relatives and friends, with little or no profit to themselves.[3]

The imperative of social obligations, including hospitality, also holds people to economic equality. At the time of the death of a relative, friend, or other kin, it is a necessity that one take time off from work, sometimes for several days, to be with the family of the bereaved. The personal expense may be considerable: from work time lost, travel expenses that are often incurred, and contributions that must be made to the bereaved. The financial obligations are greater for those who are employed. If these obligations only occurred infrequently, the burden would be supportable. But when families and kinship groups are large and deaths are frequent, these obligations constitute major expenses in time and money for wage earners and for their employers.

Public and family opinion are also often impediments to getting ahead. In traditional societies people are expected to conform to traditional thinking and ways of doing things. A friend of mine told me that early in his life he had an artistic bent. When he was still a schoolboy a couple of neighborhood restaurants asked him to draw murals on their walls. He did so to his great satisfaction, but then members of his family and his friends learned of what he had done. They criticized him unmercifully. "Who do you think you are?" "What made you think you were an artist?" "Where did you learn to draw?" "Nobody in your family is an artist so why would you want to draw?" And so on. My friend told me he gave up the idea and never again attempted to draw.

Jealousy and envy also hold people back. Delbert Chinchen describes how this manifests itself at every level of Liberian and Malawian society. It is done through what he calls "an enforced form of socialism." In this, extreme social pressure is exerted on those who have resources to share them with those members of society who have less. The effect is to prevent anyone from getting ahead and basically acts as a brake on economic

---

[3]Foster 1973:107–108.

development. What is thought of as ideals of sharing can be argued to be at least in part rules of society shaped by jealousy and distrust.[4]

There are many other leveling mechanisms, far more than can be included in this summary description. They include: threats of sorcery or witchcraft, the rule of elders who monopolize resources so that younger members of society cannot get ahead, fear of gossip, and the inescapable demands of kin and friends who lay claim to any and all resources that seem to be within their grasp.

62. The value of a development project is not to be measured by its long-term success.

An African friend of ours was given several hundred dollars by an international aid organization in start-up money for a chicken project. He had grown up in the city and had no specialized knowledge about raising chickens. The international agency gave him the money without providing any instructions or training in raising chickens. As he had no place to raise chickens, he put the baby chicks on the floor of the room he rented as a single man. So his bed was in the middle of the floor of his bedroom turned chicken coop. The chickens ate greater and greater quantities of food, and he began to worry that his money would run out before the chickens were old enough to sell. He asked me for a loan to enable him to buy chicken feed. He would repay me from the profits when he sold the chickens. When the chickens were big enough to sell, he gave some of the chickens to the woman who made his meals. He gave some to people with whom he had outstanding debts, some died, and a few he sold for cash. There were never enough profits to repay me at all, and actually, nothing was ever said to me about repayment.

At the end of the project there were no chickens and no money with which to buy more baby chicks, even though the international aid agency had provided the seed money in order for the recipient to become established in the chicken business. From my viewpoint the project came close to being a total failure because no long-term benefits were realized from it. But from the point of view of my friend, the project was quite a success. It was a success because for a few months he had cash in his pocket, he was able to settle some outstanding debts, he had chicken to eat, and he felt the respect of being a self-employed person for a time.

Another example was an attempt to establish a bottled gas dealership. Several friends had the idea of buying bottled gas directly from a petroleum company and selling the gas from a shop they would rent in their neighborhood. I queried them about the business economics of it—the profit margins that the petroleum company allowed were very low, the rent for a little shop would be relatively high, and their sales potential very limited. I did

---

[4]Chinchen 1994:87.

not see how the project could be viable in the long run. I found out that the long-term prospects were at best a minor consideration for them. If they could obtain some funding from an international agency, what would happen in the long-term was not of much concern. What was on their minds was obtaining some funding so that for a period of time they would have money in their pocket. Because of their great immediate financial needs, short-term interests were all they thought of.

This observation also applies to large-scale projects, as seen in a report in the Dakar newspaper *Wal fadjri L'Aurore*:

> Globally, the projects financed by the World Bank have had a success rate of 67% in Senegal. But the Bretton Woods funding agency and the government of Senegal have agreed on "the necessity of improving the institutional development and durability of their projects."…As regards the durability of programs, mediocre results have been brought to light, with the audit finding that only 17% of projects had satisfactory continuity.[5]

The report states that only seventeen percent of the projects funded by the World Bank continued to operate after the funding ended. Similar results could be cited for other countries. Hence, the observation is applicable even beyond the individual level.

Repayment of loans

63. A loan is eligible to be repaid when the creditor's need becomes greater than the debtor's need.

If you have the means and I have a need, you should loan me the money. When will I repay? When you have the need and I have the means. (The charging of interest would be unthinkable between friends.)

An alternative wording for this observation could be, "A loan is made with some sense of obligation of the borrower to directly repay it sometime in the future. A gift is made with no sense that it will be directly repaid; but rather, that the gift will be reciprocated sometime in the future under the unspoken rules of the culture of the people involved."

On a more formal level, loans from a bank, for example, are much less common than in the West. People of limited means cannot borrow from a bank; they cannot even afford to have an account in a bank. But even banks often go bankrupt because individuals and governments do not repay their loans, which are in effect uncollectable. Part of the problem with loans in the formal business sector is the lack of capital, but a major problem is the

---

[5]Guèye 1997:5.

collecting of monies due—practically no one repays a loan voluntarily, even if a promissory note or other document has been signed. I think there is also an underlying concept that a bank is there to provide and loan money—its coffers are full of money, it has far more money than I do, and therefore is it not a little absurd to think of me giving money to a bank? A bank, and people of means, are there to be givers, not receivers.

64. The repayment of loans is a subjective matter involving the weighing of economic, social, and time factors.

In Africa, loans between friends are not treated objectively, that is, as a binding oral contract with clearly stipulated terms that must be fulfilled, but subjectively. The number one criterion in determining whether a loan *should* be repaid or not is the financial condition of the creditor. If the creditor is well off, a loan repayment may be deferred. Of course the financial condition of the borrower is of fundamental importance (if he has no money he cannot repay a loan) but the question here is not *if* the loan can be paid back, but if it *should* be. If the creditor is judged to have means, it will be very difficult for a borrower in normal circumstances to seriously consider repayment.

A few of the subjective factors that may enter into repayment are:

1. *Economic factors*—as described in the previous paragraph, the relative economic positions of the people involved enter into the repayment of loans; major changes in the economic situation of the borrower since the loan was made; developments in the economic condition of the borrower, such as loss of employment

2. *Social factors*—the relationship between borrower and creditor; the desire for a continuing relationship; considerations of reciprocity, that is, the relative position of each vis-à-vis the other as regards past obligations, gifts, and loans; the residual imbalances in past transactions in favor of either party; the social status of each party, and their relative position in the social hierarchy

3. *Time factors*—past history of relationships and mutual attitudes; what future relationships are expected to be; what the borrower wants or expects from the creditor in the future, that is, how important it is to him to maintain a good credit rating

In sum, it is clear that the repayment of loans is far more complicated than just following the terms of a simple written contract.

64W. For a Westerner the repayment of a loan is due objectively on the terms agreed upon when the loan was made.

I had what would doubtlessly seem to Westerners to be an example of extreme "nonobjectivity." I once loaned an African friend several hundred dollars so that he could purchase land where he would build a house, dig a well, and keep a few animals. Before making the loan we had talked at length about his plans, the risks of fraud in government land offices, what level of repayments he could sustain, and such concerns. We came to an agreement which in my opinion included very generous terms for the borrower, such as not charging interest and scheduling small monthly payments that would be spread over many years. He said he would continue to make repayments even if he lost control of the land. A contract was drawn up which included all the relevant details and conditions. We both signed it and had it witnessed. Not long after closing the deal, government bulldozers moved in and just took over, without compensation, a large tract of land that included his property. My friend made two token payments, less than what was called for, and then he completely repudiated the contract. I never pursued the borrower. I believe the contract went so much against the grain of the culture, that culture won out over the legalities of the matter. He just could not bring himself to keep his word if it meant repaying a loan to a person of much greater means than he. That was just too much to expect in his culture. And if I had made an issue of repayment, which was within my rights to do, it would have meant the end of our friendship.

65. The collection of debts is primarily the responsibility of creditors, not of borrowers to volunteer payments.

Loans, rents, and other payment obligations are collected by the creditor; payments are not volunteered by the debtor. If you are a landlord and want your rent payment, or if you want your loan repaid, someone must physically go after it. The debtor or renter is not expected to go find his creditor to make a payment when it is due.

"I've come to collect the rent money." (Observation 65)

Loans are seldom repaid without reminders, repeated tries, knowing when the person gets paid, where he lives, and when he is likely to be home. In one African city we lived in, the real estate agent that came to our house the first day of every month to collect our rent told us we were his favorite renters, as collecting our rent required only one visit.

65W. The repayment of loans and the payment of rents are responsibilities of borrowers and renters.

Instead of the creditor being required to find the debtor in order to collect his money, the Westerner puts the responsibility on the debtor. The one who owes money goes to the one who is to receive the payment and is expected to do so within the time limits specified in the agreement that was established at the time of taking out the loan or of occupying the rented premises. Actually, in the West payments are usually made by sending a check in the mail, or by other means that do not require a physical movement of the payer.

For Westerners loans require that the conditions be specified beforehand under which a loan will be granted. "When will it be repaid?" is the most fundamental question. Even if a date is not required, some other indicator is given, as, "When I sell my corn crop after the harvest." Typically, the lender also wants to know what the money is to be used for, in order to judge whether or not to accept the risk of not being paid back. Also for Westerners, interest will be expected except in very personal or exceptional cases, such as within the family.

If a loan is not repaid or renegotiated, any continuation of the relationship between creditor and borrower will be strained, at best, because the Western creditor quickly loses faith in a borrower who does not keep his word and meet his obligations. Loans that are made on a commercial basis must be repaid on schedule. If they are not, the borrower faces the likelihood of legal action being taken by the creditor to force repayment.

66. Many people live with outstanding debts that they never expect to repay.

The wording of this observation could almost as accurately read never *intend* to repay as *expect* to, as it seems that must be true. I have had several African friends who were always borrowing money they could not possibly ever pay back unless they won the lottery. On a number of occasions I have been asked to loan money to enable friends to pay electric bills that were in arrears. The system is designed—purposefully or inadvertently I have never been able to determine—to create unpayable debts. It works this way. A number of families and singles rent rooms in a multiple-story building. There is only one electric meter per building, or at best one per floor. Each renter agrees to pay his share of the electric bill, and one renter is designated to receive each renter's share and take the full amount of the bill to the electric company. This involves certain risks, such as that of some renters being unable to pay their part for any given month. There was further risk in the particular city where I lived. The electric company allowed two bills to go unpaid before the electricity was cut off. This meant, in effect, most people in the city lived with six months' use of electricity unpaid (because the electric company only issued bills every two months). As renters frequently moved from one building to another, when a bill was received some of the renters who used the electrical power during the period represented by the bill had moved to parts unknown and were basically untraceable. I was approached many times for an emergency loan which would cover the overdue bills, the current bill, and the hookup charge to bring the meter back and turn on the current. All this needed to be paid because the electric company would only restore service if all charges were brought up to date. When I questioned how my loan could ever be repaid and who would do it, and why the hopeless system was not changed, I was always assured it would all be worked out just fine. The only problem was to get the current turned back on so people would not have to continue to live in the dark.

Being constantly and permanently overextended has many effects on individuals and society. One effect is to concentrate people's thinking on where in their network they can get loans for what is needed. Another is that financial planning is based on who will likely be available and willing to provide loans for what is wanted, and not just on income.

These debts seemingly do not hurt relationships in some African societies. People can borrow or loan from each other and maintain friendship with those who have long-outstanding debts. The desire for solidarity and the ties created by mutual dependency are stronger than the strains of indebtedness. In other societies this is not true, or less so, and African friends have told me that debts are frequently the source of broken relationships. For the Westerner, who is usually marginal to the social and economic systems, it is all too easy for an African borrower to disappear permanently, with the loan remaining permanently in the accounts receivable column. I have known Westerners who made loans to bothersome people knowing they would not be repaid, but also knowing that the person would no longer pester them.

67. The risk of a loan not being paid back is largely assumed by the lender.

Not only does the lender normally have to seek out the borrower if he wants his loan repaid, if the borrower is unable to pay, the lender suffers the loss. This is especially true if an act of God is involved.

I loaned money to a farmer so that he could buy sorgum seed. He said he would pay me when he sold his crop after the harvest. After the harvest he came to my house and told me, "The rainy season began well. But just when the heads of grain were ready to fill out, the rains stopped. There was nothing to harvest." No more was said, but what was meant was, "Sorry, I won't be able to repay your money."

A development project I was involved with, organized and managed by Africans, owned a team of oxen. They loaned them out to villagers for specific agricultural activities, like plowing fields. On one occasion a neighbor borrowed the oxen and kept them overnight. At the end of the working day he tied them to a tree in his field, expecting to finish the work the next day. During the night poisonous snakes bit the oxen and they both died. The project manager told me that the farmer, as well as others, knew that poisonous snakes inhabited the several holes around the tree where the oxen were tied. Still, because the man was poor he was not held responsible to repay anything at all to the project. This was not because the project was well funded, which definitely it was not, but simply because a poor man could not be held responsible for something beyond his means to pay, even if he was negligent with the borrowed animals.

When something is in use, working, available, everyone in the owner's circle has a right, and expects, to use it. But when it breaks or needs repairs, it is the responsibility of the owner to repair it. An example is the broken door handle on our car that was left in a garage to be repaired. The garageman used the car to make a personal trip of a couple hundred kilometers, using all the fuel in the gas tank and breaking a door handle during the trip.

He admitted to me that he made the trip and broke the handle. I tried very hard, unsuccessfully, to get him to replace the broken door handle.

An interesting twist to this observation comes from Ivory Coast. Philip Saunders tells of selling his mountain bike to his house helper. In his words:

> We agreed on sixty thousand francs, which he would pay off in monthly installments of five thousand francs from his wages. We shook hands on the deal, and the bike was his.
>
> Or so I thought. One fine day, he got a puncture. "Patron, the bike has a puncture." I looked at him, and he looked at me. Yes, said my inner man, so the owner should repair it. I think his inner man said the same. My outer man, responding to the expectancy on his face, fished out three hundred francs and gave it to him. Several months passed, and I forgot the incident.
>
> Then yesterday, he came to me and dolefully announced:
>
> "Patron, the gear lever is broken." "Isn't it great," I said, "that there are lots of these bikes around now, and you can easily find spare parts?"
>
> "Yes, there are lots of these bikes about now."
>
> "How much might a gear lever cost?"
>
> "Two thousand francs."
>
> "Let's see, you've been paying the bike off for six months now. Whose bike would it be?"
>
> "Yours, patron."
>
> "Ah, I thought perhaps the front wheel would be mine, and the back wheel yours."
>
> He looked at me, wondering whether this was another of my little jokes, and should he perhaps laugh?
>
> In his mind, because he sometimes uses the bike for work purposes, it is not yet fully his. Indeed it seems to be fully mine. So I should be the one to foot any repair bills. From my viewpoint, the bike is his, he's paying it off, and only if he were using it purely for work would I see any obligation to help with repairs.
>
> So I guess I have another six months of repairs to go before the hire-purchase is complete. One of those little

cultural adjustments that are hard to get used to. (Or am I being conned?)

Come to think of it, our house helper is also in the process of paying off his bride-wealth. I begin to wonder how much of his wife he actually owns...!

Caveat emptor. Caveat vendor too, I suppose.[6]

67W. For a Westerner the borrower assumes the risk of repaying a loan.

Living in Africa has made me ask myself, "Why is it in our Western society that the borrower must assume virtually all the risk when taking out a loan?" Why is the creditor allowed to require collateral so that his risk is reduced to a minimum? Are these just some of the unfair rules of the capitalist system? I think the basic, historic, reasoning must be like this: The potential borrower wants the use of another person's money. In order to induce the owner of the money willingly to allow it to be out of his possession for a given period of time, he needs to be given assurance that his property will be returned to him at the time agreed upon. If the potential borrower will not or cannot give assurance and reasonable guarantee that he will return the money, the owner will be unwilling to loan it.

The reasoning in at least some parts of Africa follows a quite different path. It seems to be this: First, there is a difference between borrowing from institutions and borrowing from individuals. When a big man borrows from a bank, his obligation to repay the loan will often be proportional to his position and influence in society. So the large risk of default on the loan is borne by the bank. The bank agrees to the loan because it may have no choice within the context of government directives or political coercion, or because management is more interested in pleasing a customer than its own long-term viability. On an individual level, loans are mostly made between people with long-term relationships. The potential lender has more than just a business relationship with the borrower, and hence is and must be lenient with the borrower in order to safeguard the advantages that the relationship has for him outside the purely monetary aspects of the loan.

68. The use of the word *loan* when requesting money from someone is often a euphemism for *gift*.

It is certainly my personal experience, and that of most of my Western friends, that loans are never repaid by most, but not all, borrowers. The same euphemistic use of the word "loan" when meaning "gift" is also employed by Africans with Africans. Yet, probably most African languages have a variety of terms that distinguish between gifts and loans, that is, between "giving" without expecting anything in return, and "giving" expecting various kinds

---

[6]Saunders 1997:5–6.

of returns, such as the precise item, or an equivalent item. In addition to local language terms, the imported European languages, usually English or French, have their own terms. These include loan, advance, credit, gift, aid, and in French *prête, avance, crédit, cadeau, aide*. With such a mix of foreign and local terms and concepts, the Westerner is advised to find out what the local terms are and what they really mean when making loans and gifts.

A friend of mine recounts an experience with an African acquaintance. The man asked to borrow money. He concluded his appeal for help, saying, "You are the only one who can help me." My friend bridled at this and retorted, "You mean that of all the people in the world, including your seven million countrymen, I am the only person who can help you?" The man then explained that borrowing money was very difficult with his countrymen. They came after their money to collect it from you, they made a scene in front of your friends when you did not pay, and so on. Therefore, my colleague was the only one who could really help him! He meant, of course, he was the only one who would not pursue him for the repayment of his money. It does not take much imagination to understand that the man had no intention of ever paying back the loan he was asking for.

69. Loans of goods or things are tantamount to gifts.

Generally, the lender must ask for the return of a loaned item if there is to be any likelihood of it being returned.

A most revealing experience of this happened to an African friend of mine. He was unemployed and had very few possessions, but a friend of his insisted on borrowing his one and only thin jacket on a chilly, windy day. This left my friend shivering for the rest of the cold season, but in spite of knowing this his friend kept the jacket, and my friend believed he should not or could not ask for it to be returned to him. The jacket never was returned to what was to me the rightful owner.

Articles loaned may be: books, tape recorders, carrying bags, articles of clothing, tools, dishes, and such items. There seems to be a strong sense that if the person believes he needs a thing more than you do, you owe it to him and should not expect it back. The greater need is defined by the one who is without the thing. And the closer the relationship between the person with such an "excess item" and the friend without it, the more true this is. Sharing and equality between close friends is the rule, not the exception.

1. Typically the borrower does not return the article unless the owner asks (repeatedly) for its return.

2. Articles may be reloaned to third parties without the consent or knowledge of the original owner.

3. A long-term borrowing (i.e., possession) of something automatically turns it into a gift.

4. Little seems to be thought of it, if the article is worn out, torn, or rendered useless, by either normal use or through apparent carelessness.

Care of property. The responsibility of maintance is a risk taken by the lender. I loaned a new tape recorder to a friend for a few weeks. When I got it back the door was broken off, several knobs were missing and the case was badly scratched. It barely functioned. No apologies were given. When a Westerner borrows an item from another Westerner, if the thing suffers excessive wear and tear, he will probably offer to pay for the damage or at least apologize for it.

Many attitudes toward possessions and taking responsibility for another's property seem to be very different in Africa and the West. Proper maintenance and preservation of things in good working order are important values in the West. The differences in the two cultures do not stem just from availability of resources.

My wife and I rented the same house for several years. The owner's agent that collected the rent expressed his amazement several times that the paint still looked clean, inside and outside the house, and things were not broken. If he experienced this at his privileged level of society, it was not for lack of resources. We considered ourselves just typical Westerners in this sense. We were also told on several occasions by African friends that it is best to not buy a used car from an African, as they frequently do not maintain them properly (as in changing the oil) on a regular schedule. Many landlords prefer to rent to Westerners because they think they will take better care of their house or apartment; some will even lower the rent in order to attract Westerners.

Another risk of lending is that if a person's possession remains a long time with a friend, in African concepts, it means that the owner has a relationship with the borrower. The object or good may well symbolize the friendship. This can mean that asking for something to be returned may be construed as if the owner is calling for an end to the relationship. I personally have not understood how this can be true, say, in loaning books, even when I am told it is true. Over the years I have loaned books to my research associates. Almost invariably two things have been true: One, I have had to ask for the books to be returned when I needed them; and two, the associate knew in many instances that they were books I was in the process of using, yet seldom returned them of his own volition, even when I had given a specific time period at the time of making the loan.

70. **The response, "No," to a request for money, a loan, or a material object, is understood as an insult, indifference to need, a lack of respect, or a sign of rejection of the petitioner.**

The word *no* often trips up foreigners living in Africa. To Westerners *no* is simply the antonym of *yes*, although even Westerners realize that tact in many situations requires that the answer *no* needs to be softened with gentle qualifiers. In many, probably most, African cultures, the use of *no* and other negatives is an area strewn with booby traps for the Westerner. A direct reply, "No," to a request will probably be perceived as an insult. A direct negative response is an indication that the person so responding does not care about the person he or she is responding to.

There are alternatives to a direct and confrontive no when responding to a request. Examples are, "Maybe later," "Not today," "I'm interested but am not able to buy today." Also, one may suggest another person who might be interested; in effect, it is better to use any response that does not in effect slam the door on the person.

Just how far apart African and Western cultures can be in their use of saying no and otherwise communicating negative information is shown in a personal experience. I first give a brief summary of an incident from my own viewpoint. Then I give the description of the same incident from the viewpoint of one of the African participants.

Western version (written by the author). I was working in a particular city when an aged man, Mr. B, came to ask for my help in getting several manuscripts of his published. He had learned of my interest in African languages, origin myths, and ethnic histories from one of my research assistants. Before his retirement he had been a schoolteacher. He came with a collection of perhaps ten manuscripts, some handwritten, some typed. The subject matters included a grammar of his language (a major African language with published grammars readily available), folk stories, and tribal origin myths. I tried to tell him it was very difficult to get manuscripts published as the market for such materials was very limited. But in an attempt not to be rude, I said he could leave the manuscripts with me for a little while, and I would examine them and see if I could find a publisher interested in them. He left to return to his village, which was located in a distant part of the country.

I examined the papers. The grammar was very traditional and not of a high quality. Besides, he did not have the qualifications to write such a grammar, or at least to get it published. I looked at the folk stories; they looked quite typical of the scores that are available from many publishers. And finally, I looked at his history of his own people and their language, which is a major one in West Africa. To my amazement he claimed that Adam spoke this language, as did Abraham and other ancients. He also said that French was based on this language, and on and on. Well, in my opinion these ideas discredited everything he wrote, and I could in clear conscience put them aside.

I thought that when Mr. B returned for my verdict I would just politely say that I was unable to help him, especially in light of having many of my own manuscripts unpublished. I would meet with him personally and explain all this to him. But I would give him back his manuscripts, expressing my regrets at not being able to help him, so he would not need to use his very limited resources to travel in poor health yet a third time to the capital.

When I told an African friend of all this, he was horrified. This somewhat surprised me, so I asked another African friend his opinion of the matter. He completely sided with my first African friend. At that point I turned the whole matter over to them, to deal with Mr. B in the manner they thought best.

African version (written by an African).[7] In Africa, in Europe, and elsewhere, people render service to each other. Even in societies that cultivate individualism, no one can stop someone from helping a third person from time to time, or stop a person from soliciting something from another. The problem is not therefore there. It rather resides in the attitude to adopt if one asks us for something that we are not able or willing to grant.

In Europe and in North America if someone is solicited for help that he cannot give, he answers directly in the negative, without any embarrassment. The one that is making the solicitation understands the frank attitude, and without resentment may go knock at another door. Here in Africa it is different. A categorical refusal is understood to show a lack of tact and diplomacy. To answer a request in a negative and direct way is an offense, and shows an absence of respect vis-à-vis the other.

It does not mean that Africans make promises that they will not keep. Not at all. As people do all over the world, they put off those that come to ask them for a service they cannot perform. However, there is a way to do it without offending the other and without adversely affecting future relations between them.

If Africans cope in this world, it is because many of them have a double culture and a large capacity to assimilate the customs and cultures of others. But they do so without disowning their African values. This explains how they manage to live in other countries of the world without experiencing cultural stress.

But, at least it appears to be true, Westerners do not have this capacity, or they do not make the necessary effort, to understand the other. Those among them who do make the effort, report it on the cold pages of a book that the overwhelming majority has no interest in reading. Thus, this understanding, to the extent it exists, remains purely theoretical. In the field

---

[7]This section, called "African Version," was written by one of the participants in the episode who, at the author's request, wrote up his viewpoint of the event.

therefore, that is, in practice, at the intersection of the two cultures, sparks are often produced. This is as we should expect where there is such great incomprehension which is far more cultural than circumstantial.

Take this case of Mr. B, a retired teacher who is dedicating the rest of his life to write books of folk tales, of grammar, of the history of his ethnic group, and of the origin myths of his clan. But he has had problems finding a publisher that is interested in his work. After having made the rounds of the publishing houses of the capital city in vain, he decides to go to see one of his acquaintances—a Westerner—for a possible bit of help. But he finds that this Westerner also has a whole mountain of manuscripts that he also wants to publish. Nevertheless, he takes the time to examine the manuscripts of Mr B. He leaves his manuscripts with the Westerner for him to examine as he has opportunity, and he returns to his home in a distant part of the country.

Some time later Mr. B returns to see the Westerner, to find out if his manuscripts had finally found a taker. His Western friend, knowing that he would not be able really to do anything for him, decided he would give the manuscripts back to him. With his inability to find a publisher for his own work, finding one for someone else would be utopian.

Dialogue or communication? (Written by the same African.) The Africans on the scene made the Westerner realize that if he proceeded in his brusque way he risked hurting the old man. This realization caused a lot of questioning of the conduct to adopt. Should the manuscripts purely and simply be handed over to Mr. B with a smile at the corner of the mouth?

In the West this is what would have been done. But it happens that we are in Africa. Therefore to solve the problem, and there is one, it is necessary to demonstrate far more understanding and diplomacy. An African in such a situation would know how to handle it without causing offense to the old man. Of course, it would take whatever time was necessary, but the problem would be resolved. But the Westerner who would want to resolve such a problem in one minute and with a handshake without dialoguing, would leave a residual feeling of animosity.

Dialogue is the solution to such a problem. Some people say that Westerners *communicate* but do not *dialogue*.[8] In communication a no is no and yes is yes. What counts is that the other person comprehends the message that is being transmitted. In dialogue, on the other hand, the heart of the matter is looked for, going beyond the words to address the feelings and the passions. Dialogue is therefore stronger than communication because it

---

[8]Although the word dialogue is used here, I believe the author is pointing out the difference between one-way "communication" that he believes Westerners use, for example, informing Mr. B that the Westerner cannot help him, to the two-way dialogue which he believes is used by Africans. This is virtually negotiating an answer, taking into consideration the needs and desires of both parties for the sake of avoiding hurting the feelings of Mr. B, even though there is no intention of helping him.

permits one to put himself in the place of the other, to understand from the interior and not just the exterior.

Putting oneself inside the other to understand from the inside (written by the same African). The Westerner goes from the surface toward the interior while the African puts himself inside the other, going from the interior toward the exterior. This is the core difference in the conception of things, and above all, of the understanding of people. This, therefore, is the start of solving the equation before us, of accepting dialogue in place of mere communication.

The two Africans (my friend and I) spoke to Mr. B of the interest that his work would have for present and future generations. They also made him understand that his Western friend had a large number of manuscripts which will never be published due to a lack of financial means. However, they told him his Western friend had told them to tell Mr. B he should not lose hope, because doors sometimes open up overnight.

At that point Mr. B, who is African and understands the subject, left part of his manuscripts for further consideration and took the rest with him hopefully to show to another publisher. Thus, the manuscripts left with the Westerner will be returned to him at his next visit.

Returning to the subject of the gentleman B and his Western friend—their good relations were preserved and nothing stops them from collaborating in the future. If this is true it was made possible by Africans of the same culture as that of Mr. B, who acted as mediators in playing an important socio-diplomatic role. To carry this out it was necessary to know the workings of a whole culture. And on this precise point, it proves that Africans know Westerners better than the latter know them. If there is a problem of comprehension between Africans and Westerners, it is cultural and not epidermal (personal communication, 1997).

Western viewpoint of the African viewpoint. In the "Western version" above, I report how I had wanted to handle the situation with Mr. B. My assistants very strongly disagreed with the way I proposed to deal with him. (I was gratified to have them express their objections to me. That they would feel free to do so, I took as an accomplishment. I had long worked to encourage them to express their opinions, which many Africans do not do with foreigners, especially when they are employees.)

As my viewpoint of the matter was very different from that of my assistants, I asked one of the Africans to write up the episode from their point of view. The result was the "African version." To conclude the discussion, I will make explicit some of the cultural differences the whole episode seems to reveal.

Some Western cultural clashes with the African viewpoint are:

1. I did not think that I would be acting offensively if I politely and respectfully told Mr. B that unfortunately, I was unable to see to

the publication of his manuscripts. To tactfully be clear about it would be simple courtesy. It would also free him to pursue other publishing possibilities. I would be doing him a disservice to pointlessly hang onto his manuscripts.

2. The African approach was to me insincere, hypocritical, and even dishonest, requiring me to feign interest in his writing. In fact, I believed: (a) it to be unpublishable; (b) he should know that I was not in the publishing business and, therefore, really unable to help him; and (c) it would be a disservice to Mr. B to falsely raise his hope of seeing his writings published.

3. I disagree with the interpretation given by my African colleagues to my inability to help Mr B get his manuscripts published. They understood it as being a refusal to help him. For me, to give Mr. B the impression that I could help him when in fact I could not, would be misleading and a misrepresentation of what I was capable of doing and not doing. It cannot be a refusal, when a person tells another of what he is incapable of doing. A refusal can only be an unwillingness to do what is possible to do, in my culture. It is something else to make someone believe you can do something when you cannot, in the name of not hurting his feelings. What they saw as the correct way to proceed, was for me to hide my inability to help, while pretending to help Mr. B, all in an effort to not discourage him. To me this was supersensitivity carried to the extreme. Adults should be able to confront reality, if it is gently presented to them. An extreme need to hide normal realities from normal people, and the need to keep normal adults from feeling even the slightest personal misfortune, seems to me to create a make-believe world in which unreality necessarily becomes indistinguishable from reality.

4. The Africans believed their handling of the situation did not involve making a promise they, or I, could not keep. To me it did at least implicitly involve promises. Mr. B thought I was promising to try to find a publisher, that I was promising to work with the manuscripts, etc. In fact, my African assistants and I knew perfectly well that all this was not true.

5. The African writes that answering a request in a negative and direct way is offensive and will adversely affect future relations with that person. My opinion is that this is very unfortunate, if true. And, in fact, it does seem to be true in many African cultures. The alternative to giving a straight answer is to just tell people some form of what they want to hear. In my cultural

understanding, this will create problems in the long run that will render it counterproductive.

6. My African colleagues believed that Africans are far more attuned to other cultures than are Westerners. I cannot agree, but find the viewpoint interesting. It is very possible that if Africans seek to avoid clashes on an interpersonal level, more than do Westerners, this could be construed as being "more attuned." But this also reflects another basic contrast between Africans and Western cultures. It is arguable that Africans often seek surface harmony at the expense of letting deeper differences remain unresolved.

What the African writer calls being "attuned" to other cultures is less a case of understanding others than seeking to not offend people of other cultures. This is different from crosscultural understanding. Take this situation between my African assistants and me. They dismissed my desire to deal with Mr. B in a polite yet direct manner. Of course, they could correctly consider my approach as being offensive in their culture. I can accept that in fact it was. But that does not mean that I am insensitive in my own culture, or that Westerners are objectively more insensitive than Africans. Those from one culture who see particular behaviors as insensitive may be seen by those of the other culture as supersensitive.

I was categorized as being uncaring and insensitive. A more understanding opinion on their part would have been to recognize that sensitivity is defined relatively. What would be insensitivity and wounding of others' feelings in one culture, could be perfectly normal frankness in another. A different interpretation would be that I as an individual was insensitive, but that this did not mean that all Westerners are insensitive. Instead, judgment was made on general terms of "Africans are sensitive, Westerners are insensitive." Of course, Westerners too frequently make the same kind of unjust generalizations of Africans as in this case Africans seem to have done with Westerners.

7. I do not, of course, agree with the put-down directed at me: "Apparently, Westerners don't have this capacity (to assimilate the customs and cultures of others), or they do not make the necessary effort to understand the other. Those among them (meaning me, his employer at the time) who do make the effort, report it on the cold pages of a book (meaning this book, *African Friends and Money Matters*) that the overwhelming majority has no interest in reading."

Finally, a short summary of the whole episode with Mr. B: My African colleagues considered my opinions to show that I was insensitive, uncaring, and lacking in basic human feelings and diplomacy. To the extent that I am a typical Westerner and my colleagues are typical Africans, this reveals that there is a wide cultural chasm between us in the area of interpersonal relations.

70W. The simple response "No" is meant to tell the petitioner in the most economic terms possible that the request is denied, for whatever reason.

No is thought of by the Westerner as an immediate response that gets to the heart of the matter without wasting the time of either the petitioner or the potential giver. Although in the West softeners are often added to a *no*, such as, "No, not yet," I think usage of the word *no* itself, and other such negatives, whatever they actually are in local African languages, are much more delicate than equivalent negatives in the West.

Because negative or contrary opinions and disagreements are such delicate matters in Africa, Westerners need to pay special attention to them.

> [They] should probe gently for specificity and details until they are reasonably satisfied that they understand what is meant even if not stated.

> The challenge is to determine whether the true response is really affirmative or negative. As British businessman Peter Biddlecombe explains:

> "You ask a question or make a proposal. The African disagrees or is uncertain, but doesn't want to offend you so he agrees. But it's a formality, he uses symbol words or codes. Like a diplomat saying *yes* when he means *perhaps* and *perhaps* when he means *no*. He has observed the rules of courtesy, but has conveyed his true feelings. The problem, of course, is interpreting the signals."[9]

Africans have assured me that they understand one another, and that what appear to Westerners to be unclear meanings are to them perfectly clear. I have had reason to doubt that this is always so. On one occasion some African friends of mine planned to make a presentation in a village some distance from the capital city in which they lived. They obtained the agreement of the village chief's son to sponsor their visit. They all agreed on a date and a time when the son would be in the village to receive them and present them to the chief. At some personal expense the friends hired a vehicle, borrowed equipment, and traveled to the village. They waited and

[9]Richmond and Gestrin 1998:45.

waited, but the son of the chief never showed up. The presentation could not be made. They had misread his agreement to meet them and wasted their time and money through the misunderstanding.

Summary: loans and debts

The misuse of someone else's things is a sensitive issue with Westerners. Things are valued, and taking good care of them is considered necessary. Many times Westerners are unwilling to lend their things to others because they believe the other person—whether an African or fellow countryman—will not take good care of them, either from neglect or misuse. Therefore the wear and tear on these things will be excessive.

Westerners have found from experience that many Africans do not take care of their own things. They fail to understand how it is that Africans seem to value things as much as Westerners do but that they do not take care of them. Even when Africans have little, it is inexplicable that they do not carefully maintain what they have, in the Westerner's thinking.

This subject overlaps with the Westerner sense of hospitality. Westerners have very rigid rules that govern the use of toilets and bathrooms and other areas of their houses. They are very fussy regarding hygiene and the procedures to follow in these places. When the rules are not followed by African guests, it is easy for their sense of hospitality to suffer. Africans widely interpret Westerner attitudes toward loaning their things and their lack of hospitality as stemming from racial prejudice. In fact, they usually have nothing to do with race and everything to do with the proper care of and respect for property. The Westerner would resent the improper use, say, of his toilet, just as much from a fellow Westerner as from an African.

In the United States, anyway, people that do not maintain their houses, yards, automobiles, furniture, and personal possessions in neat and good working order are looked down upon as wastrels and a priori, part of the social underclass. These feelings and their underlying values carry over to their adopted lands in Africa, where attitudes toward possessions seem to be radically different.

8

Business Matters

Introduction

Reference was made in chapter 3, "Use of Resources," to a certain African ambivalence toward money. It can also be said that many Africans have misgivings about business. Business has historical and emotional ties to foreign intrusions into Africa, the growth of cities, the unbridled quest for profits, and the loss of traditional life and values. The words of the Cameroonian writer, Jean-Marc Ela, eloquently describe the attitude:

> For the African, the rustic village is a place of security that comes from being rooted in a homogenous, fissureless, world. The move to the city marks the end of the world. It marks the collapse of the verities of existence and the rupture with all community ties to traditional life. The city is where youth are lost, exposed to all the dangers and temptations of the "corrupt" world that is in contact with "civilization." When all is said and done, the urbanization of Africans brings about a detachment from traditional society and community and a rejection of the past way of life. Deprived of participation in his rituals, having abandoned his ancestral beliefs and practices, the African is but a disoriented city dweller. He is an anonymous individual, available, even while keeping up his guard. He often lives as a single man, precariously attached to a scrap of kinship or to a group of comrades. He lives isolated among strangers, disoriented by the mixture of customs, the unfamiliar way of life, and the many temptations.[1]

---

[1]Ela 1983:187.

For the Western reader a few other introductory notes are needed:

1. Business is very much connected to social issues. Business and social relations are not separate compartments of life in Africa.

2. At least to a Westerner, African business culture seems less direct or factual, less explicit about certain problems, overly diplomatic in telling customers what they supposedly want to hear, and less forthcoming about problems.

3. Lastly, business in Africa is a reflection of economies that are often less tuned to competitive market conditions than is typical in the West.

Following are twenty observations (numbered 71-90) about business matters in African culture.

Role of relationships

71. Before attempting to do business with an African, it is essential to establish at least a minimal personal basis for carrying on the transaction.

This applies even to the simplest of business transactions, such as asking directions of a stranger on the street or along a rural road. Basic African courtesy requires that a person be greeted first, before any other interaction can take place. If greetings and a personal basis are needed for such trivial and fleeting encounters such as asking for directions, they are much more needed in substantial dealings.

> Africans lead materially simple but socially complex lives. Within that complexity, interpersonal relations take precedence, in everything from working with government officials to making purchases from vegetable vendors.
>
> In relating to Africans you must first connect with them on a human basis. Talk about family, theirs and yours. Go out of your way to develop a good relationship so that you don't seem like the usual businesslike, distant foreign visitor.[2]

Jon Arensen tells of a man who came to visit him in the Sudan. He was offered tea, and Jon and the visitor "talked and drank tea for over an hour until he finally asked if he could have a few nails. He felt it was rude to just ask. First he had to establish a relationship with me" (unpublished notes, n.d.).

---

[2]Richmond and Gestrin 1998:90.

A proper ending to a meeting is also important. Often leave-taking is done in two stages. First, the one going away says, "I need to be going," and after a suitable delay says, "I am going now."

Clothes can also affect relationships between people, including Westerners. In the West the way people dress is usually thought to be their personal business. Employers frequently dictate acceptable dress for employees, but outside of the workplace, people mostly dress according to their personal tastes. In Africa the general rule is that people dress for others, not for themselves. Being improperly dressed is not so much a reflection on the invitee as on the host. Being properly clothed honors the other person, and they feel dishonored if someone is improperly dressed in relation to his status and position.

72. The relationship between a seller and buyer may well affect the price asked and the price paid for a good or a service.

A client with a relationship to the seller may be asked to pay more than an unknown client or a stranger, or he may be legitimately taken advantage of, that is, have liberties taken with him.

The complex factors include the following:

1. A known client may be asked to pay more, or less, than an unknown client or a stranger; closeness and trust are major factors in the equation.

2. He may also legitimately be taken advantage of, that is, have liberties taken with him.

3. The seller will size up the potential buyer, inferring nationality, noting the kind of dress and general appearance of prosperity or want, and adjust the asking price accordingly.

4. If the client does not bargain, or does not complain about a high price, or is well off, he or she will generally be expected to pay more.

This observation is true especially if the client has means, whether a foreigner or an African. This is not a universal rule, but I have found it true in enough cases that I am not surprised when it is encountered. Rationale: You naturally help your friends if you are able when they have needs. So if a client is a friend, he is in your network and you naturally expect him to help if he is able to.

I was taking my car to a mechanic who did good work at reasonable prices. After a few months I said to him, "It seems to me your prices have increased since I first came to you." He replied, "Of course, you're my friend."

"My last price is three kudos." (Observation 72)

If you leave your car with a garageman for repairs, and he has a need to use it during the day, he will frequently do so. Sometimes it will be used until the gas tank is just about empty. I learned to take my car in for repairs with only a minimum of fuel in the tank. Once I had taken it with the tank almost full, and when I picked it up the next day I noticed the tank was registering empty. I asked the shop owner where he had gone with the car. He said he had gone to a nearby city, but if I did not want him to use my car that way, from then on he would not do so in the future. I made no further fuss, but never again tested him on the point by leaving the car with anything but a minimum amount of fuel in the tank.

But these business practices are not just for use by sellers. The buyer can also take advantage of relationships developed through being a regular customer, or otherwise going beyond minimum transactions. The customer can ask for favors: "I have looked all over and can't find okra, could you find some for me?" The shopkeeper will probably send a boy to get some for you, or find that there is none for sale that day. Or if you have confidence in the shopkeeper, you may leave your bags with him or her while you shop or run an errand.[3]

---

[3]Hungerford n.d.:5.

73. Bargaining for a better deal in any transaction involves important social as well as economic factors.

Walter Ong understands the dynamics of bargaining relationships as especially being a feature of oral, or face-to-face societies:

> In primary oral cultures, even business is not business: it is fundamentally rhetoric. Purchasing something at a Middle East bazaar is not a simple economic transaction, as it would be at Woolworths' and as a high-technology culture is likely to presume it would be in the nature of things. Rather, it is a series of verbal and somatic (bodily) maneuvers, a polite duel, a contest of wits, an operation in oral agonistic (combat).[4]

Some helpful points to remember when involved in bargaining in Africa:

1. When shopping, buyers are not just purchasing an item, they are relating to and communicating with sellers. Often the social value of African market interactions outweighs the commercial value.

2. Bargaining is part of the game of life. The buyer should go to the market with adequate time for interaction with the sellers.

3. Paying the first price disrupts the dynamics of market relationships. Asking higher beginning prices is not usually an attempt to cheat the buyer or an attempt to make a high profit, but is a normal expected, and agreeable aspect of life. Trading and bargaining involve social interactions, with the bargaining routine designed to prolong the time of interaction.

4. The desired results of traditional bargaining are satisfied buyers and sellers and an enhanced relationship between them. Vendors will have made a reasonable profit and buyers will have paid a price commensurate with their social and economic statuses.

5. Some vendors in markets frequented by tourists or foreigners become greedy, manipulative, and unethical. The behavior of such individuals should not be taken as typical of traditional African market behavior. Some of these vendors become adept at making foreigners feel that they have paid less than a fair price, or the price required by their status.

6. There is nothing unethical or unchristian about negotiating over the price to be paid for something. It is unchristian if the buyer becomes angry or upset during the process.

---

[4]Ong 1982:68.

7. There are two ways to bargain while shopping. One is to seek a lower price. A second is to seek superior merchandise at the price the vendor is asking. The latter ploy allows the buyer to pick out the very best items the vendor has to sell; otherwise, the vendor may make the choices.

8. Foreigners will be respected if they bargain reasonably; it shows they know how to buy and know the real value of what they buy. Conversely, not bargaining, but paying the first price asked, lowers the respect the vendor has for the buyer. It is also one of the contributing factors in encouraging the unethical behavior seen in markets frequented by tourists.

9. African market people will usually not be cheated. If they cannot make a fair profit they will ordinarily not sell. Sometimes, especially at the end of the month, vendors will sell at a loss if they are desperate to raise cash for an urgent financial need.

10. Westerners should not fret when they realize sometime after making a purchase that they have paid too much. Africans also sometimes lose. The best strategy is to do one's reasonable best and then not look back, realizing that it takes time to develop bargaining skills, and mistakes will always be part of buying, anywhere.[5]

74. Employers are expected by society and even by governments to provide advances to employees in certain family situations and for certain holidays.

It comes as a surprise to many foreigners working in Africa that they are expected by employees to provide cash advances before special holidays. Organizations are required by law in many countries to provide such loans. Individuals are not required in the same way to do so, but it is so expected and counted on by employees that it becomes in fact an inescapable obligation. These requirements are fair, to my knowledge, as employees typically do not have cash on hand which will enable them to finance the heavy expenditures so often required at special occasions by family and peers. Employees are usually given some two or three months to repay the advances, or have them deducted from their monthly salaries.

Examples of mandated advances include those made before employees' annual vacations, at the time of a newborn child's naming ceremony, at the time of funerals of close family members, and in Muslim areas, advances to prepare for the annual *id al-Adha* sheep feast.

---

[5]This section has borrowed heavily from Hungerford, "A Crash Course in Cameroonian Etiquette" (n.d.).

Other types of advances against wages are very frequently requested by employees, not just for the holidays mandated by governments. Policies are needed in every organization and by individuals who employ national citizens, so that employees will be able to plan their lives and have reasonable expectations of what their employer will do for them when certain needs arise that cannot be met from current income. These policies are needed in order to maintain good and fair relations with the employee and good relations with the public who know the organization or people working for it.

Negotiating

75. Final payment is final settlement; any subsequent business or adjustment is considered to be a new transaction.

A contract or a bill paid in full before the service is completed is money lost, with few exceptions.

A Westerner engaged a man to trim some trees in his yard. After they had settled on a price, the tree trimmer was paid in full. The Westerner never saw the man again. A similar experience happened with a tiling contractor. He was paid for the complete job before he finished, and he left the work half done, never to be seen again.

Local customs will determine how to handle payments. My experience in several countries has been that payments are first of all divided into those for materials and those for labor. Advances for materials are made as is reasonable to buy materials and have them transported in an efficient way. For labor there is usually an agreed-upon amount to finance the start of the job, and one or more payments made during the execution of the work. And always, a substantial amount is reserved for final payment to be made once the job is completely finished, inspected, and approved as satisfactory by the person having the work done. Once final settlement is made, there is little ground for complaint or rectification of problems.

76. Any financial matter is subject to renegotiation until final settlement, that is, until final payment is offered and accepted.

A foreigner may think that once a deal is struck, it has been settled finally. In some parts of the world this is the rule, but it does not seem to be true in much of Africa, where any transaction is subject to renegotiation until the final payment is made and accepted. Informal or oral contracts for various kinds of goods or services and all sorts of business matters fall under this rule.

It is common in many parts of Africa supposedly to settle on a price with a taximan before entering his vehicle, yet have him try to renegotiate the price all the way to the destination. In Wolof this is simply *waxaale*, bargaining for a better deal. With taximen the claim that the previously agreed price was unjust will be based on the amount of "extra" baggage the passenger has, the distance being longer than was understood, the street having potholes that will damage the taxi, or any other pretext that comes to mind (Hungerford, n.d., 5).

77. A request for money from a government functionary or other provider of services may be a request for a "pretip" rather than for a bribe.

There are differences between pretips, posttips, and bribes. Pretips are called "dash" in some countries of West Africa. The Nigerian journalist Peter Enahoro explains pretips in seriocomic terms:

> In Nigeria, by the time a waiter brings your change, you are on the verge of calling the police. Hence the origin of "dash" which is a "service charge" preceding the service.
>
> We have the sweetly quaint custom of expressing gratitude in anticipation of services about to be rendered...
>
> Because it is a favour when he does his job. I mean, he might well refuse to attend to you. So, what do you do about that? Go to the boss? Rubbish. The boss probably received a "dash" before employing him...
>
> Thus, while tipping is reward, the "dash" is an incentive. But if certain evil persons offer it as inducement, accept it with the rational conviction that had you received it *after* and *not before,* it would have been a tip instead of a bribe. Many people have accepted patronage for lesser reasons.
>
> I recommend the "dash." It reduces hostilities to the barest minimum.[6]

---

[6]Enahoro 1996:30–31.

A request for money. (Observation 77)

In the West the standard way to show appreciation for and encourage good service, for example in a restaurant, is to give a tip to the waiter. This is a posttip, and in the West is considered to be entirely legitimate. But in some societies the provider of services wants the tip before the service is provided, for a variety of reasons, including a lack of confidence in the person served that he or she will indeed give a tip even after good service is rendered. This is the pretip. Bribery, on the other hand, in its most unambiguous form, is paying someone for rendering a service that is illegal.

Then there is the gray area between a pretip and a bribe. This is when, for example, a government functionary refuses to execute a document that is entirely legitimate, and which the functionary is paid to perform for qualified petitioners, but which he will not do without a special payment being given to him. The request for service and the procedure are entirely legal, but nothing will be done unless the one who needs the document makes a special, personal payment to the functionary. Is it a bribe to pay him or her? This is a very sticky area and one for which I do not have a clear answer. My practice has been, for whatever it may be worth to readers, basically to follow one criterion: If the functionary will provide me with an official receipt, I am willing to pay. If payment must be secret, under the table, or otherwise suspect, I will not pay. This may fall into the category of extortion, but I want it to at least be quasi official extortion, or I do not pay.

An example of this was encountered at the time of getting a shipment out of port. I had obtained all the required documents, signatures, and stamps.

All was in order for me to bring in my truck, have the shipment loaded onto it and clear the guard at the gate. All was ready just after lunch. I showed all my documents to the man in charge, and expected immediately to be told to bring in my truck. But nothing happened, while many dockworkers just sat around doing nothing. Finally, just after five p.m., when the port closed down, the supervisor told me to bring in the truck. Port workers were still on duty, so the truck was quickly loaded. Just as I was about to leave, I was given a bill for loading the truck—at double the normal rate, as the dockworkers had had to work overtime! The whole process was a scam, but an officially sanctioned one. I was given an official customs agency receipt for my payment. To me, although such proceedings involve fraud, they are at least done within the framework of unofficial policy, and not just at the whim and for the benefit of one official. Supposedly, in my case at the port, all the employees benefitted from the scam, and higher government officials were involved to the point of restraining excesses.

Occasionally, a policeman will stop a vehicle, check the papers, hand them back to the driver, and then ask that he be given something. I interpret these as not being requests for a bribe, as the officers have returned the papers, indicating the vehicle is authorized to move on. Sometimes I have asked, "Am I free to leave?" upon hearing their request for money or perhaps for something they see in the vehicle. If they say yes to my query, I am disposed to give them something. It seems that frequently policemen, border guards, or other officials, may actually be hungry or otherwise in financial need (as they are frequently underpaid or are months behind in receiving their salaries), or just simply being askers of rich Westerners. (Cf. observation 46 in chapter 6.) On trips through rural or border areas, some Westerners carry small loaves of bread or extra small fruit to give out as need or opportunity arises. They do not consider them as bribes, but as elements of public relations and demonstrations of generosity to officials who, after all, are out there for the benefit of travelers.

Many ethical and moral questions arise when dealing with paying for services rendered or to be rendered. It is beyond the scope of this discussion to review them in detail. The only goal is to call attention to some essential differences between bribery, pretips, posttips, and pseudoextortion. Understanding the basic differences between these types of payments (or payoffs) is sometimes helpful in finding a way through what is often an ethical thicket.

Business strategies

78. Many people will choose a sure and immediate benefit over a potentially larger long-term benefit.

This observation is especially applicable when the future benefit is at all doubtful or if it requires more input, such as the spending of money or time.

The Westerner living in Africa frequently runs into examples of this behavior. In the African cities I have lived or traveled in, vehicles trailing smoke from their exhaust pipes are almost the rule. This is seen with private vehicles, taxis, and trucks. Why? Basically because vehicle maintenance is not given attention. I have even had Africans advise me never to buy a used vehicle from Africans because so few of them change their engine oil on a regular basis or otherwise spend money and time to keep their vehicles in good condition.

I once hired a carpenter to build a couple of simple doors. The handsaw he used was the dullest I had ever seen. Sawing a small board took many minutes with a great deal of effort, and the cuts were very rough. Besides, he sometimes sawed into concrete or against steel pipes, further dulling it. Clearly the carpenter was not concerned about efficiency or doing his work faster, as sharpening his saw would only require a simple file, which was not beyond his financial capabilities to buy.

On several occasions I have had tires go flat, ruining the inner tube. (Tubeless tires are typically outfitted with inner tubes in Africa, as a precaution against not finding repairs for tires without tubes.) At these times I needed to buy a new inner tube, or at least a used one. The tire repairmen have tried to sell me inner tubes that did not match the size of my tires. Sometimes the inner tubes were of a very different size. When I have said I wanted a tube that matched the size of the tire, the response has been, "That isn't the way we do it here—the size of the inner tube doesn't matter."

Business people frequently take the short-term approach with customers. I had been using a mechanic for many months when my car developed problems with the front half-axles. I took the car to my mechanic, but soon found that his repairs were not right. I returned the car to his shop. After he fixed the problem I took the car home and put it in my garage. The next day I found two mounds of tar just behind the front tires. The mechanic had filled the axles with tar, which leaked out onto the garage floor. The mechanic had preferred to make an immediate profit, even knowing that I would find out and doubtlessly stop taking my car to him.

Other frequent, if trivial, examples are the sandals, shoes, or flip-flops that people wear. Very often the footwear is far too large or too small, with the wearer's feet hanging over the front or the back. Is it of no importance to wear correctly fitting shoes? It is certainly people's personal business

what size footwear they choose to wear; I only mention it because it ties in
with wider cultural patterns.

**79. People tend to accept immediate, cheap, or even quasi-legal solutions
when dealing with business matters, rather than take care of matters
properly, deal with technicalities or delays, or incur additional
expenses.**

A common example relates to the burying of garbage. We have rented
houses with space for a garden in the yard. And frequently when we want to
plant the garden, we find that it is full of buried garbage, including plastic
bags, tin cans, and all kinds of refuse. Once we hired a plumber who did
his work quickly and disappeared before we expected him to be gone. We
found the answer to his efficiency: He had buried broken concrete, tiles, and
old pipes in our yard!

I have a number of times had the experience of taking a taxi, and either
having the driver go immediately for gasoline and buy only a couple of lit-
ers, or else running out of gas before I got to my destination. To a Westerner
it is puzzling behavior when a taximan will repeatedly put tiny amounts of
fuel in a vehicle he will be driving all day.

Another taxi example was told to me by a taximan himself. He said most
taxis in his city do not buy a taxi license. Rather than buy the annual license
at the equivalent of thirty-five U.S. dollars, they prefer to be stopped and
pay a fine of twenty or thirty CFA francs each time. He said that he once
made some calculations, and found that not buying a license cost the average taximan about seventy-five U.S. dollars a year. So he said he not only
has the satisfaction of obeying the law but is money and time ahead by getting the license. He has explained this to many of his taximen friends, but
few, if any, have been convinced by his analysis.

Recently we had a recurrence of a small plumbing problem at home.
Our sink had just been repaired by a professional plumber, but was again
leaking. Being something of a fix-it man, I decided to do the job myself.
When I took it apart I found that the problem connection had been jerry-
rigged—stuffed with string—and was bound to leak. I went to a hardware
and bought the proper part for less than two U.S. dollars. When I engaged
the plumber I told him I wanted the work done right, but he was so used
to making do that he had done a job that had no assurance of holding up.

A spirit of just getting by. We lived for some time near a city market.
We had a garage that opened onto the street. We told the vendors we wanted the entrance clear, which was our legal right to claim. We clearly painted
"No Parking" signs on the garage doors, but that did not stop vendors from
locating on the sidewalk in front of those doors. Every time we took our car
in or out, the vendors had to move out of the way. In the meantime they lost
business or had a sale in progress interrupted. When they moved out of the
way of the vehicle, they did so by centimeters. We had to drive extremely

slowly, so as to not run over them, the children that were around, or their merchandise. We had to insist on every centimeter in getting them to pull back. This of course made the exits and entrances take much more time than they otherwise would have taken.

This spirit of just getting by is quite pervasive. It is in evidence with masons, carpenters, electricians, and other tradesmen who do not come to work with even the basic tools they need to do a job properly. It is far more than just a question of financial means: it is largely an attitude of mind. It applies to the driving of automobiles and other vehicles. The roadways will often be almost so blocked that two vehicles cannot pass, and even one vehicle can only pass very slowly, just barely squeezing through. When a vehicle breaks down, it is often repaired right in the middle of the road or street where it stopped, with other vehicles passing with difficulty. Sometimes traffic is backed up for blocks. No attempt is made even to push the vehicle out of the middle of the street. Repairs on vehicles are minimally done, just enough to get by for a short time rather than make a repair that will last indefinitely. Even educated people typically do not pay attention to punctuation and proper spelling, even when they have had years of university study. Souvenirs in many tourist markets are poorly made, revealing a lack of pride in fine craftsmanship.

This section may read like an intemperate attack on Africa, or a venting of past frustrations. I believe this is not at all the case. My intention in bringing up these examples, many of them trivial, and with which I have lived quite contentedly for many years in Africa, is to point out some differences in Western and African cultures. They are pointed out because they reveal some fundamental attitudes that are worth noting. I believe that much development in the West is due to taking the long-term approach to many situations and problems. So although the examples may be quite insignificant in themselves, they reveal characteristics of the cultures that are deepseated and significant. More weighty examples could have been given that reveal the same tendencies. An illustration would be the insistence of one government that multilateral aid agencies fund a large irrigation dam. After detailed study, qualified specialists pointed out that if the dam was constructed, there would be a net loss of agricultural land. The government still insisted that the dam should be built.

Observations 78 and 79 are related. They both involve short-term approaches to life, rather than long-term. That people should seemingly live and behave in ways that favor the present rather than the future may be a reflection of a basic incertitude about the future. Perhaps experience has taught individuals and society that the future is so unsure that the best strategy in life is to seize the advantages of the moment, with little regard for the future. Whatever the reasons may be, society as a whole is the loser.

A final word is needed for the above paragraphs. Although there certainly is a widespread tendency by many people to act in ways similar to those described in the examples given, there are also many Africans who do quality, professional, competent, and careful work. To leave an impression that this is not true would be a gross injustice.

80. **When an occasion provides the opportunity to make a large profit, it is typically seized upon. There is little concept of a reasonable, or just, or ethical price, or of price gouging; rather, the accepted practice is to charge whatever the buyer will pay.**

This observation applies to those business transactions and markets where Westerners are the usual customers. Observation 73 deals with traditional African business situations.

In the business dealings in focus here, it is totally the buyer's responsibility to know what is reasonable, normal, or affordable for him or her. And it is totally normal for the seller or provider of services to obtain as much as he or she can.

Westerners often think that African sellers are greedy or price gougers, but I think the main problem is that they are not used to bargaining for purchases that in their home countries would have set prices. Certainly price gouging, or charging as much as the market will bear, is a long-established Western practice. It is as American as apple pie. In the West most lawyers, dentists, and doctors, to name a few Western experts at charging high prices, seem to show little reasonableness in price setting, except in terms justified by their self-interest associations. Yet they are given prestige and places in the higher levels of society. If most Western businessmen follow reasonable pricing policies, it has far more to do with competition than with their great sense of fairness and just profits.

81. **Inaction or delay in carrying out a matter may constitute a well-considered, unverbalized message, and not just be the result of mere inaction, inertia, or delay caused by unforeseen events.**

When an African fails to perform an agreed-upon service, to fulfill a promise, or to meet a deadline, it may be because a problem has arisen that makes him or her unwilling to do what is expected. The Westerner will rarely be told directly of the problem with a straightforward answer. The cause usually comes from either (1) a hope that the unfulfilled action will be forgotten about; or (2) if the Westerner queries the delay, the African will inform him that some important factor or condition has changed and that new terms must be agreed upon before the work can be reinstated. But (2) may only be made clear by going through a third party who will be able to get to the root of the problem.

An example of the first situation would be an agreement with a man to collect so many kilograms of a certain kind of oil-bearing seedpods, on which you want to do research. For whatever reason, he does not collect any seeds and does not say anything to you. It is up to you to discover the cause of his inaction. He might be unhappy with the price you said you would pay, or the rains may have been too meager to produce a plentiful supply of seeds this year, or...For whatever reasons, he leaves the fulfillment of the agreement vague, and even after querying him about it, you are not sure what is going on. So you are kept in doubt for weeks and months, until you finally realize it is very doubtful he will ever bring you the seeds you have counted on.

The second situation could arise with a contractor. You make an agreement with a painter on painting your house. He will paint the house for a set amount with the cost of the paint and other materials being separate. He begins to paint, with an advance on the contract price, but then stops. Days go by and he does not show up. You know something must be wrong, but he has said nothing to you. You query him why the job is not finished. He then informs you there was a mistake. The price you gave him was too low and he cannot continue unless you increase the amount you will pay.

Handling problems

82. Once money is exchanged in a business transaction there is very limited recourse in such matters as mistakes, damaged merchandise, breakdown, and not meeting contractual stipulations.

"Satisfaction guaranteed or your money back" is not only *not* a business principle in Africa, it is a laughable idea when explained to many Africans. Contrary to what is stated in this observation, Westerners will actually often be allowed to return merchandise, but I believe this is due to their perceived economic power and their position in society. It does not come from a generally accepted business philosophy.

83. When a problem is encountered in trying to complete or carry through with a transaction involving finances or other matters, the problem will seldom be clearly admitted at the outset, but will typically only be revealed over a period of time.

This observation applies not only to financial transactions, but to appointments, business and committee meetings, dealings with government officials, political matters, and other areas of individual and institutional relations.

A classic example of this happened in Senegal. Although the law clearly does not allow political parties based on religion, an Islamic party has for many years tried to gain recognition. In 1991 during the time the Organization of the Islamic Conference was holding its big conference in

Dakar, leaders of the unrecognized Islamic Liberation and Democratic Party (PLDI) tried to win official recognition. It was obvious that they thought the presence of top government officials from all over the Muslim world in Dakar would pressure the Senegalese government to allow their registration.

The Secretary General and members of his National Secretariat, along with a number of journalists, went to the large building of the Ministry of the Interior, to register their constitution. After a relatively short wait, they were allowed into the building. They were taken to the head of the Division of Political Parties and Unions of the Directorate of General Affairs and Territorial Administration. The division head told them he did not have the authority to accept the registration of the PLDI; rather, the prefect was the correct authority to see.

At the prefecture the prefect himself received them, but told them he in no way was authorized to deal with the PLDI. He told them they would need to return to the Ministry of the Interior. He said that only the ministry had the authority to deal with such political matters. Back at the ministry, the delegation was emphatically told that only the prefect had the necessary authority. Finally, the secretary general told the journalists that between the Interior ministry and the prefecture, someone was not telling the truth. He said the attitude of the authorities was unacceptable. He called for national and international public opinion to support their efforts in the "unjust and unacceptable treatment shown their party."

Note that the Islamic party was never told, "No, you cannot register your party—it is illegal." Which it was and is, and to a Westerner would have been the clear, straightforward way to respond to the PLDI. But nothing like that was done. The answer from the government only emerged with time. After years of effort, and finally trying a direct approach at what they thought was an auspicious moment, they had to draw their own conclusions, that the answer was an unspoken, "There is no way we will officially recognize the PLDI."

Delegation going to register the Islamic Liberation and Democratic Party.
(Observation 83)

On an individual level I had this experience. In one African country we lived in, I tried to get a telephone installed. I went to the telephone offices, filled in a form, paid my application fee, and was told to come back in two weeks. I went back, was told all was in order, but not ready, and to come back in two weeks. I did this, and continued to return as I was always politely told to come back. When I asked what the impediments were, I was told there were none. I never did get a telephone. Whether the problem was my failure to offer a bribe (which African friends told me was the case), or whatever the reason, I was never told what the obstacle was, at least in a way that a Westerner could understand.

The previous cases came from the experiences of those requesting a service. The following example shows how the observation plays out for those offering a service. When an NGO, for instance, offers a training course and opens registration, many people will register but fail to come to the course or notify the NGO that they are not coming. This presents very difficult organizational problems. If the NGO overbooks the course, as airlines do with their flights, and more people show up than can be handled, bad will is created when they are turned away after having accepted their registration. Yet if registrations are closed as soon as the number of applicants equals the places available, there will doubtlessly be vacant places in the course. The problem would be greatly alleviated if people could be contacted just before a course began, but large numbers of people have neither a telephone nor a mailing address.

83W. Westerners find it very frustrating to have Africans appear to be unclear, indirect, and uninformative.

Westerners think that the reluctance to take clear positions on common things, but rather to let time solve so many matters, is horribly inefficient and a serious impediment to getting things done in the modern world. Philosophically, they think that getting to the heart of the matter is a positive way to act. They think that putting off decisions that need to be made usually makes matters worse in the long run, and that through delay many irreplaceable opportunities will be lost.

I made an innocuous observation, very much in jest, about another Westerner who was at that moment driving out of a parking lot, raising a cloud of dust. I observed to my friend that he "revved his engine like a race driver." The African friend that I happened to be conversing with at that moment commented, "You talk just like a Westerner, speaking directly about things."

For many Africans it seems that they believe there is such a danger of offending others that they prefer silence, indirectness, the solution of time making opinions clear, and extreme tact. An African friend told me this is one reason that Westerners are often misled, interpreting silence to mean that all is well. And of course to many Africans the Westerner comes across as insensitive, callous, indifferent to how others think and feel, and as having a great lack of human sensitivity and tact.

A fundamental difference between the typical Westerner and African lies is their respective attitudes toward criticism—whether of governments, organizations, officials, or individuals. Disagreements seem very frequently to be taken as criticisms of the persons, rather than as just another viewpoint that is not directed against any person. In many situations I have experienced in Africa, it seemed that disagreements were a priori defined as personal attacks. This of course also happens in the West, but even though it is easy to take criticism personally, people in the West are taught not to do so unless there is strong evidence to the contrary. Perhaps there is no sharp boundary between Western and African behavior in the area of criticism, but there are cultural differences that the Westerner frequently encounters and gets into that make for sticky relationships.

It may be that Westerners criticize by means of face-to-face encounters believing that, although it may hurt, people and society in general are better off in the long run than if problems are hidden or ignored. If this represents a traditional value in regard to disagreements and criticism, change seems to be in the air. Political correctness is a very important concept at many levels of Western society, where individuals and organizations are careful not to utter words that may give offense to individuals or groups, especially in relation to minorities and others outside the established power structures.

The reluctance to inform interested parties of problems and developments applies to many areas of life in Africa. The pattern can be seen at all levels of society. Governments follow policies and practices that are never made known to their citizens. Businesses follow policies not communicated to their clients. For example, banks may impose fees on depositors that depositors find impossible to have explained. Even within many families information is not shared, so that children are not told about many matters that would seem natural to Westerners to share or reveal, and wives are not informed about their husband's business, or even of personal matters.

84. When a customer is told that an ordered article or service will be ready on a specified time or date, it is unlikely to be ready at that time.

It would seem that when an African furniture maker, mechanic, or government functionary gives a date for doing or finishing something, he thinks of the earliest possible date it could be ready, if everything went according to plan: no interruptions, no illness, no funerals to attend, no holidays. And as life never proceeds so smoothly, of course the date is unrealistic, but will make the customer feel good to hear it, and who knows, something miraculous might happen this time and it will be ready. Everyone in the society knows this is what a set date means. Another element is probably the African way of tending to tell people what they want to hear.

84W. The Western customer expects to be given a reasonable date, and that barring extenuating or unusual circumstances, the thing or service will be ready as specified. Consequently, when it is not, the Westerner considers the service provider to be unreliable or even untrustworthy.

The Westerner expects that he or she will be given a realistic date for something to be ready. The Westerner does not want an overly optimistic date, as plans will be made that depend upon receiving the thing ordered at the time promised. If a service provider is found not to keep his word, that is, does not meet his assumed deadlines, the Westerner will seek another provider who will do so.

Some African service providers do finish things on schedule. In many cases foreigners gravitate to them, if they also provide quality service and otherwise fulfill their obligations. Word will be passed around the foreign community that so-and-so is a good person to do business with.

85. Admissions of a personal lack of knowledge or resources, or admissions of personal shortcomings are considered to show weakness and should be avoided if at all possible.

> In Côte d'Ivoire vulnerability is often perceived of as a weakness. In general, people will say anything to cover up the fact that they don't know the answer to your question. Or if a landlord doesn't have the money to do the necessary repairs on a house, he won't tell you that outright. That's a direct admission of weakness. He'll tell you he'll do it tomorrow, or next week. If this happens successively, there might be a problem that he can't admit openly without losing face. People would rather 'lie' than to incriminate themselves publicly. So, folks here aren't direct in their relations with others, but also they are not direct with their own shortcomings and problems. The guiding principle is to save face for everyone involved, including yourself.[7]

In the quotation just given, reference is made to the fact that Ivorians (people from the Ivory Coast, or in French, Côte d'Ivoire) "will say anything to cover up the fact that they don't know the answer to your question." I have had countless experiences of this in several countries. For instance, I go into a hardware store looking for a certain object. The clerk will say, "We don't have any of those, but the hardware store two blocks up the street has them." At the hardware two blocks up, I get the same sort of answer, and will get it at each succeeding hardware for as long as I want to believe there is some basis to what they are telling me. A variant of this happens when asking for directions. The asker cannot tell if the directions are accurate or a cover-up for ignorance. Probably the best way to solve the problem is to ask at least two people and compare their responses. When, as often happens, someone volunteers to go with you to lead you to your destination, it is very likely he knows where you want to go. But in rural areas even this is not sure, as children or even sometimes adults, just want a ride in a vehicle, no matter where it is going.

Another experience of this reticence to admit any shortcomings involved an employee. He was hired as a typist to keyboard documents into a computer. I pointed out to him, when we were alone, that his typing speed was below the professional minimum, that I would pay him to practice typing to increase his speed using a computer program I provided, and that his salary would increase as his typing speed increased. He was grossly offended that I had, so he thought, criticized him. I had thought that as an employee and with my offer to pay him more as he improved, I would not

---

[7]Hill 1996:9.

have to, in my thinking, treat the situation with kid gloves, but could deal with him in a direct manner. This proved not to be the case.

The voice of experience

86. The amount shown on a receipt (*facture,* in French) may not correspond with the amount paid for goods or services.

It is common for the seller and the buyer to agree on how much a receipt will be made out for. Even professionals, like medical doctors, sometimes ask how much the client wants shown as paid on the receipt. After paying a well-known doctor in a major city in cash for a consultation, I asked for a receipt. He responded nonchalantly, "In what amount?"

Having doubts about the amount shown on a receipt. (Observation 86)

The application of this observation is obvious. When receipts are presented by an employee for reimbursements, it behooves the employer to be informed about prices, and to verify from time to time that the amounts being reimbursed accord with local market prices.

87. Change is frequently a problem in business transactions.

Small-time vendors and businesses start their business day without a supply of change, so the first customers to arrive after the start of business can expect to have delays if they do not have the exact amount of their purchase.

Often a storekeeper will send someone out on the street to get change while the client waits. Even clerks in larger businesses frequently ask the customer to pay the exact sum of the purchase, to avoid giving out their smaller coins and notes.

The problem of making change is most acute in rural areas. Westerners are advised to take a supply of coins and small bills with them when traveling to rural areas, or even smaller urban areas. This will often serve to avoid delays and difficulties when making purchases or paying for services rendered. The problems are encountered more in some countries and localities than in others.

Frequently, vendors claim to have no change when they actually have it. I once paid for a tire repair, handing the repairman a one thousand franc note, four US dollars at the time, for a two hundred franc repair bill. He asked me if I had change, as he had none, he said. I said no. So he sent an apprentice off in one direction for change. After about five minutes the boy came back, with the one thousand franc note still in hand. The repairman himself then set off in the opposite direction, and he also came back after some minutes, still with the one thousand franc note in hand. Well, perhaps because he saw my patience wearing a bit thin, he went to the back of his shop, with me following him, and opened a steel box in which was a substantial hoard of both bank notes and coins.

"There is no change." (Observation 87)

Another time I was in a large, prosperous shop to make a purchase. I only had one five-thousand franc note with me for a one-thousand franc purchase. The cashier told me she did not have a bit of change and asked if I could not provide it. I told her that was all I had, and even showed her my empty wallet. She sent a clerk out for change but he came back without any. So she casually reached into her cash drawer and handed me four one thousand franc notes.

Why do shopkeepers continuously play such games with change? It is quite natural, given that many banks do not offer the service of providing, in terms of American banking, rolls of coins, even to their customers, nor do they provide banknotes of any denomination as change. The most that I have understood banks to offer is a department where old and tattered banknotes may be exchanged for newer ones. So with no official or public place to obtain change, and with people always trying to get it for themselves or their businesses, it is natural that shopkeepers jealously protect what they have. On a personal level I do the same thing!

Another good reason for starting the day without change is that it simplifies bookkeeping, eliminating the need for arithmetic. All the money that is in the till, whether a cash register or a folded cloth, represents the total receipts of the day. There is another, hard-to-believe, reason that affects cashiers in a number of countries. One African friend told me the reason many shops do not like to keep large banknotes around is that some of them are believed to be magic money. Many people believe that there are certain practitioners of magic who are able to change the face value of banknotes into larger notes, like changing a one thousand franc note into one of ten thousand francs. The problem is the transformation is not permanent, and after a time they revert to their original amount. So you do not want to have large bills around in case some of them revert to smaller amounts while in your cash drawer. When I asked if this sort of thing really happened, he said people say it does and the proof is that often at the end of a business day, there is less money in the cash drawer than there should be. Many cashiers claim that this kind of money disappearance has happened with them!

88. Having the correct amount of money for a business transaction is the responsibility of the buyer; it is not the seller's responsibility to provide change.

This observation is less noticed now than in the past but is still encountered. The most common form it now takes is the very frequent experience of a store cashier or other business person not giving back quite all of the change the customer is due. Change is made, but the last five, ten, or twenty-five francs are not given. This may happen even when the cashier has small coins in the till. If you ask for all your change you will get it, but it may be with a rather surprised or pained look. If there really are no small coins you will be told to wait until a customer making a purchase provides them.

89. When giving a tip to several people, e.g., baggage handlers at an airport, the donor should apportion it out. Giving a lump sum to one person expecting him to divvy it up with the others is unfair and unsatisfactory.

Frequently, a Westerner will pay several baggage handlers that have helped him with just one banknote handed to one of them. The Westerner tells the one baggage handler that the large bill is for all of them and that he is responsible for distributing a fair share to the others. This is basically unsatisfactory to the others who may well immediately clamor for their own tips, understanding that in their culture, whatever is given to someone is his to keep. Even if they are willing, there are no rules governing the distribution, so they will have to negotiate with each other or one will exercise his power over the others to do it his way. The Westerner may think it is obvious that they should share alike, but that is rather a Westerner's idea of fairness, and is not necessarily that of the baggage handlers. Another problem is that of obtaining change, and their losing business while trying to sort it out.

90. People of all cultures act logically unless they are mentally retarded or mentally disturbed.

The final observation of the book applies to people everywhere—in Africa, the West, and elsewhere. Both Western and African readers may find some of the experiences and observations that have been described to be illogical, strange, or incomprehensible. This observation points out that all people are logical and act in accord with their society's rules. The outsider finds it strange or misunderstands only because he or she doesn't understand the people's logic.

So if you see an otherwise normal person do something incomprehensible, take it as a sign of your lack of understanding, not of his strangeness, stupidity, or insanity. Assume that a friend, an employee, or even an unknown person, is acting logically according to the rules of his culture until you have very good reason to believe otherwise.

For example, a couple was having quite a bit of trouble with their household help in the Ivory Coast. In talking about it, one big issue was that despite the instructions given by the wife, the employee kept washing the dishes in cold water. The couple was horrified: imagine washing dishes in cold water! When told that Africans always wash dishes in cold water, they were surprised. This did not solve their problem, because they still wanted their dishes washed in hot water, but it did help them perceive their employee as intelligent and logical.[8]

A seemingly illogical episode happened to me in the early 1980s in an African capital city. Telephones were rare and difficult to obtain. Public

---

[8]Hill 1996:10.

telephone booths were just being installed in a few scattered locations in the city. An intelligent young man, whom I will call Mbanwi, was working for me. He had always done very well in school but had to leave before finishing high school. One day I needed information about arrival times for Sabena Airline flights. I told Mbanwi that he would not need to go all the way to the Sabena office, as there was now a telephone booth just a couple of blocks from where my office was located, so he could get the information by phone. I gave him some money and he set out early in the working day. Hours passed and Mbanwi did not return. I was afraid he might have been in an accident, not a rare thing in that city. Lunch time came and no word from Mbanwi. Finally, in the middle of the afternoon, he arrived back. He told me that he had tried to use the phone near the office but it was out of order. Consequently, he took the bus to the center of the city, found a telephone booth on the main square, and proceeded to phone Sabena. He had continued for all those hours to reach the airline by phone, dialing and redialing, but never getting through. All this time he was within sight of the Sabena office which was located across the square about one hundred yards away. I was dumbfounded. How could he be so stupid? The information he was trying to obtain by phone was available just a two-minute walk away! I knew he was honest, so I believed his story. I also knew he was intelligent, so there had to be a reason for his apparently bizarre behavior.

The reason for this seeming inexplicable behavior was, I believe, that I had during the months he had worked for me, asked him to do many things that were for him senseless and meaningless. I was not particularly aware of this, but realized it in retrospect. I had not taken the time to explain the reasons behind many assignments, so he was accustomed to just trying to follow my instructions without understanding my purposes. This episode was just one of a series. Telephones were new to him, airlines were unfamiliar, the need to obtain flight information and where it came from was new. In his mind my emphasis on telephoning meant that I wanted him to obtain the information by telephone, thinking that was important to me. For me, on the other hand, I had only emphasized the telephone aspect because I wanted to minimize the time his errand would take. My only real interest was the Sabena flight information, but he did not know this.

Summary: business matters

Business matters in Africa are carried on differently in cities than in rural or more traditional areas. Even in city markets and neighborhoods where there are few tourists or other expatriates, traditional values and practices are generally followed. In places where tourism and related businesses flourish, local behavior will approach those followed along other international tourist routes. Tourists are well advised to consult guidebooks that focus on the specific countries they will visit.

There are a number of features of doing business that will probably surprise a Westerner who is new to Africa. Bargaining is one area that is different. In the United States, at least, bargaining is known in business, but with very limited kinds of transactions, such as buying a house or automobile. So for a Westerner going to a market and being expected to bargain over the price of carrots, for instance, is a new experience. Though bargaining in Africa is not a completely new business concept for the Westerners, what is especially different and unknown is what things are supposed to be bargained for, and what are not. Even in Africa there are many things that have fixed prices. Meals at restaurants is one. I know of no place where a customer bargains over the price of a meal, whether in a very simple canteen located along a street, or in an upscale restaurant catering to tourists. Add to this problem the frequent situation where the currency is different from that of the home country, the local value of goods and services is unknown, the salesmanship of vendors seems intimidating, and finally, that the transaction must be carried on in a language unknown to the buyer. The result is that bargaining seems to many Westerners to be a much more difficult matter than might be expected.

Another area to note is that of the importance of personal relationships. Certainly, in the West they are crucially important to the conduct of much business. Getting to know business associates by playing golf or going to lunch with them are standard ways, among many others, of developing personal relationships. So the principles are not so different, but the practice of how, when, and what to do to cultivate friendships are the crucial matters. They may be very different from those practiced in the West. During one period of time my duties in one African city required that I frequently went to one particular bank to check on foreign currency exchange. This involved going to one floor of the bank where some fifteen to twenty men and women worked. I often had to wait quite long periods for my business to be handled. In the process I was able to observe an example of the importance of personal relationships. The department manager arrived for work about ten o'clock. His glassed-in office was located at the far end from the entrance. Every day it took him fifteen to thirty minutes to traverse the distance from the door to his desk. He went to the desk of every employee, greeted him or her, enquired about the family, and carried on small talk for a brief time before moving on to the next desk. This manager was just doing the normal thing: putting people ahead of business.

Also often different in Africa from what Westerners may expect are the expectations of buyers and sellers. The Westerner probably has a mental attitude generated from Western, or at least North American, business practices that make the customer king. Merchandise must be perfect. If it is found to be damaged or defective, the vendor is expected, within thirty days at a minimum, to return the customer's money, upon complaint and return of the goods. In Africa the *vendor* is much more likely than the customer to be king. This may not be evident to Westerners because they and other people of presumed social and economic standing are treated with more care than those who appear to be lower on the social ladder. But basically there are fewer customer protections in Africa than in the West. It is well for the Westerner to follow the old maxim, "Let the buyer beware." Caveat emptor.

A last word for business in Africa is that it can be a very positive experience. With Africans in business situations being open to developing relationships, treating people like people and not just as customers, being willing to take some time for *you* in the midst of their business day—all this can make business in Africa much more than just getting a job done.

9

Toward a Conclusion

In the preceding chapters I have recounted many experiences from across Africa that involved the use of personal resources. Related experiences were brought together so that the underlying generalities of behavior could be seen. Ninety observations are the result. These observations are presented as the approximate unwritten and unexpressed behavioral paths that guide Africans when they are dealing with the use of their resources, including money. Like all paths, there are forks along the way, providing many behavioral choices. They are not rules, as individuals have many choices in how they will act. They may choose one path today and in the same situation tomorrow choose a different path. Some individuals will choose one path in one situation and another individual will choose another path in similar circumstances. The purpose in formulating these observations is to help Westerners better understand African economic behavior. With better understanding of what may seem at first to be puzzling practices, Westerners will hopefully develop more understandable, comfortable, and satisfying relationships. No judgment has been intended, and no criticism implied.

In talking with a large number of Westerners who work or have worked in Africa, I find it is clear that the use of resources, and especially the question of money, is a major concern for virtually every one. Expatriates run into problems and questions related to finances practically every day they are in Africa. The problems are confusing, pressing, and often distressing. From the African side, many who work with Westerners also find much of their behavior confusing, unintelligible, or even disagreeable. Hence, it is hoped this book will be of assistance to Africans who work with Westerners or Western-based organizations.

How can we summarize this general difficulty with money in Africa? First, it is not a problem related to racism. I have known African-Americans who were traveling in Africa as tourists and who did not want to even leave their hotel rooms to encounter Africans because their dealings with money matters had been so difficult for them. Obviously, their problems were not related to race. Rather, they were those of cultural differences that centered on matters of money. I believe this also applies to white visitors in Africa. Their problems in dealing with money and other resources are best explained as cultural differences, not as racial.

Nor are the problems connected to a dislike of Africans. On the contrary, I believe most Westerners traveling, living, or working in Africa find Africans very friendly, personable, and enjoyable. Basically, there are few problems involved in meeting, getting to know, and having casual relationships. Of course, there may be problems of communication because of language and other cultural differences, but such problems are not caused by people-to-people differences. The problems and conflicts that arise come from a deeper level of misunderstanding.

The most obvious problem is the great difference in access to resources between the average African and the average Westerner who is in Africa. To put it simply: the African sees the Westerner is rich while he is poor. This creates many difficulties in interpersonal relations. Some comments I have heard from recently arrived volunteer workers illustrate the difficulties:

> I was a poor student all my life until I came to Africa, but since my arrival here I am considered to be rich. I don't have any more money now than I did then, but I am seen as a rich person. It is uncomfortable and I don't like it.

> Even if I don't have much money, I have a lot more than the people here (personal communication, 1994).

> To us, we have left such a lot behind, and yet the little we seem to have makes us look very rich here. This will probably be a constant struggle while we are in Africa.

> I certainly never wanted to be rich and famous at home; so it is hard to be "rich" here!

> At home we feel quite poor; it is uncomfortable to feel so rich here (personal communications, 1999).

Ordinary Africans are, on average, the poorest people in the world.[1] There are wealthy urban Africans, of course. The fine houses in upscale neighborhoods and the many luxury cars on city streets testify to their existence, but they are very much the exception. The average foreigner working in Africa is far more likely to come into contact with the less affluent members of society. Although there are many poor people in Western countries, few of them travel to or work in Africa. This means that the typical

---

[1] *The New Enclyclopædia Britannica,* 1988.

relationship between African and Westerner involves great economic inequality. The African if employed may be earning one hundred dollars per month while the Westerner will have an income of at least two thousand dollars, and more likely over three thousand dollars per month, and double if husband and wife both receive salaries. If the African is unemployed—and it is safe to say that at least fifty percent of Africans are not meaningfully employed—the income gap is infinite in mathematical terms, and grievous in human terms. These facts are at the heart of the tensions and misunderstandings that are discussed in this book.

Imagine that you are a Westerner and work in the same project as some Africans, or you are at least in regular contact with some. They could be office workers, drivers, cleaning people, sellers at the market, night watchmen, waiters, and many others. What do they think of you? Let us assume you are polite and treat them with respect. There are therefore no particular problems in relating to them in a normal, casual way. They see you as an okay human being, but of course a rich one. Your riches cannot for a minute be forgotten or disregarded. After all, your household income is some thirty to sixty times greater than theirs. It would be faintly similar for you, if you rubbed shoulders with someone with an annual income of one to two million dollars, which is approximately thirty to sixty times the average household income in the U.S. In reality the gap is greater than even these ratios indicate. The Westerner, with an income that is but a fraction of the millionaire's, lives vastly better than his African counterpart who receives the same fraction of the Westerner's income.

The Egyptian economist Samir Amin describes the income gap between Europe and its offspring in historical terms. Prior to the year A.D. 1000, the most productive areas of the world were two to three times more prosperous than the poorer areas. Europe and Africa were on an approximately equal level economically. The situation began to change dramatically with the Industrial Revolution. Today the ratio is about sixty to one, and the economic gap continues to widen dramatically. This means that the average Westerner will have access to sixty times more wealth in a lifetime than will the average African.[2]

It is widely recognized that cultural differences exist between Africa and the West, which create barriers to understanding. But economic disparities create another set of barriers that have received less attention than they deserve.

Two factors contribute in a major way to the disparity: (1) the Westerner has a much higher income and lives among people who are equally well off; (2) the Westerner lives in a society that is focused on the individual, and therefore is free to make economic decisions according to purely personal criteria. He is free to choose his own life style, within the limits of his

---

[2] Amin 1997.

finances. He has few constraints on his use of resources from his extended family, friends, or community. Others in his peer group have very similar incomes and make virtually no demands on his resources. All people are able to cover their needs and they do not look to any other individuals for economic support. (Again, I note that the discussion refers to Westerners who work and travel in Africa; not all in their home countries live so independently.)

For the average African the situation is reversed. He has a much lower income that at best meets minimal personal and family needs. Among his extended family, friends, and neighbors are many people who are unemployed and are virtually without income. Often these people cannot even meet their own survival needs. In addition to these economic facts of life, the society itself demands that its members live in community, not just as autonomous individuals. Community life is in fact a high value that is inculcated in every individual, so that they do not even consider being autonomous. They grow up wanting to be a valued member of society, fully participating in it. This means that each person feels close to others and sensitive to their material needs.

So the average African, unless he withdraws from being an active and valued member of society, is always looking outside himself when considering material resources and needs. Those who have more, share with those who have less. Those who have less expect to receive material and financial benefits from those who have more. The rules of society constrain both the haves and the have-nots. This is not utopia or true communism, but a system that has been worked out over hundreds of years of difficult existence. The vagaries of life, climate, disease, colonialism, slave raiding and interethnic conflict have meant that those with resources today may be lacking them tomorrow. People have learned that it is good insurance to share their relative prosperity today, as they themselves may well be in need tomorrow. Survival has depended upon living in community and sharing resources.

When the Westerner arrives in an African community or workplace, this is the invisible context of life that he enters. He is immediately and automatically placed in the category of the "haves," although he is unaware of it. The only other category available is that of the "have-nots" and he obviously does not fit there. As a "have," he will be drawn into the system to the extent he allows. The consequences are that he will soon be approached by one or more people who want help. They will ask him to share his resources with them in some specific way.

People asking for help can be divided into two groups. First is that of individuals entirely unknown to the Westerner. They are the Unknown Askers, or UAs. They may be Africans, usually men but sometimes women, who knock on the door of a residence, or those who accost foreigners on the street. The UA usually asks for money, sometimes for employment. He may have a prescription for medicine in his hand, or he may tell of his own plight or of that of his family, often in pathetic detail. The Westerner does not know what to do. He does not know if the story, and therefore the need, is genuine or not. In the end, he may give the person some money, but is discontented, not knowing whether he has really helped someone in need, or has merely been duped.

Sometimes this kind of UA can be very difficult to deal with. There are many UAs in Africa. Among them are professionals in the art of telling heartrending stories and manipulating foreigners to give them money or other resources. Some can even produce real tears when and as needed to make their stories truly believable. There are many talented actors and clever operators in this category. Early in our African experience my wife and I were taken in by a UA. We met him at a Catholic conference center. He volunteered to help us with French. He said he just wanted to help us and did not expect to be paid. We accepted his help a few times. One day, I received a summons from our district police commissioner, ordering me to appear before him. No reason was given. I asked a well-placed African friend to accompany me. It turned out that our volunteer friend had been jailed by the police on a particular charge, and he had given my name as a character witness. He was a rogue and had attempted to establish a clean record with us so that he could have a good reference. When I explained our relationship to the Commissioner, he thanked me and did not require my presence at the trial. My African friend who had accompanied me to the police station did not let me off so easily. He severely reprimanded me for my behavior. He said I was typical of too many foreigners in Africa, who are taken in by rogues and confidence men. They accept at face value what they are told by unscrupulous Africans whom they do not know personally, or know where they live, or what kind of people they are. He said people like me are very misguided in their actions to help Africans. He said many people need help, but the foreigner should find out about the person, his family, and social circle, before getting involved. I appreciated his admonition as that made by a wise friend.

The second class of petitioner is that of Known Asker, or KA. These persons are known through long-term contacts. They become known in the organization where the Westerner works, at the church they both attend, in the club where the Westerner is a member and the KA works, or in many other ongoing situations. The Westerner gets to know the Africans over a period of months or years. Sometimes the Westerner gets to know these individuals fairly well, but the knowledge is almost entirely based on job performance and what the Westerner is told by the person himself. Little first-hand knowledge of the person's family or home environment is obtained. The Westerner rarely visits any of these people at their homes. The relationships developed in this way are quite similar to relationships developed between fellow workers in workplaces in the home country. But the relationships are also fundamentally different, as the economic status of the foreigners and Africans is so radically different. This is highlighted in table 9.1, where access to the desired things of life is contrasted between the average employed African and the Westerner. Although Westerners are generally aware that a gap exists between their life style and that of most of their African fellows, it is safe to say that Africans are acutely aware of this gap, which to them is virtually a gulf that they constantly confront in all of their relationships with foreigners. Yet the Africans described in this chart represent the fewer than fifty percent that are employed. A chart that contrasted the concerns of life of those without employment would be even more dramatic.

Table 9.1 Comparison of Western and African access to
the good things of life

Concerns of Life	Westerner	African
Residence	Lives in large house in upscale neighborhood	Lives in small quarters occupied by many family members; crowded
Food	Eats wide variety of local and imported foods; has a balanced diet; eats often in fine restaurants; invites friends to meals	Eats local affordable foods; has a very limited diet; provides food and meals to many relatives and friends; food budget is always under stress
Clothing	Buys clothing as needed; is well dressed according to chosen life style	Dressing well is a high value, but extremely difficult to afford; shops for used clothing that comes from the West; has one or a very few good outfits
Transportation	Has efficient private vehicle to go to work, church, club, for shopping, outings	Uses inefficient public transportation; walks

Concerns of Life	Westerner	African
Social life	Has wide variety of social events; entertains at home; socializes with friends; has sizeable entertainment and recreational budgets	Social life largely centered on visiting and receiving kin and friends, with food and drink; may attend sporting events
Vacations	Typically takes vacations in home country	If employed "officially" will have government-mandated annual leave, probably thirty days long; takes vacations in country
Educational background	Has had university education	Has had limited educational opportunities in ill-equipped schools
Educational resources	Has many books, subscriptions to magazines, TV, videos; keeps up with the world	National radio is probably listened to, may watch TV; daily newspaper is sometimes read; owns almost no books or magazines
Children's education	In good, well-equipped schools, with well-trained teachers; relatively small classes; up-to-date curriculum; attending university is expected	Will be difficult to ensure minimum schooling for all; large classes with practically no equipment; university will be possible only for brightest and luckiest
Telephone	Has access to a telephone at home and at place of work	Can use a public telephone; employer may allow use at the place of employment

Concerns of Life	Westerner	African
Computers	Has an up-to-date computer, e-mail, and access to the Internet	Computers are used in offices by a minority; almost none can afford their own
Medical situation	Has access to well-trained doctors, dentists, specialists, hospital care; fills all medical prescriptions	Can barely afford marginal quality care in a very limited local clinic; well-trained doctors are beyond reach; may consult traditional healers and use traditional medicines
Discretionary income	Has much money to spend for nonessentials	Is very hard pressed to meet monthly needs for food, housing, electricity, water, and clothing
Retirement expectations	Is preparing for retirement with investments and house ownership in home country; goverment-provided social security	Is paying into government-run social security fund with marginal prospects of ever receiving its limited benefits
Economic security	Is little concerned about being unemployed long-term and becoming destitute; may be slightly concerned about maintaining a well-paying job	Is very much concerned with obtaining or maintaining long-term employment; job loss would probably mean very hard times and perhaps becoming destitute along with many dependents

Concerns of Life	Westerner	African
Physical security	Construction is solid protected by iron bars, residence and office guards employed in insecure locations	Construction is less than solid; subject to neighborhood insecurities

The end of the story is that the Westerner gets to casually know Africans. He finds them friendly, personable, and approachable. He begins to develop friendships. Then a newly made African friend unexpectedly asks for a loan of money, or asks to borrow something. The first few times it happens it may be accepted, because the Westerner is new and wants to believe the best of his African acquaintances. Money is given or loaned, but the Westerner feels the friendship has been abused. When the loan is not paid back as promised, he doubts the honesty of the person. After several such experiences he begins to generalize, wondering if all Africans are dishonest, or at least, if they do not keep their word when it comes to money matters. Soon, the Westerner is tempted to conclude that "the only reason Africans want my friendship is for what they can get from me. They don't care about me, but about my money." One Westerner put it this way, when asked what she found most challenging:

> The main challenge at the moment is whether it's possible to make relationships without feeling that people are hoping for financial gain from it somehow. Is a foreigner just a fund-raiser for projects, to be flattered and honored so as to get his money in the end? The differences in wealth are unavoidable, so it's a difficult hurdle to overcome (personal communication, 1997).

Westerners are rather shocked to find Africans seeking material benefit from friendships. It seems to them almost abusive. Yet, I believe it is not so strange and alien to their own conceptions and uses of friendship as their reactions indicate. The shock comes from the form it takes in Africa, not from the principle. They largely overlook the widespread mixing of the two in their own culture. The organization and functions of friendships are very different in Africa and the West. The main reason Westerners do not see how friendship and material interest go together in their own culture is that there is such a sharp division between *personal* friendship and *business* friendship.

In personal friendship material interests are ruled out, except for disastrous happenings, such as life-threatening illness, death, and other very major unexpected events when a friend in need is a friend indeed. In business friendships, material interests are of paramount concern. Consider friendship among businessmen, professional people, and politicians. Why are there so many service clubs in the U.S. and around the world? Examples are Rotary, Kiwanis, Chamber of Commerce, and countless others. In these clubs business and professional men and women mix friendship, social events, and personal material interest. Then there are professional associations, such as the American Society of Civil Engineers or the American Medical Association. Meetings are held on a regular basis, where technical presentations are made in an environment of social interaction, but where the real business is to make contacts that will result in professional advantage or advancement, or other personal benefits to the members.

Also consider politicians. Why do many people seek political office, or at least seek to be associated with political leaders? Is civic duty, disinterested service to the public and advancing the common good uppermost in their minds? Should we believe that politicians serve disinterestedly? Or is their motivation significantly self-seeking, to influence enactment of laws and regulations which will result in personal benefits to themselves, to their friends, and to those of their social class? Imagine members of a city council in the U.S. One makes a forceful presentation of a plan for a new highway bypass, which includes the exact routing the proposed road will take. The councillor does not explain to the council that he owns a large tract of land that will be greatly enhanced in value if the highway passes next to it. His councilmen associates question the proposal on technical, environmental, and other grounds, but do not ask personal questions, and ultimately vote for its enactment. Later, a different councillor makes a proposal for some other city project. She will expect the first councillor to vote for the measure on the basis of repayment for her support of the highway bypass. Again personal questions are avoided. Friendship, loyalty, and self-interest require this kind of behavior for the smooth functioning of the city council. Even if such crass behavior is typical of only a small percentage of politicians, civic duty is usually mixed with self-interest. Certainly, a majority of Americans hold the opinion that it is.

In all of these business, professional, and political activities, self-interest is intimately mixed with social interaction and friendship. We do not so much think of them as such because they are institutionalized and impersonalized. We can therefore conclude that the mixing of friendships and material interests is not alien to Western culture. The mixing done in Africa is not so much related to the concept as to the level on which it is carried on. In the West it is largely institutionalized; in Africa it is personalized.

Finally, what should the Westerner do? I conclude with what we have worked out on a personal basis:

1. Be respectful. This includes being courteous, patient, and understanding with everyone. (Exceptions to patience may be necessary with persistent vendors who will not take any form of no for an answer!)

2. Be generous. This does not mean you have to give to everyone who asks for something. Find out locally acceptable ways of refusing people. It does mean that you budget for a certain amount to give away, and that you expend some effort in determining to whom and how you will give. It may also mean developing mid- to long-term relationships with a limited number of worthy, promising, yet needy people, to invest in their lives.

3. Make friends. Get to know some Africans well, going to their homes, getting to understand them and their lives, sharing experiences with them, enjoying their friendship. The closer these friends are to your socio-economic level, the easier it will probably be to have mutually satisfactory relationships. Note that African friends may have quite different expectations from friendships than what you are used to, for instance as to the incidence, and frequency of spending time together. Make friends with people with whom you can talk over your questions, doubts, and lack of understanding about particular matters.

4. Be reserved with unknown people. *Unknown* means people you only know in one context, say at the office, market, club, or other locale. Certainly be leery of people who approach you on the street or in other public places, asking for something from you, or even seeming to ask only to be your friend. Do not put them off in an unfriendly or hostile way, but with the realization that until you know them, you should limit what you say to them and the degree of confidence you put in them.

5. Use references. Ask African friends about unknown people you are interested in for any reason. Find out about their character, reputation, families, and history. By no means hire someone whom you do not know or for whom you have no references.

6. Cultivate African counselors in whom you have confidence and to whom you can go for advice whenever you need it. Use them to help you understand normal and unusual situations and behavior. Include men and women, and people from the middle and lower social levels as well as some from high levels. Let them know you want and need their advice, and even criticism when your speech or actions seem to them to be offensive.

7. Inform yourself about Africa and her cultures. Africa has produced many fine novelists, playwrights, producers of films, poets, and other classes of intellectuals. Many of them focus on African subjects that inform as well as entertain. Much African music is world class. Then of course many foreigners in many fields have produced helpful and interesting works on Africa.

Last of all, *experience* Africa. Be a participant as well as an observer.

References

Amoako-Agyei, Erika. Amin, Samir. 1997. *L'Afrique et le développement*. Interview by Mamadou Barry, Xavier Theulet and Jeanne Tietcheu. *Jeune Afrique Economique* (February 3).

AOC Lecture Notes. 1999. *Pastoral economics*, Yaoundé: Summer Institute of Linguistics.

Arensen, Jon. n.d. How to deal with begging and requests. Unpublished notes. Yaoundé: SIL International.

Barclay, William. 1971. *Ethics in a permissive society*. New York: Harper and Row.

Barley, Nigel. 1983. *Adventures in a mud hut*. N.Y.: Vanguard Press.

Barnes, Sandra T. 1986. *Patrons and power: Creating a political community in metropolitan Lagos*. Bloomington: Indiana University Press.

Bayart, Jean-François. 1989. *L'etat en Afrique: la politique du ventre*. Paris: Fayard.

Besteman, Catherine 1996. Violent politics and the politics of violence: The dissolution of the Somali Nation-State. *American Ethnologist* 23(3):579–596. August.

Biddlecombe, Peter. 1993. *French lessons in Africa: Travels with my briefcase through French Africa*. Boston: Little, Brown

Bohanan, Paul, and Philip Curtin. 1971. *Africa and Africans*. Rev. ed. Garden City, N.Y.: The Natural History Press.

Bosch, David J. 2001(1979). *A spirituality of the road*. Eugene, Ore.: Wipf and Stock Publishers.

Bouba, Bernard. 1982. Reflections on the life of the European. In Philip A. Noss (ed.), Grafting old rootstock: *Studies in culture and religion of the Chamba, Duru, Fula, and Gbaya of Cameroun*, 27–32. Dallas: International Museum of Cultures.

Brinkerhoff, Derick W. and Arthur A. Goldsmith. 2004. Good governance, clientelism, and patrimonialism: New perspectives on old problems. *International Public Management Journal* 7(2):163–185.

269

Britan, Gerald, and Bette S. Denich. 1976. Environment and choice in rapid social change. *American Ethnologist* 3(1):55–72.

Bryan, Ashley. 1999. *The night has ears: African proverbs*. N.Y.: Anthenum Books/Simon and Schuster. (no page numbers)

Burmeister, Nancy. 1995. Murphy's law. *Ethno-Info* 34:14. Abidjan, Ivory Coast: Summer Institute of Linguistics.

Chabal, Patrick, and Jean-Pascal Daloz. 1999. *Africa works: Disorder as political instrument*. Bloomington: Indiana University Press.

Chinchen, Delbert Clifford. 1994. The patron-client relationship concept: A case study from the African Bible colleges in Liberia and Malawi. Unpublished Ed.D. dissertation. Biola University.

Clasberry, Emma Umma. 2010. *African Culture through Proverbs*. Indianapolis, Ind.: Xlibris Corp.

Corbett, Steve & Brian Fikkert. 2009. *When Helping Hurts: How to alleviate poverty without hurting the poor & yourself*. Chicago: Moody Publishers.

Crawford, John R. 1981. Stewardship in younger churches: Observations and caveats from an African perspective. *Missiology* 9(3):299–310.

Cribier, Jacqueline, Martine Dreyfus, and Mamadou Gueye. 1986. *Léébu proverbes Wolof*. Paris: ACCP, CELF, and EDICEF.

Crickmore, Mary. 2011. Gift-giving etiquette in the global village: Bread, stone, or snake? *Banner*, January 18. www.thebanner.org/features/2011/01/gift-giving-etiquette-in-the-global-village. Accessed April 15, 2015.

Cruise O'Brien, Donal B. 1989. Africa. *Journal of the International African Institute* 59 (4):528–529. http://www.jstor.org/stable/1159950, accessed Jan. 27, 2014.

Dealy, G. C., (1977) 1992. *The Public Man: an Interpretation of Latin American and other Catholic Countries*. Amherst Mass.: University of Massachusetts Press. Quoted in Hansen 2003, p.204.

De Jong, Ferdinand. 2007. *Masquerades of Modernity: Power & secrecy in Casamance, Senegal*. Bloomington, IN: Indiana UP.

Devine, Elizabeth and Nancy Braganti. 1995. *The travelers' guide to African customs and manners*. N.Y.: St. Martin's Press.

Dowden, Richard. 2009. *Africa: Altered states. Ordinary miracles*. N.Y.: John Wiley & Sons.

Ela, Jean-Marc. 1983. *La ville en Afrique noire*, 106. Paris: Editions Karthala. (Quoting Balandier, G. *Afrique ambiguë*. 1957. Paris: Plon.)

Enahoro, Peter. 1966. *How to be a Nigerian*. Ibadan: The Caxton Press [West Africa].

Enahoro, Peter. 1966. *How to be a Nigerian*. Lagos. The Daily Times of Nigeria.

Escher, Marilyn. 1998. A linguist faces culture. unpublished ms.

Etounga-Manguelle, Daniel. 2009. *Vers une société responsible: Le cas de l'Afrique.* Paris: L'Harmattan.

Fatton, Robert Jr. 1986. Clientelism and patronage in Senegal. *African Studies Review* 29(4): 61–78.

Foster, Dean. 2002. *The global etiquette guide to Africa and the Middle East.* N.Y.: John Wiley and Sons.

Foster, George M. 1973. *Traditional societies and technological change.* Second ed. New York: Harper and Row.

Geschiere, Peter. 1997. *The modernity of witchcraft: Politics and the occult in postcolonial Africa.* Charlottesville, Va.: University Press of Virginia.

Guèye, Ousseynou. 1997. *La pérénité, le tendon d'Achille. Wal fadjri L'Aurore* [Dakar] (July 3).

<http://www.jstor.org>, accessed Sept. 12, 2013.

Haibucher, Irene. 1999a. *Learning the hard way.* Unpublished ms.

Haibucher, Irene. 1999b. *Showing respect.* Bangui: Central Africa Republic. Self-published.

Hall, Edward. 1966. *The Hidden Dimension.* N.Y.: Anchor Books/ Doubleday.

Hall, Edward T. 1990. *Understanding cultural differences.* Yarmouth, Maine: Intercultural Press.

Hall, Edward T. and Mildred Reed Hall. 1990. *Understanding cultural differences: Germans, French and Americans.* Yarmouth, Maine: Intercultural Press.

Hammond, Dorothy, and Alta Jablow. 1976. *Women in cultures of the world.* Menlo Park, Calif.: Cummings Publishing.

Handlin, Oscar E. Peasant origins. 1967[1951]. In George Dalton (ed.), *Tribal and peasant economies: Readings in economic anthropology,* 456–478. Garden City, N.Y.: Natural History Press.

Handwerker, W. Penn. 1987. Fiscal corruption and the moral economy of resource acquisition. In Barry L. Isaac (ed.), *Research in economic anthropology,* 307–353. Greenwich, Conn.: JAI Press.

Hansen, Ketil Fred. 2003. The politics of personal relations beyond neopatrimonial practices in Northern Cameroon. *Africa* 73(2):202-225.

Harden, Blaine. 1990. *Africa: Dispatches from a fragile continent.* New York: W. W. Norton.

Harries, Jim. 2000. The magical worldview in the African church: What is going on? *Missiology: An International Review* 24(4):487-502.

Hawkins, Christy. 1998. Campers get lesson in paying bills. *Dallas Morning News,* July 5.

Hill, Brad, and Ruth Hill. 1990. On borrowing from the Mondele. In *Slivers from the cross. Adaptation,* 57–59. Chicago: Covenant Publications.

Hill, Harriet. 1996a. Patron-client systems. *Ethno-Info* 37:4. Abidjan, Ivory Coast.

Hill, Harriet. 1996b. Employer-employee relations in West Africa. *Ethno-Info* 37, October, 9–11.

Hungerford, Marian. 1998. Begging, loans, and requests. Unpublished lecture notes. Compiler Yaoundé: Summer Institute of Linguistics.

Hungerford, Marian, ed. n.d. A crash course in Cameroonian etiquette. Unpublished notes. Yaoundé: SIL International.

Hutchinson, Sharon. 1992. The cattle of money and the cattle of girls among the Nuer, 1930–1983. *American Ethnologist* 19(2):294–316.

Irvine, Judith T. 1989. Strategies of status manipulation in the Wolof greeting. In Richard Bauman and Joel Sherzer (eds.), *Explorations in the ethnography of speaking*, second edition, 167–191 (and footnote 9, *sa waa ji, sa waa ji, gacce a nga ca, ndam a nga ca).* New York: Cambridge University Press.

Jacobson, David. 1973. Itinerant townsmen: *Friendship and social order in urban Uganda.* Menlo Park, Calif.: Cummings.

Lasswell, Harold D. 1958(1936). *Politics: Who gets what, when, how.* N.Y.: Meridien Books.

Laye, Camara. 1954. *The African child. Isle of Man.* UK: Fontana/Collins.

Lemarchand, René. 1972. Political clientelism and ethnicity in tropical Africa: Competing solidarities in nation-building. *The American Political Science Review* 66(1): 68–90.

Le Temoin (Dakar). 1997. January 21.

LeVine, Robert A. 1970. Personality and change. In John N. Paden and Edward W. Soja (eds.), *The African experience: Volume I: Essays,* 276–303. Evanston, Ill.: Northwestern University Press.

Maathai, Wangari. 2009. *The Challenge for Africa.* N.Y.: Anchor Books.

Mabry, Marcus, and Alan Zarembo. 1997. *Newsweek,* July 7, 42–43.

Mandela, Nelson. 1994. *Long Walk to Freedom.* N.Y.: Little Brown and Co., quoted in Yale Richmond and Phyllis Gestrin, 1998, *Into Africa: Intercultural Insights.* Yarmouth, Maine: Intercultural Press.

Mani, Joseph Mani. 2010. Cultural Patterns from the Kamba Culture. United States International University, Nairobi, citing Hofstede, Geert, and Gert Jan Hofstede. 2005. *Cultures and Organizations of the Mind: Intercultural Cooperation and Its Importance for Survival.* New York: McGraw-Hill. <www.kenya-information-guide.com/kamba -tribe. html> accessed 4/2/2010.

Mann, David P. 1990. Toward understanding gift-giving in relationships. *Missiology* 18(1):49–60.

Maraniss, David. 1995. *First in his class: The biography of Bill Clinton.* New York: Simon and Schuster.

Maranz, David E. 1993. *Peace is everything: The world view of Muslims and traditionalists in the Senegambia*. Summer Institute of Linguistics and the International Museum of Cultures Publications in Ethnography 28. Dallas.

Marsden, Carolyn and Philip Matzigkeit. 2009. *Sahwira: An African friendship*. Somerville, Mass.: Candlewick Press.

Mbiti, John S. 1989. *African Religions & Philosophy,* 2nd ed. Oxford and N.Y.: Heinemann Educational Publishers.

Mboya, Paul. 1938. Luo Kitgi gi Timbegi. Kisumu, Kenya: Anyange Press.

McNee, Lisa. 2000. *Selfish Gifts: Senegalese women's autobiographical discourses*. Albany: State University of New York.

Mogre, Salifu. 1982. A report on my first few weeks a cross-culture experience in America. Unpublished manuscript. Norman, Okla.

Morgan, Timothy C. 2000. Have we become too busy with death? *Christianity Today* 44(2):36–44, Feb. 7.

Muchena, Olivia N. 1996. Sociological and anthropological reflections. In Tetsunao Yamamori, Bryant L. Myers, Kwame Bediako, and Larry Reed (eds.), *Serving with the poor in Africa*, 169–180. Monrovia, Calif.: MARC.

Mungai, Eddie. 1997. Asking as a way of life. *Ethno-Info* No. 40, July.

Nelson, Harold D. et al. 1974. *Area handbook for Senegal*, Second edition 250. Washington, D.C.: U.S. Government Printing Office.

Newsweek. 1995. Questions without answers. May 15.

Nydell, Margaret K. 1996. *Understanding Arabs: A guide for Westerners*. Yarmouth, Maine: Intercultural Press.

Nzemen, Moïse. 1993. *Tontines et développement ou le défi financier de l'Afrique*. Yaoundé: Presses Universitaires du Cameroun.

Ong, Walter J. 1982. *Orality and literacy: The technologizing of the word*. London: Methuen. Hutchinson.

Owin, Dan. 1995. Cheating death the Suba way. *Ethno-Info* 34:4–5. Abidjan, Ivory Coast.

Parker, Shipton. 1995. How Gambians save: Culture and economic strategy at an ethnic crossroads. In Jane I. Guyer (ed.), *Money matters: Instability, values and social payments in the modern history of West African communities*, 245–276. Portsmouth, N.H.: Heinemann.

Pennington, Dorothy L. 1990. Time in African culture. In Molefi Kete and kariamu Welsh Asante (eds.), *African culture: The rhythms of unity*, 123–140. Trenton, N.J.: Africa World Press.

Phillips John E. 1999. A Bekwel folk tale sheds light on sharing. *Ethno-Info* 44:2–4. Dallas, Tex.: Summer Institute of Linguistics.

Pipes, Daniel. 1984. *In the path of God: Islam and political power*. N.Y.: Basic Books.

Richmond, Yale, and Phyllis Gestrin. 1998. *Into Africa: Intercultural insights.* Yarmouth, Maine: Intercultural Press.

Rose, Laurel L. 2002. African elites' land control maneuvers. Études rurales163/164:187–213. http://www.jstor.org/stable/20122941. Accessed Jan. 21, 2014.

Rosen, Lawrence. 1984. *Bargaining for reality: The construction of social relations in a Muslim community.* Chicago: University of Chicago Press.

Samovar, Larry, Richard E. Porter, and Edwin R. McDaniel. 2007. *Communication between cultures,* Sixth edition. Belmont, Calif.: Thomson Wadsworth.

Saunders, Philip. 1997. Caveat vendor. *Ethno-Info* No. 40, 5–6.

Savage, Andrew. 1997. Proverbs Applied. *Ethno-Info* No. 39. Abidjan, Ivory Coast, SIL International.

Savage, Tom J. 1996. An Insulting Compliment? *Ethno-Info* No. 35. Abidjan, Ivory Coast: Summer Institute of Linguistics.

Schmeltzer, Sue. 1997. Soninke values: Responsibility, work, respect and shame. *Ethno-Info* No. 39, May.

Schraeder, Peter J. 1994. *Elites as facilitators or impediments to political development? Some lessons from the 'third wave' of democratization in Africa.* The Journal of Developing Areas 29(1): 69–90. http://www. jstor.org/stable/4192413, accessed Jan. 21, 2014.

Schwartz, Glenn J. 2007. When Charity Destroys Dignity: Overcoming unhealthy dependency in the Christian movement. Lancaster, PA: World Mission Associates.

Shawyer, Richard. 2009. Wisdom of the Wolof sages: A collection of proverbs from Senegal, translated and explained in English <wolofresources.org/language/ download/proverbs.pdf>, accessed Mar. 24, 2013.

Shenai-Khatkhate, Deodatta V. Insightful quotes from Africa on friendship and learning, <www.dshenai.wordpress.com>, accessed Jan. 17, 2014.

Shipton, Parker. 1995. How Gambians save: Culture and economic strategy at an ethnic crossroads. In Jane I. Guyer (ed.), *Money matters: Instability, values and social payments in the modern history of West African communities,* 245–276. Portsmouth, N.H.: Heinemann.

Smith, Donald K. 1984. *Make haste slowly: Developing effective cross-cultural communication.* Portland, Ore.: IICC.

Stanley, Thomas J., and William D. Danko. 1998. *The millionaire next door: The surprising secrets of America's wealthy.* New York: Simon and Schuster.

Stewart, Edward C. 1972. *American cultural patterns: A cross-cultural perspective.* LaGrange Park, Ill.: Intercultural Network.

Stewart, Julia. 1997. *African proverbs and wisdom*. N.Y.: Kensington Publishing Corp.

Sub Hebdo, Dakar. 1991. La banque des exclus. Dec. 26.

Sud Quotidien (Dakar). 1997. *Le «Neeral," un système d'aide à la famille*, and *Vers une protection sociale des pêcheurs*. March 10. Also: *Sud Quotidien*. 1997. *Le «mboole," un modèle de solidarité entre pêcheurs*. Mar. 11.

Sud Week-end (Dakar). 1996. December 14.

Sylla, Assane. 1978. *La Philosophie morale des wolofs*. Translation by the author. Dakar: Sankoré. Talla, Blaise-Pascal. 1997. Cameroun *Gangstérisme financier à Yaoundé*. Jeune Afrique Economie number 244, (July 1).

Szeftel, Morris. 2000. Clientelism, corruption and catastrophe. Review of *African Political Economy* 27(85):427, citing *The Times*, London, February 15, 1999.

Talla, Blaise-Pascal. 1997. Cameroun Gangstérisme financier á Yaoundél *Jeune Afrique Economonie*, number 244 (July 1).

Tembo, Mwizenge S. 1990. The concept of African personality: sociological implications. in Asante, Molefi Kete & Kariamu Welsh Asante, eds. *African Culture: The Rhythms of Unity*. Trenton, N.J.: Africa World Press.

The Herald. 1999. Yaoundé, Cameroon, Feb. 26–28.

The New Enclyclopædia Britannica. 1988. Africa, Asia, Australia, North America, and South America. Fifteenth ed. Chicago: Enclyclopædia Britannica.

Thornton, Robert. 2005. Four principles of South African political culture at the local level. *Anthropology Southern Africa* 28(1&2):22-30.

Unseth, Carole. 1995. Maryam's 'Thank-you.' *Ethno-Info* No. 34, 3–4 October.

Van Chi-Bonnardel, Régine Nguyen. 1978. *Vie de Relations au Sénégal: La Circulation de Biens*. Dakar: Institut Fondamental d'Afrique.

Venkatappiah, B. 1968. Misuse of office. *International Encyclopedia of the Social Sciences* 2:272–276.

Walle, Nicolas van de. 2003. Presidentialism and clientelism in Africa's emerging party systems. *The Journal of Modern African Studies* 41(2): 311–312.

Wikipedia, The politics of the belly, accessed Jan. 27, 2014.

Index

SIL International Publications

Additional Releases in the Publications in Ethnology Series

42. **Ensnared by AIDS: Cultural contexts of HIV and AIDS in Nepal,** by David K Beine, 2014, 358 pp., ISBN 978-1556713507.

41. **The Norsk Høstfest: A celebration of ethnic food and ethnic identity,** by Paul Thomas Emch, 2011, 121 pp., ISBN 978-1-55671-265-4.

40. **Our company increases apace: History, language, and social identity in early colonial Andover, Massachucetts,** by Elinor Abbot, 2007, 279 pp., ISBN 978-1-55671-169-5.

39. **What place for hunters-gatherers in millenium three?** by Thomas N. Headland and Doris E. Blood, eds. 2002, 130 pp., ISBN 978-1-55671-132-9.

38. **A tale of Pudicho's people,** by Richard Montag. 2002, 181 pp., ISBN 978-1-55671-131-2.

37. **African friends and money matters,** by David E. Maranz, 2015, 237 pp., ISBN 1-55671-117-4.

36. **The value of the person in the Guahibo culture,** by Marcelino Sosa, translated by Walter del Aguila, 1999, 158 pp., ISBN 978-1-55671-085-8.

35. **People of the drum of God—Come!,** by Paul Neeley, 1999, 310 pp., ISBN 978-1-55671-013-1.

34. **Cashibo folklore and culture: Prose, poetry, and historical background,** by Lila Wistrand-Robinson, 1998, 196 pp., ISBN 978-1-55671-048-3.

SIL International Publications
7500 W. Camp Wisdom Road
Dallas, Texas 75236-5629 USA

General inquiry: publications_intl@sil.org
Pending order inquiry: sales_intl@sil.org
www.sil.org/resources/publications